THE MAJOR

THE MAJOR

The Biography of Dick Hern

MICHAEL TANNER

PELHAM BOOKS

PELHAM BOOKS

Published by the Penguin Group
27 Wrights Lane, London W8 5TZ, England
Viking Penguin, a division of Penguin Books USA Inc
375 Hudson Street, New York, NY 10014, USA
Penguin Books Australia Ltd, Ringwood, Victoria, Australia
Penguin Books Canada Ltd, 2801 John Street, Markham, Ontario, Canada L3R 1B4
Penguin Books (NZ) Ltd, 182–190 Wairau Road, Auckland 10, New Zealand
Penguin Books Ltd, Registered Offices: Harmondsworth, Middlesex, England

First Published 1991
1 3 5 7 9 10 8 6 4 2

Copyright © 1991 by Michael Tanner

Typeset in 11/13½pt Old Style
Printed and bound in Great Britain by
Butler & Tanner Ltd, Frome and London

A CIP catalogue record for this book is available from the British Library.

ISBN 07207 1963 1

Contents

Author's Note

Unlike Shakespeare's Mark Antony I *did* come to "praise Caesar". In such circumstances it was all the more disappointing that Dick Hern chose not to co-operate in the writing of this book. No biographer rejects the thoughts, views, memories and asides of his subject. Fortunately, I was able to unearth a fair amount of interview material, and in this regard I am particularly grateful to William Heinemann for permission to use extracts from John Rickman's lengthy conversation with Dick Hern included within the book *Eight Flat-Racing Stables*.

Non-participation of the subject, however, does have its advantages. The biographer is allowed a degree of independence, and therefore objectivity, which might otherwise have been jeopardized by an obligation to please. For authorized biography frequently read sanitized biography.

Consequently, I adopted the same approach to researching my subject as would (of necessity) be employed by any biographer of a historical figure. Effecting a meaningful balance between the printed word, which has borne public scrutiny, and the spoken word, which has not, was my sole criterion. My aim was to settle for nothing less than an honest, even-handed treatment; there would be no genuflexion and no digging for dirt – any clods deemed to have been thrown up are the result of legitimate research practices. I did not set out with the avowed intention of trying to "bury Caesar".

In the quest for balance the verbal testaments of numerous

individuals drawn from every phase, and covering every aspect, of Dick Hern's life have been used to supplement rather than automatically to supersede published sources. To all those who agreed to speak to me I offer my sincere thanks in the hope that they do not consider their confidence to have been misplaced. At the very worst I can find some solace in the words of Mark Twain: "Biographies are but the clothes and buttons of the man – the biography of the man himself cannot be written."

Michael Tanner
Sleaford
October, 1990

Chapter One

THE ENIGMA

'Few men are of one plain decided colour'

ACCORDING TO THE American poet and essayist Ralph
Waldo Emerson "All persons are puzzles until at last we find in some
word or act the key ... straightaway all the past words and actions
lie in light before us." Where, one wonders, would Emerson have
found the 'key' to William Richard Hern, or even begun the search?
A man once dubbed the Howard Hughes of racing, Hern has somehow
contrived to keep the secrets of his personality safely guarded despite
occupying a place at the top of his chosen profession – one with a
high public profile, no less – for over thirty years. In the eyes of
many involved with the 'great triviality' that is the Turf, Hern has,
to all intents and purposes, thrown away the key, an action crying
out for some kind of explanation. "All is riddle," continued Emerson,
"and the key to a riddle is another riddle."

Somerset may never be worthy of Churchill's description of Russia
as "a riddle wrapped in a mystery inside an enigma", but, even so,
Dick Hern grew to manhood in an area proud of its folklore replete
with stories of mythical places and legendary characters. From
Glastonbury's links with Joseph of Arimathea, the Holy Thorn and
the Holy Grail via Arthur's Avalon to the blood-stained fate of
Monmouth's rag-tag army of pike-waving peasants, Somerset's heri-
tage is enshrined in prose, painting and song, bequeathing a cultural
legacy every bit as hypnotic as the county's physical landscape.
That, too, embraces powerful emotions. Windswept moorland and
wood-clad hills lie cheek by jowl with vast stretches of milk-rich

meadow and barren mudflats. On a misty morning high in the Quantocks it is not impossible to imagine oneself nearer the past than the present. The paradoxical elements which characterize Somerset are personified in one of its most famous sporting sons. The countryside is loath to give up its secrets. To a boy raised where the Quantocks spill across the flats of the Severn estuary these were no mysteries, merely the facts of life.

Once Hern had passed through the introspective and, to many, the equally mysterious world of public school and the Army those Somerset foundations were fortified with a formalized code of conduct which brooks few compromises and tolerates little or no criticism. Indeed, there are grounds for suggesting that Hern is a man born – or at very least living – out of his time. "The Major's a 1930s man," says Willie Carson, his stable-jockey since 1977. "It's about discipline and about loyalty and getting on with the job. The military thing shows through all the time." In the pre-war era of Butters, Darling and Boyd-Rochfort, Dick Hern's autocratic approach to training racehorses would not have received a second glance.

Any privacy someone in the public gaze could have expected by right in the 1930s, or even as late as the 1950s, rapidly began to be eroded in the wake of the massive social changes stimulated by the 'Swinging Sixties'. The private lives of the rich and famous – politicians, pop stars and, regrettably perhaps, sportsmen – became public property. Journalists found little difficulty keeping abreast of these changing attitudes. Simple and accurate reportage of a match or race gave way to the post-event quote, the exclusive and the in-depth interview. As the trainer of over 1,500 winners (including fifteen English classics, a total unmatched by any of his countrymen currently holding a licence) encompassing household names such as Brigadier Gerard, Troy and Nashwan, Dick Hern has increasingly found himself centre-stage beneath the unrelenting glare of a spotlight he would rather was pointed elsewhere.

Leading trainer on four occasions, he has, since the retirement of Noel Murless, constituted the role model for any trainer with ambitions of becoming THE classic trainer of the century's last decade. In the forty-five post-war years to 1990 only six horses have won the 2000 Guineas on their seasonal reappearance; Hern trained two of them. When Sun Princess won the 1983 Oaks Hern became the first trainer in thirty-three years to win an English classic with a maiden. Hern was also the first trainer to reach another milestone: in 1980 he rewarded his owners with over £1 million in win and place prize money. "I think I've trained with some of the greatest trainers in the world," says Her Majesty the Queen's racing manager Lord Carnarvon, "and Dick must be one of the best of them all."

Any reticence in Hern's dealings with human beings is not repeated when he is confronted by horses, for he is blessed with the horse-master's equivalent of green fingers. So the story goes, when Hern and his brother officers of the North Irish Horse visited Vienna's renowned Spanish Riding School toward the end of the war and indulged in a spot of carefree exercise, one of the resident staff was moved to observe: "There's only one who can ride – him." He was motioning toward Hern. This empathy with the most graceful of God's creatures forms the mainstay of Hern's career with horses, first as an instructor at the Porlock Vale Riding School and then as a trainer. "He could see what very few can see within a horse," says European and Olympic Three-Day Event gold medallist Bertie Hill, who came under Hern's tutelage during pre-Olympic training at Porlock in the winter of 1951–2. "It's God's gift. The first time I went to Porlock he taught me the rules of the dressage ring. He's a master of all aspects of horsemastership."

Hern's achievements will be challenged, and possibly surpassed, by the likes of Henry Cecil, Michael Stoute and Guy Harwood, but as Stoute, three times leading trainer himself, replied when quizzed about his own deeds: "The Major's got a better record than any of us." Significantly, Stoute then added: "He's not only a great trainer he's also a very special man." Such unsolicited praise from another master of his profession merely serves to underline the indisputable truth of Willie Carson's instant assessment of his guv'nor's status within the racing sphere: "Well, he's just the most respected trainer in the land, isn't he? He understands horses. He thinks like a horse. His LIFE is the horse. He's a master trainer isn't he?"

A mark of that respect is to be gleaned from the way Dick Hern's reputation has emerged unscathed from a number of causes célèbres which, however mundane to outsiders, initiated quite a few ripples on racing's pond. The departure from West Ilsley of stable-jockey Joe Mercer in 1976 and, to a lesser degree perhaps, the unsavoury rumours which followed the inexplicable performance of Gorytus,

3

red-hot favourite for the 1982 Dewhurst Stakes, generated enough
newsprint to have easily damaged Hern's standing within the sport.
More recently, in the spring of 1989 it was confirmed that his lease
on West Ilsley stables would not be renewed by the Queen. With
virtually the entire racing community on his "side" – no mean feat
in one of the few sports which continues to place royalty on a lofty
pedestal – Hern maintained a dignified silence, whereas all those
around him seemed intent on making capital of the situation. Such
sang-froid could be expected of a 1930s man. "We were brought up
to say little; don't draw attention to yourself," says Harry Thomson
Jones, an old friend of Hern's and another soldier turned successful
trainer. However, for a man who had suffered a broken neck, which
had confined him to a wheelchair for the past four years, and who
had recently overcome heart surgery, Hern's resiliance was nothing
short of astonishing.

Despite gradually being overtaken by the inexorably rising tide
of media attention Hern comfortably avoided a thorough soaking,
even if his toes did get a bit damp. Throughout these ordeals the
mask seldom slipped and today he remains as much an enigma as
ever. Sir John "Jakie" Astor, a lifelong friend, knows him better
than most. "He is the most loyal friend you could have. The adjective
which comes to mind when you think about him is 'reliable' but that
doesn't say anything about his very good, quiet sense of humour.
He may seem a bit terse with the Press but he's totally dedicated to
his horses. It may seem incredible but the first thing that he wanted
when he came round after breaking his neck was to find out about
evening stables. He's extremely good company. Most of the jokes
we share are rather 'in', so there's no point in describing them. But
he's a very amusing man, and given the right evening he'll recite
some long poem like 'The Man from Snowy River' or the one about
the 'Green-Eyed Yellow Idol' after dinner and bring the house
down."

One documented example of Hern's occasionally off-beat sense of
humour that would not be misplaced in a P.G. Wodehouse novel
surfaced after Troy won him his first Derby. A considerable champagne celebration back in the yard inadvertently included six bottles
of a rare vintage. "Don't be cross," an anxious Sheilah Hern
beseeched her husband, "it's a lovely time for the champagne to be
opened – we've just won the Derby." An exasperated Hern, for all

the world Jeeves incarnate, spluttered, "I know we've won the Derby but, dammit, it's not even been chilled!"

During fourteen years as Hern's stable-jockey Joe Mercer was given ample opportunity to savour the Major's sense of humour and penchant for rude stories. "When racing he is very diplomatic but afterwards he is completely the opposite. He's a fun-loving person and a lovely party-man. He's a great wit and story teller, can recite poems as long as your arm – it's wonderful how he does it – and sings magnificently."

David Murray-Smith, who spent six years at West Ilsley, the last two as an assistant, says of Hern: "He is quite a shy man, though once you've got to know him he's good company. People say he's very stern but when he's about his business he just likes to get on with it and I couldn't have worked for a better or fairer person. He is a man with a great sense of humour – on any kind of subject – but he doesn't suffer fools gladly. Unfortunately for him he is a private man in a public business."

Conversing with monarchs, sheikhs, lords and ladies has done nothing to cure Hern's innate reserve, which is not eased by the deafness he suffers in one ear. He has always taken time to thaw. Bertie Hill again: "He's a terrific character. At the same time one had to know him and as time went on, like so many characters, you did get to know him. We all used to meet up in The Ship, at Porlock, and Dick was always there on duty with us. He was a great one to make light of problems that arise in a crisis. And he was a great singer."

To outsiders, though, Dick Hern cut a formidable figure, straight-backed and straight-talking, a Captain Ahab stalking winners instead of a white whale. "He's a queer man, Captain Ahab – so some think – but a good one. Oh, thou'lt like him well enough; no fear, no fear. He's a grand, ungodly, god-like man Captain Ahab; doesn't speak much; but when he does speak, then you may well listen."

However, the officer mentality of addressing subordinates as one pleases when one pleases is an unpleasant habit for anyone – even a trainer – to carry over into civilian life. In distinct contrast, Ian Cocks well remembers driving over to West Ilsley one balmy summer evening in 1979 to be 'interviewed' for the position of assistant trainer. "I was very, very worried and sat in the car for a few minutes

5

beforehand having a cigarette. We had a drink in the garden. I had to keep biting myself and telling myself that this was a very important interview because he made it all so very easy. I never found him daunting at all. He has this amazing memory for ditties, songs and poems, and loves to quote little bits of text or insert a little story in general conversation." Seldom is this softer side of Dick Hern unveiled in public.

Hern's standards are exceedingly high. As a result he can be an exacting man to work for. Hardly surprising for a man who barely a month after his 22nd birthday, and newly arrived in the North African desert, was controlling a Churchill tank and the destinies of its four other occupants, when circumstances suddenly decreed he assume command of the entire squadron of eighteen tanks during a fierce enemy counter-attack.

History has frequently observed that for a man "to command efficiently he must have obeyed others in the past." The qualities of leadership and personal courage forged in the young Hern that day at Hunt's Gap and honed in numerous other engagements later on throughout Tunisia and Italy would forever stand him in good stead, notably after his fall while hunting.

"I thought he was immensely brave after his accident," says Lord Carnarvon. "Every time I went to see him I was struck by the marvellous way in which he handled it. Although he couldn't move, he wanted to know everything about the yard and he would assimilate in his mind everything we were telling him. He'd know every horse, every box and every detail we described to him." Jakie Astor agrees: "He's been really quite extraordinary about his accident. He's an iron-willed man and I am absolutely amazed at the way he's gone on in spite of it. I can't think of anyone else who would have had the guts to do it. He's a very disciplined man in many ways. I have never once heard him complain."

For Dick Hern to be loved, admired and respected among his peers of the officer class is understandable enough. If it be thought, however, that his seemingly aloof and rather remote mien has contrived to hammer an implacable wedge between himself and his subordinates let the sceptic think again. Hern's staff, from lads to jockeys, have consistently demonstrated tremendous loyalty and won't hear a word said against him. One who knew him in his early days at Newmarket makes no bones about his admiration for the

Hern approach to training and man-management. "He was a very astute horsemaster and you couldn't talk rot to him. What came out of his mouth he meant and there was only one way to do things and that was the right way. And there's one other thing. No one can ever say Dick Hern did them a dirty trick and there's not many people in the racing world you can say that about." Alan Bond, Hern's second jockey in 1977, echoes these sentiments: "He's a real gentleman and there is definitely some kind of aura about him. He put me at my ease straight away, making it plain he was pleased to have me at West Ilsley. A genuinely honest person. You always know where you stand with him."

Restricted opportunities obliged Bond to head for Newmarket. Another whose stay at West Ilsley was relatively brief is Rodney Boult, head-lad to David Elsworth and work-rider of the redoubtable Desert Orchid, but like Alan Bond he is quick to refute suggestions that his departure had anything to do with his treatment at the hands of Dick Hern. "He was a great man to work for, a charming man. You got praise when you deserved it and a rollocking when you deserved one. He is so dedicated. You'd be up there on those Downs in the cold weather with your hands and feet near dropping off and I can only remember once when we came in early – and that was after $1\frac{1}{4}$ hours. You've got to admire a man if he's up there with you. Then, when we'd come in, he'd go back out to school his hunter. He's a real man's man but has another side to him. I remember taking a horse to France. We'd only been at West Ilsley nine months and he took the trouble to think of my wife and popped round to tell her I'd arrived all right and when I'd be expected home."

Dick Hern would gladly shout from the rooftops his adherence to the old maxim "an ounce of loyalty is worth a pound of cleverness" were it not for the fact that his staff broadcast it for him. Head-lad Geordie Campbell and, until his tragic death in March 1990, travelling head-lad Buster Haslam supported Hern throughout his tenure of West Ilsley which began in the autumn of 1962. Brian Procter arrived as chief work-rider in 1969. "You can get the wrong impression of the man. You can think, 'Oh, Oh, he's in a bad mood' – and he's not. His main concern is for the horses and he never misses a trick. He's a very fair man, you play the game straight and honest and he's as straight and honest with you, which is fair enough." As one of Ahab's crew reassured a new shipmate: "It's better to sail

with a moody good captain than a laughing bad one." Lastly there's
the testimony of Willie Carson, who states emphatically, "He's the
most loyal person to a jockey I've ever known. His jockey is his
team. And if you're as one, you've got to be better. It's total, total,
total. His accident was a big blow to us all, but when we got the
vibes from him that he wanted to continue, that gave us all the
incentive we needed to do even better than we'd done before. He
was the sort of man who used to walk round the yard every night
with his little stick. Horses would have to stand to attention. He
used to love touching them, feeling legs to detect whether any
problems were arising. The accident robbed him of that finger-tip
touch and he has had to adapt from his wheelchair. His eyes, I
suppose, are a lot sharper now than they were; he never misses a
thing. He likes me there twice a week to ride work and if I'm not
there, he's on the phone to tell me what went on. Every time horses
have worked, he speaks to every lad in the yard afterwards and likes
to hear what they have to say. The Major desperately wants to know
what you think about a horse because, as he always says, there's
nothing to compare with the feel a jockey gets from a horse; there's
no substitute. He knows, because he was a great horseman himself."

No wonder George Wigg called Hern the 'Mayor of West Ilsley'
after experiencing at first hand the community spirit and together-
ness of the trainer's domain.

Thus a picture emerges, hazily perhaps and a trifle indistinct
round the edges, of a man universally acclaimed by peers and
employees alike. How accurate a portrait is it? "The followers of a
great man often put their eyes out, so that they may be the better
able to sing his praises," wrote Nietzsche; in other words, there are
none so blind as those who will not see. The racing public has never
viewed Dick Hern in a favourable light until, that is, the misfortunes
of accident, illness and eviction induced both a sense of genuine
sympathy for the man's plight and heartfelt admiration for the
courageous manner in which he defied each successive blow. The
responsibility for much of Hern's hitherto unattractive public image
lay squarely on his own shoulders, however.

There is one story that captures perfectly the way in which Hern's
image has been manufactured. It is a Pimms-sipping summer's day
at the Newmarket July course and a young stable lad is walking his
charge round the pre-parade ring in splendid isolation. Dick Hern

chances to pass by. He stops and stares at the pair circling beneath the swaying beech trees. The lad is tugging self-consciously at the horse's lead-rein. Perhaps recognizing the interested spectator, he begins tugging all the harder. Hern's stare becomes a glare. His eyes narrow and turning on his heel he barks, "Why don't you pull a bit more and yank his bloody head off!" An incident which could have led to an inexperienced stable lad receiving quiet words of advice from a master trainer that would have stayed with him forever, instead left an impressionable young man crestfallen and a number of eye witnesses disillusioned. Though driven by the noblest of motives – his love of horses and zeal for doing things by the book – Hern's delivery still left a lot to be desired.

Moments akin to that one have wreaked havoc with Hern's image in the eyes of the public – and have continued to do so. What conclusions does the onlooker draw about a person's character from the unedifying spectacle of seeing, and hearing, that person berating an ageing gateman from his wheelchair in one breath, only to assume, on the sudden appearance at his shoulder of his principal patron Sheikh Hamdan Al-Maktoum, the demeanour of a saint in the next? A man is judged on the basis of how he is seen to act; and this is how Hern has been seen to act by all too many people on all too many occasions. All that has mattered to him are his owners, horses and staff – not necessarily in that order. The man in the street who helped support Hern's lifestyle with his interest and, frequently, his wager was superfluous it seemed; a point soon picked up and sometimes ruthlessly exploited by certain sections of that self-elected voice of the people, the Press.

After a lifetime spent surmounting every obstacle placed before him – not without effort – the vicissitudes of the 1980s finally brought Hern face to face with the vulnerability of the human condition. With the harrowing confirmation of man's physical frailty came the brutal realization that not even he was indispensible. Since the day he took out his licence as private trainer to Major Lionel Holliday in 1957 Hern had never enjoyed the luxury of being, literally, his own master. Astor, Sobell and Weinstock, and the Queen had all held the keys to his yard. To be able to train the racehorse – improving him and nurturing his development – was the only motivation Dick Hern required: the purest form of motivation. He was no wheeler-dealer. The almost venal obligation of the modern trainer to insist on his cut from every deal involving the horses he has manufactured into valuable economic properties ran contrary to Hern's inclinations. This reluctance – lack of business acumen some would call it – left him vulnerable, financially and politically. He could no more save himself in 1989 than he could Joe Mercer thirteen years earlier.

He began to change, ever so slightly to loosen-up. The media received more assistance in 1989 than for many a long year. Raised within the strict, hierarchical regimes of public school and the Army, Hern had always shown displeasure at the instant accessibility associated with the modern age. The Racing Press tend not to follow the military principles of putting requests in writing and/or going through specified channels. They prefer ambushing a trainer outside the weighing room or telephoning him at all hours of the day. Neither prospect excited Hern. In the first place he is not a natural interviewee: words do not come easily. Secondly and equally, if not more, importantly he believes the Press have no divine right to information he deems confidential. Nor had Press coverage of Mercer's sacking and the Gorytus 'affair' been designed to please. On the latter occasion Hern resorted to calling in Racecourse Security Services to track down the source of 'leaked' information, and in 1986, for much the same reason, made it perfectly plain to Willie Carson that giving fulsome television interviews was not a good idea. After Henbit won the 1980 Derby television crews were denied the customary access to film celebrations. Yet in the aftermath of Nashwan's 2000 Guineas victory in 1989 the Major consented to an interview being transmitted live on Channel 4 from the winner's enclosure (albeit with the proviso that he would not discuss the West Ilsley tenancy row). Only those with a good memory could recall the last time this had happened. Moreover, Hern was expansive: words did not have to be prised from him like the lid off a pot of paint.

Throughout the summer of 1989 a stream of communiqués flowed from West Ilsley in anticipation of, and in answer to, Press inquiries about Nashwan's health and future plans. The trainer even allowed himself to become associated with a publicity scheme devised by one of the leading bookmaking firms. Hern's metamorphosis was as remarkable, and understandable, as Scrooge's dramatic character transformation after he had been confronted with a similarly bleak vision of the future. "Ghost of the future," Scrooge exclaimed, "I fear you more than any Spectre I have seen. But as I know your purpose is to do me good, and as I hope to live to be another man from what I was, I am prepared to bear you company and do it with a thankful heart." Life, complete with all its undesirable traits, suddenly became very sweet.

In spite of this mutual harmony between Hern and the Press, the Major's elevation to the status of racing folk-hero struck one or two journalists as decidedly odd. As Dickens said of Scrooge, "Some people laughed to see the alteration in him, but he let them laugh and little heeded them." Bruised by Hern's off-hand manner in the bad old days, perhaps, they were difficult to convince, though wise enough to keep such a view off the printed page. Considering Hern "an unpleasant piece of work, the product of another era," they saw no reason to alter their opinion. References to loyal servants like Buster Haslam, and even Carson, being publicly and loudly rebuked after incurring his wrath were resurrected and cited as corroborative evidence. "If you don't bloody well do as you're told, you'll not ride for me very long," Carson was informed as he brought his mount back down Sandown's rhododendron walk one evening in 1977. If such an incident did occur, and one would be surprised if some such words were not occasionally spoken in the heat of the moment after a close-fought race, it is certain they would have been instantly forgotten by the two principals. "He's not like other people," insists Carson. "If I make a mistake, it's discussed and that's the end of it. There's pressure on me not to make mistakes but there's less pressure because he's so easy to ride for. We know the horses, know what they want, and it's down to me to do the right thing in a race. He'd never tie you down to orders. If we have a disagreement over a horse, you won't read about it in a newspaper, like you do with some people. He's a man so understanding of one's faults and who restores everything to proportion. I have been lucky that my main jobs have been for gentlemen like Sam Armstrong, Bernard van Cutsem and the Major." However intimidating he may be, or caustic he can be, disparaging his employees in public is not Hern's style. Rodney Boult came to West Ilsley from a stint out of racing, working in his father's Liverpool club where hair long enough to warrant a rebuke from any officer-of-the-day was the norm. "He just called me in one morning and quietly told me it would be more suitable if it was cut shorter and I wore a cap. He's too much of a gentleman to bawl you out in front of the men.''

If the haughty Garboesque persona has softened a mite since 1984 one can be sure it owes more to the unseen hand of God than the heavy hand of the Press. It took a succession of bodyblows to begin to show the world at large what kind of man Dick Hern really is, to scratch away, however imperceptibly, that tough, no-nonsense veneer and reveal traces of the more considerable presence obsessively secreted beneath. ''Few men are of one plain decided colour,'' wrote the eighteenth-century statesman Lord Chesterfield. ''Most are mixed, shaded and blended.'' An understanding of the genuine article, warts and all, becomes a more viable proposition the moment one accepts that William Richard Hern is not merely a trainer of the old school, whom Messrs Butters and Darling would have recognized and admired, but also a man of the old school, the kind of man who once upon a time built empires.

Chapter 2

BOYHOOD

'Youth is the Lord of Life'

THE SURNAME HERN, HEARNE, Hurn or Harn almost certainly derives from the Old English 'Hyrne' denoting someone who lived by a bend in a river or in a recess in a hillside, although it may also be a variation of 'Heron', the nickname for a tall, thin person resembling the bird of that name. Consequently, entire families might have drawn their name from a settlement such as Hurn on the Hampshire Stour, for example, and taken it with them on any migration along the south coast. There is a Hurne recorded at Axminster in 1361 and a J. Newton Hearn became a noted Devonian poet, writing "The famous game of bowls and others" and the song "O Devon Fair Devon."

For a family bearing this name there could be no more apt place to live than on a hill overlooking a bend in a river. It is in just such a spot, on Chuley Hill above the River Ashburn, barely a mile south of Ashburton in south Devon, that Dick Hern's forefathers were domiciled at the turn of the nineteenth century. Of the numerous Herns to be found living on the fringes of Dartmoor, William and Charlotte Hern of Chuley House were among the most prosperous. When William died on 31 October 1832 his will ran to six pages and contained substantial bequests to his two sons George Augustus and John. Most of these bequests took the form of land or other items dear to a yeoman farmer – gold and silver watches, silver teapot and tankard, family bibles – but, significantly, William Hern also set aside £1,000 for John's education. The money was clearly put to good effect and the desire for educational fulfilment, so redolent of the Victorian age, was not lost in successive generations of the Hern family. When John Hern died in May 1914, aged eighty-six and quite blind, the *Mid Devon Advertiser* described him as "one of the most highly esteemed and respected townsmen". All three of his sons had graduated to the medical profession. The eldest, another John, became an ophthalmic surgeon, spending some years in Darlington before settling at South Nutfield in Surrey. He died in 1936, aged eighty-one, leaving over £17,000 to his three children. George, the youngest of old John's boys, also prospered as a surgeon. When he passed away in 1935 his will, proved at £122,350, demonstrated his gratitude to the medical profession by including bequests to the NSPCC, the Middlesex Hospital, Dr Barnardo's and the Mission of Hope – as well as £1,000 to his brother William.

William Hern, two years younger than John, was born in 1857. After Ashburton Grammar School and a private education, William opted for dentistry and won a Saunders Scholarship at the Royal Dental Hospital in London. In 1882, when he was still only twenty-five the publication of his work on "Fractures of Maxillae and Treatment" in the British Journal of Dental Science heralded the start of a brilliant career in dentistry. He became lecturer on Dental Surgery, Demonstrator and House Surgeon at the Royal, and was appointed the Consulting Dental Surgeon to the Middlesex Hospital and the London Military Hospitals; all of which led to him being awarded the OBE. Although William had forsaken life in the country, the rustic pursuits of shooting, fishing and golf remained his favourite forms of relaxation, particularly the former. He was a crack shot, as witnessed by a collection of silverware won at Bisley. In 1889 he had married Laura, daughter of the Reverend L. Herschell and four years later, on 27 April 1893, their first child was born. Named William Roderick Herschell, though commonly known as Roy, this son was to become the father of Dick Hern, trainer of thoroughbred racehorses.

Educated at Rugby School, Roy Hern belonged to a generation that would make a fearful sacrifice for its country. Commissioned as a 2nd Lieutenant into the second line of the Glamorganshire Yeomanry on 29 October 1914, he got no closer to action than coastal defence duty in East Anglia until the grievous losses sustained by every unit in the British Army demanded that many officers of the home reserve be seconded to other regiments for active service. Sixty percent of Glamorganshire Yeomanry officers fought with other regiments. Roy Hern went to the South Notts Hussars, whose three squadrons of horse, numbering less than 350 men, were among the Allied forces pushed into Salonika during 1916 in another futile attempt to turn the German flank after the failure to do so at Gallipoli. The Germans referred to Salonika as their "largest internment camp" because it kept half a million Allied soldiers locked up without the trouble of taking them prisoner. The campaign was no more instrumental in bringing about the defeat of Germany than Gallipoli had been. The Regiment's greatest loss, however, came at the very moment of victory. On 27 May 1918 the troopship *Leasowe Castle* was sunk minutes after she cleared Alexandria harbour, claiming the lives of fifty-six Hussars *en route* to the western front. Fortunately for Mrs Winifred Hern her husband of seven months did not meet a watery grave.

Roy Hern and Winifred Mullens, both aged twenty-four, were married on 27 October 1917 in the village of Chedzoy, just outside Bridgwater in Somerset. Winifred was the daughter of a clergyman, as were her mother and her mother-in-law. Her father George performed the ceremony in St Mary's Church overlooking Sedgemoor where Monmouth's peasant army was so pitilessly crushed in 1685. In the cornfields south of the village scores of the Duke's fleeing supporters were hacked to pieces by royalist cavalry: a scene chronicled by Andrew Paschall, one of George Mullens's predecessors as rector. George Richard Mullens succeeded his uncle George Oakman Mullens in 1891. Between them uncle and nephew tended the Chedzoy flock for the best part of a century, from 1855 to 1940. Winifred's father was the archetypal Victorian cleric. Learned and monied, he owned two farms and employed butler, cook and gardener to maintain Chedzoy Rectory in the style of someone who saw his role as embracing both the spiritual and temporal needs of his parishioners. Mullens ensured that they met their spiritual responsibilities to God; by way of temporal reward he provided Chedzoy with a village hall. A black top hat crowning a six-foot frame lent physical credibility to the lofty opinion of him held by the villagers. His wife Ethel presented him with no less than seven daughters, but no son. As befitted vicar's daughters all seven were well-educated and well-mannered, not to mention well-heeled.

Roy Hern's 'wedding present' from the Army was his promotion to Captain. The newly-weds settled into Chedzoy Rectory where, almost a year after their marriage, on 5 October 1918, Winifred was delivered of a son, christened William John Roderick. Tragically, the baby boy died of acute laryngitis when he was only sixteen months old. However, within twelve months the Herns had a second son, born on 20 January 1921, whom they decided to name William Richard.

Shortly after William Richard was born – at Holford, ten miles or so the other side of Bridgwater on the road to Minehead – the Herns moved into Wick House, a farm nearer Bridgwater which William Hern had purchased for his son. Standing beside the lane from Stogursey to Stolford where it fords the Stogursey Brook, the property is one of half a dozen forming the hamlet of Wick. A large, stone structure of considerable age Wick House constituted the perfect residence for a gentleman farmer of leisurely inclinations.

In this evocatively described "forgotten corner of Somerset, and inscrutable, silent, fen-like wasteland", Dick Hern had little alternative but to grow up nurturing an air of mystique and an adoration of the countryside and its ways. Men are like plants: the goodness and flavour of the fruit proceeds from the peculiar soil in which they grow. To the west loomed the Quantocks where Wordsworth "roved unchecked or loitered 'mid her sylvan combes" during his sojourn at Alfoxton, and it was in Nether Stowey that his friend Coleridge composed that most enigmatic of poems "The Rime of the Ancient Mariner". Legend insists that strange sounds emanate from Wick Barrow, or Pixie's Mound as the locals refer to this alleged meeting place of 'the little people'.

Here, around Wick Barrow, on 200 acres of lush Somerset grass, Roy Hern lived the life of a gentleman, keeping hunters for his own pleasure and ponies for Dick and his two younger sons Rupert George (born in 1922) and Michael John Sydney (born in 1925). "I cannot remember being unable to ride," Dick Hern recalled during the course of an interview with John Rickman in 1978. "I think my father probably sat me on a pony before I could walk. He was the greatest influence on the course of my life. He instilled in me his own passionate love of horses." The sight of the Hern boys patrolling the byways with legs secured by ropes beneath their ponies' bellies was a familiar one to neighbours. By 1990 Wick House had undergone conversion to a nursery and garden centre, but the stables remain, as does the tack room whose wall still bears testimony to the lessons Roy Hern drilled into his sons. Two dozen rosettes recall successes at West Somerset Hunter Trials and Pony Club Gymkhanas and a certificate dated 4 August 1934 records Second Best Rider at the Lydford Show & Sports. Adorning the wall of a derelict privy is a large and beautifully detailed pencil drawing of a horse's head.

If Roy Hern was not the original 'hail-fellow-well-met', the description was coined with characters like him in mind. Even twenty years after his death tales of Roy Hern's escapades are legion in the villages around Bridgwater, and in their retelling have all but won the Cap'n, as he was known to the locals, a niche in Somerset folklore beside King Arthur and Judge Jeffries. There was the day he was observed riding a Jersey bull around his orchard purely for the devilment; the morning he reduced traffic in Bridgwater's North Street to a standstill when he abandoned his car in the middle of the road – engine running, naturally – so that he might deliver some eggs to a grocer; the afternoon he vaulted his hunter across the wide and treacherous Manor Rhine, otherwise referred to as the Black Ditch, for a bet. Fondly remembered as what the Edwardians used to call 'a card', he found it easier, by all accounts, to spend money than to accumulate it. Invariably resplendent in boots, breeches and trilby with a roguish twinkle in his eye and a word for all and sundry, he was every inch the retired cavalry officer. One picture from the old days still hanging in Wick House depicts a foxhunter in full cry and is entitled: "A good 'un to follow and a hard 'un to beat". This motto seems an apt comment on the challenge that faced Roy Hern's three sons. His was a dominating presence, a hard act for any son to follow and quite possibly a daunting prospect that discouraged any attempt. Allowing oneself to be overawed was the easier option. With the union of Roy Hern, cavalryman, gentleman farmer and horseman *par excellence*, and Winifred Mullens, the genteel, refined vicar's daughter, two elements fused: fire and ice. Who can say in what ratio they filled their sons' veins, but in the character and personality of Dick Hern both are self-evident.

Once proficient in the saddle, the next test for the Hern boys was the hunting field. Their father had long been a fanatic. Before the war he had hunted with the Quorn; after it his loyalties lay with the

West Somerset Foxhounds and the Bridgwater Harriers. For the latter he was very much a driving force, acting as Master between 1930 and 1932. They hunted fox and hare alternatively across territory stretching from the River Parrett to the River Brue. The Master enjoyed every minute of the chase. One December afternoon the hounds cornered and killed their fox in Sedgemoor Drain. Refusing to surrender the 'trophy' Hern swam the drain and just managed to secure the brush before it was swept away. He was a fearless rider and remained so all his life.

"He was a very brave horseman," remembers Jack Hosegood, who hunted alongside him with the West Somerset in the 1950s. "Well-built, ruddy-faced, strong-shouldered – a real goer with no nerves at all. He usually rode a goodish hunter which he had schooled at home and he would stand back, at the gallop, at some of the rhines – the drainage ditches – and cross from top to top rather than go down and across."

The Quantocks also offered staghunting which, unlike foxhunting, say those who know, "is a science". A traditional meeting place nearby was the Castle of Comfort at Over Stowey, where in 1797 the body of charcoal burner John Walford was hung in chains after his execution for the murder of his half-witted wife. All in all, Roy Hern and his sons could hunt four days a week during the season: Monday and Thursday with the Quantock Staghounds, Tuesday and Friday with the West Somerset Foxhounds.

"Youth is the Lord of Life, the one thing worth having," remarked Oscar Wilde. This idyllic Somerset lifestyle certainly made it so for Dick Hern. "That was a wonderful part of the world in which to live if you were keen on hunting. Not only could you go out in the autumn and winter but also in the spring and summer when there was staghunting. We used to go up into the Quantock Hills which we adored. I have marvellous memories of that very sporting part of England."

Shooting was also plentiful. When George Hern died in 1935 he had willed a gun to his great-nephew and on William Hern's death in 1939 all three brothers received some of their grandfather's guns and trophies (and his fishing rods). Most of William Hern's estate (£64,599 all told) was divided between Roy and his sister Eileen. By establishing a trust fund for Roy's future income and presenting him with Wick House, William Hern ensured the continuation of a carefree rustic existence not only for his son but also for his grandsons.

School can always be relied upon to invade Elysium. Dick was sent to Norfolk House in Beaconsfield, a preparatory school adjacent to his grandfather's home, Alfriston, at Knotty Green, doubtless protesting in the manner of Mr Jorrocks, "all time is lost wot is not spent in 'unting." Then, in September of 1935, he was despatched to Monmouth School, which faced Stogursey from the Celtic shore of the Bristol Channel. Founded in 1614 by William Jones, a Monmouth-born merchant of the City of London and a Liveryman of the Worshipful Company of Haberdashers, the school waiting to greet the 14-year-old Hern was nowhere near the size it is today. He was one of only eighty or ninety boarders – compared to 210 nowadays – and his house, New House, was one of just two – there are currently six. One of his contemporaries in New House, 'Dan' Daniels, describes the young Hern as: "A quiet, unremarkable boy who was well liked and who mixed easily with people. He was academically average or a bit above – he was on the 'A side' and did Greek."

Dick Hern lit no academic bonfires during his four years at Monmouth but two portentous beacons as to his future were evident. He frequently went riding at Troy Farm, on the outskirts of the town, which belonged to Will Coldicutt, a local Justice of the Peace and President of the Monmouth Show. Coldicutt maintained a stable of hunters and point-to-pointers and took the horse-mad schoolboy under his wing. In the Easter holidays of 1939 Dick Hern tasted the excitement of riding between the flags. On 8 April he had two mounts during the West Somerset & Quantock Hunts' fixture at Dytche. In the Hunts' Cup he was obliged to pull up his father's Happy Days III, but later in the afternoon he finished second on Mr C.T. Hutchings's Sheba Brown in the Farmers' & Members' Maiden. The following Saturday he partnered Happy Days III again (unplaced) at the rain-lashed Devon & Somerset Staghounds' meeting held on Exmoor.

Secondly, Hern was a committed member of Monmouth's Officers' Training Corp, listed in the school magazine as a lance-corporal. He had decided that the Army was to be his immediate career; more specifically, the Indian cavalry, which would accommodate his love of horses. Leaving Monmouth in the summer of 1939 he went to Millfield Tutorial College (as it was then called), where his father had been riding instructor since vacating a similar post at the Porlock Vale Riding School – an institution destined to play a not insignificant role in Dick Hern's own equestrian education.

Hern had barely begun cramming for the Sandhurst entry exams when war broke out and all arrangements were cancelled. He and a friend promptly borrowed the headmaster's car, drove to Bristol and enlisted. "They said we were OK because we had School Certificate and Certificate A which was a school Officers' Training Corps proficiency certificate. Of course, we thought we would be going off the next week but they told us that we would be on reserve. They didn't really want us till we were nineteen."

The callow youth was on the brink of vindicating Thomas Fuller's assertion that "A wild colt may become a sober horse."

Chapter Three

THE ARMY

'A fine officer and a natural leader of men'

> If you want to smell hell
> If you want to have fun
> If you want to catch the devil
> Join the cavalry.

THE CALL-TO-ARMS favoured by that charismatic Confederate cavalryman General J.E.B. Stuart was a clarion that Dick Hern was unable to answer in the autumn of 1939, but Roy Hern could, and did, respond to the call. He joined the North Somerset Yeomanry and can still be visualized standing in the centre of Weston-Super-Mare's rugby ground allocating horses to the troopers in his capacity as horsemaster and dispensing a word or two of advice about each animal to its new partner. Some of the mounts selected by Roy Hern participated in the last cavalry engagement in British military history, a skirmish with the Vichy French in Syria, before the regiment was dismounted in 1942. The Yeomanry sailed for the Middle East with the 1st Cavalry Division in February 1940. However, Roy Hern, 46 years old at the outbreak of hostilities, was invalided home and was aboard the *Empress of Britain* when she was attacked by German bombers sixty miles off the Irish coast on 26 October 1940. Set ablaze and subsequently finished off by a U-boat, the liner sank with the loss of forty-five lives. Roy Hern emerged hale and hearty.

His eldest son, meanwhile, kicked his heels back in Somerset, running the farm and using the hunting field to syphon off excess steam. Eventually he was assigned to the 55th Training Regiment at Farnborough and, on 11 October 1941, commissioned into the North Irish Horse, joining them at Westbury on Salisbury Plain. The North Irish Horse was a comparatively young regiment. Originally raised in 1902 as the North of Ireland Imperial Yeomanry, it assumed the present title three years afterwards and bore it with distinction throughout World War I, from Mons to Cambrai, winning forty-seven decorations including a Victoria Cross. Dismounted in 1917 and disembodied after Versailles, the North Irish Horse was reconstituted as a light armoured regiment of the Supplementary Reserve at the start of World War II. Its battle role had been upgraded from armoured cars to tanks – the new Churchill variety – by the time Dick Hern arrived in late 1941.

Following intensive training in Wiltshire, an anti-invasion function was undertaken in East Anglia and Hern had to tolerate the same sort of frustrating 'phoney' war that his father endured with the Glamorganshire Yeomanry. However infuriating, the delay helped forge a valuable camaraderie among the raw recruits who, contrary to the regiment's Ulster origins, came from all over Britain. Michael Pope, son of a West End estate agent, was gazetted to the North Irish Horse a month after Dick Hern and the two became firm friends, "I never wanted to do anything else but horses. I was hunting and point-to-point mad and at the age of eighteen went to Robin Reed at West Ilsley as a pupil trainer. When war broke out I joined the Royal Horse Guards as a trooper – they still had horses – and then, on the advice of David Dawnay, who was later Clerk of the Course at Ascot, joined his regiment, the North Irish Horse." John Behr, on the other hand, had been a trooper in the City of Londonderry Yeomanry prior to switching allegiance. He first clapped eyes on the rather gangly, gaunt-faced figure of Dick Hern in the mess hall at Thetford. Any notions of a soldier existing on a starvation diet soon proved illusory. "We were queuing up for the hot lunch, a stew. A dollop on each plate and help yourself to potatoes. My first memory of Dick was of this chap who put fourteen new potatoes on his plate. I'd never seen anyone eat so many in my life! He always has been a great nosher!"

After two months beet-pulling in the fields round Wickham Market the NIH was celebrating Christmas 1942 when it was ordered to

North Africa. Under the command of Lieutenant-Colonel David Dawnay the regiment sailed out of Liverpool in the SS *Duchess of York* on 22 January 1943 and arrived in Phillipville, via Algiers, on 5 February, where it became part of the 1st Army, whose task was to link up with the 8th Army and squeeze the enemy out of North Africa. The NIH immediately marched to the sound of the guns. During Rommel's "Fruhlingswind" offensive, designed to breach the Allied lines by forcing the Kasserine Gap and driving on northwards to Bone, a strong German attack with tanks had been launched against Sidi Nsir, some sixty miles west of Tunis. This thrust posed a grave threat to the British positions at Hunt's Gap. If the Germans succeeded in forcing the Gap their armour could sweep on through rolling terrain and take the key town of Beja, necessitating the withdrawal of the Allied line by up to fifty miles. The North Irish Horse was given the task of defending Beja.

Dick Hern's Churchill was in A Squadron which occupied "The Loop", the nub of the town's defences. At first light on 28 February his squadron leader's tank was hit by an anti-tank gun, killing two of its crew and badly wounding its commander. Regimental policy was for all seconds-in-command to be kept out of the front line. Accordingly, Captain Robin Griffith was back in Beja. In this moment of crisis for an untried and untested body of men command devolved for the time being upon Lieutenant W.R. Hern. Nearly 100 men – eighteen tanks with five men in each – were depending on Dick Hern. It was only thirty-nine days since he had celebrated his 22nd birthday. Yet meeting this onerous responsibility he acquitted himself splendidly until relieved later that morning.

In the afternoon enemy activity increased as their tanks constantly manoeuvred for an opening. Hern was itching for some action. Robin Griffith recalls the scene:

> We were in a very good defensive position. There was very little need for us to do anything, except wait for the Germans to come over a ridge in front of us, when we could have decimated them. Of course, this can seem a rather boring activity, though basically and tactically sound in that situation. Since we appeared to be doing very little Dick Hern came over to my tank and said something like, 'Griff – the Colonel is always telling us to show initiative. I think that we should get up on the ridge and have a shot at a German tank.' I was a bit doubtful,

this being the very first battle situation we had been in, but agreed that he could try if he wished. I said that I would adjust the position of my tank, which happened to have a 3″ mortar mounted in the driver's compartment, so that I could drop smoke in front of him should he get into trouble. Of course, I should never have agreed. The Germans were waiting. They probably saw the aerial moving up. However, they were stupid to fire when they only had the top of the turret to engage. Their shot bounced off.

Hern was struck by a ricochet and wounded in the back of the neck, though not before he had taken his pot-shot at a Mark VI tank and holed it through the turret.

Hern was immediately evacuated. The North Irish Horse remained in the Beja sector, holding firm, until the 6 April offensive directed at a number of strategical highpoints such as Mergueb Chaouach and 'Longstop Hill'. On 9 April Hern was back in command of two troops (six tanks) during a fierce counter-attack at Chaouach, and on the 22nd A Squadron supported the infantry assault on the western flanks of Longstop. The Germans, astounded at tanks being deployed on this high ground, were suitably demoralized. By the 26th Longstop had fallen. The final push toward Tunis began at 4.30 am on 6 May and within two days tanks of the North Irish Horse rumbled through the city with the enemy in disarray. A quarter of a million German and Italian troops were captured.

From the successful completion of the Tunisian campaign until late March 1944 the North Irish Horse remained in North Africa, near Bone, awaiting further orders. On 7 April the regiment began shipping to Italy where its initial assignment on 23 May was to support the 1st Canadian Infantry division in a frontal attack on the Hitler Line around Monte Cassino, one of the strongest defensive positions ever conceived. The defences included anti-tank and machine gun emplacements of steel and concrete combined with tactically laid minefields and wire to draw the tanks into specially cleared 'killing fields' amidst the dense woodland. The Line was pierced but at considerable cost, particularly to the Canadians who sustained 1,000 casualties. In that single day the North Irish Horse lost twenty-five tanks and thirty-four men – more than the entire Tunisian campaign. Two of Hern's tanks in 4 Troop A Squadron were immobilized in the attack near Forme d'Aquino and two of his men killed. In appreciation of the support they received, the Canadians asked the NIH to wear the Maple Leaf.

Hern was promoted to Captain and put in command of B Squadron Echelon. An echelon's importance cannot be overestimated. Its responsibility lay in nightly replenishment of petrol, ammunition, lubricants and rations to the lead tanks. Hern warmed to his new task, which was just as well, because on occasion it got very hot indeed. On 3 September, while accompanying the 1st-4th Hamps in an attack on the Gothic Line near Pesaro, his tank was fired on by self-propelled guns and received a direct hit. All the crew were wounded except Hern. A month later, during torrential rain on the night of 7–8 October, Hern experienced, as the Regimental Battle Report phrases it, "a very warm time getting his jeeps and trailers through some very heavy harassing fire" at Monte Farneto. Continuous rain and harsh terrain hindered progress but the forward tanks were always replenished every night thanks to the sterling work of Hern's echelon and Captain R.H. Bowring's A Squadron equivalent. Finally, having been relieved by the 12th Battalion Royal Tank Regiment at the beginning of December, the NIH took a thoroughly deserved rest at Riccione. The stuffing had been knocked out of the enemy and subsequent fighting was far less exhausting. On 23 April the regiment was the first 8th Army unit to reach the River Po; hostilities in Italy largely ceased and, a week later, the order to stand down was given.

The officers and men of the North Irish Horse had come through with flying colours; none more so than Dick Hern. The "wild colt" had come of age. Regimental Padre Captain Elwyn Hughes was in a wonderful position to witness this transformation.

> Dick Hern matured in times of stress into a fine officer and a natural leader of men, without any fuss or arrogance, just by being himself. The word 'morale' is bandied about a great deal these days but I know that it is the key to survival of any community and I know that Dick Hern in his way contributed positively to the morale of the men under his command. He was friendly and unassuming. Although our backgrounds were different and we literally spoke different languages, we were both countrymen, and he and I shared a common interest, namely a love for the poems of John Masefield, not a fashionable poet even then, but we could quote passages from the Everlasting Mercy,

Sea Fever, Ark Royal and, of course, Reynard the Fox or The Ghost Heath Run.

However traumatic, the experience of war failed to obliterate Hern's idea of life's priorities. Hughes relates: "We were in the Officers' Mess at Rimini listening to the General Election results as they came through on the radio, one Labour gain after another, and suddenly Dick, unable to restrain himself, exclaimed loudly, 'I know very well what the buggers will do, they'll stop foxhunting'."

Scores of racing folk might detect something of the latter day Dick Hern in that anecdote, as they would in John Behr's recollection of a week's leave in Hern's company. "Dick and I went to Amalfi or Positano, I can't remember which. We stayed in a small, luxury hotel next door to the house where the King of Italy was living. We walked into the hotel bar, which was empty, and Dick said to the little barman, 'A glass of sherry and a thin captain.' Of course, the barman hadn't a clue what he was talking about – he didn't know a captain was a biscuit. Well, Dick started shouting at him and the little Italian was petrified. Dick was a hard man; very hard on himself, his horses and other people. He was absolutely meticulous – the Army probably developed him there – but he loved a joke, the ruder the better."

While the North Irish Horse was recuperating at Riccione in December 1944 they received an unlikely Christmas present from the departing King's Dragoon Guards in the form of ten horses, which not only gave incalculable pleasure to officers like Hern and Pope who missed their hunting and racing but also opened up all sorts of possibilities for the near future. South of the Po many more horses – abandoned by a pack transport unit – were acquired, and at Ravenna there was a trotting track which, though badly shelled, could be made raceable with a little ingenuity and much elbow grease. Hern, Michael Pope, and his brother Barry, were put in charge of the project by Tony Llewellen-Palmer, another racing enthusiast, who now commanded the regiment.

"First of all we had to clear the mines," Hern recalled years afterwards. "We got the German prisoners out of the cage to do that. We filled in the shell holes and harrowed the ground. It was in fact quite a passable dirt track, four furlongs round. The stands were already there." Hern and the Popes eventually rounded up over 100 horses, which included some ex-racehorses, a German show jumper (White Cloud) and a grey mare from the King of Italy's stables called Farina that was rumoured to have been Mussolini's personal hack. The string was stabled at Rimini, where Hern and Michael Pope trained them on the seemingly endless stretches of hard sand. "I can remember riding out at 4.30 in the morning," says John Behr, "and doing three lots before breakfast. My main job, however, was to go to Bologna and get the racecards printed – in green naturally. You can imagine what it was like trying to explain all this in Italian. We drew enormous crowds of Italians, all waving these big pink 500 lire notes, eager to bet."

On 12 July 1945 Ravenna staged its first Army Race Meeting. David Dawnay (by then a Brigadier) was Senior Steward; the opening race on the card, the Fairyhouse Maiden Chase over $1\frac{1}{2}$ miles and worth all of 1,000 lire in Allied Military Currency (about £5), was won by Michael Pope riding Red Sails from Dick Hern on Birdcatcher. Pope reminisces: "The NIH organized a Tote and the proceeds went to the regiment's benevolent fund but after three or four meetings some of the operators found a way of milking the till and a loss was made, much to the horror of the brass-hats."

The North Irish Horse was demobilized in June 1946. For Dick Hern, as with all his brother officers, the joys of peace were tempered by the realization that a civilian career had now to be carved out of next to nothing. He may have left the regiment with the rank of Major but he also departed with a sense of loss. The North Irish Horse had been his family for nearly five years. It provided a close community and a warm atmosphere that would be difficult to rediscover outside the military. Hern knew one thing: he wanted to work with horses. Before the war Roy Hern had worked as an instructor at the Porlock Vale Riding School run by Tony Collings, with whom he later served in the North Somerset Yeomanry. What more sensible and logical step could his recently demobilized son take than to enroll on one of Porlock's courses and acquire an instructor's certificate?

Chapter Four

SORCERER'S APPRENTICE

'His strength was his great horsemanship'

THE AIMS OF THE Porlock Vale Riding School were to impart instruction in equitation, training the young horse and stable management along the most modern and scientific lines. A three-month course led to the British Horse Society's Preliminary Examination; there were also numerous short courses dealing with topics such as dressage or children's riding, and specialist courses like hunting. To this end, Porlock possessed three covered schools, three junior paddocks complete with every type of fence, a lecture room and a theatre.

Satisfying the Porlock examiners involved no undue strain for a horseman of Hern's proven calibre. The result was that Tony Collings requested he stay on as an instructor. To Hern the benefits of this move were twofold. First, he came under the influence of a supreme equestrian; secondly, living at Porlock provided access to a society of like-minded individuals which rekindled the corporate identity he had enjoyed in the Army.

Joseph Anthony Collings descended – like Hern himself – from a long line of West Country yeomen. The family business dated from 1826 when his grandfather began leasing harness horses and carriages in Exeter. By World War I Tony Collings's father, J.C., had expanded the firm's scope to include the provision of hunters for the tourists who were now flocking to Exmoor – "the riding playground of England," in the words of Cecil Aldin. The uninitiated also needed tuition, so in 1931 J.C. Collings welcomed the first visitors to his

Riding School at Porlockford House that would soon win inter-national acclaim. Tony Collings picked up the reins after the war. A man, according to *The Times*, "possessed of a personal charm that was almost a handicap," Collings had demonstrated his prowess in every aspect of equitation: eventing, showing, point-to-pointing, polo and hunting (he had ridden with no less than fifty different packs) – it was all the same to Collings. "Through sheer personality," said *Horse and Hound*, "Tony Collings built the reputation of the Porlock Vale Riding School until it became recognized as one of the leading establishments of its kind in this country – indeed in the world." Moreover, Collings was a sportsman in the noblest sense of the term who "could take the hard knocks of life and still come up smiling." Once he started preparing top-class eventers for inter-national competition he also appreciated the importance of owners. Without their co-operation and financial support he and his riders were out on a limb. All of these traits could not fail to leave their mark on as willing, able and enthusiastic a pupil as Dick Hern.

Set in a green bowl presided over by the brooding Dunkery Beacon, Porlock has always bewitched its visitors. "Thy verdant vale so fair to sight," penned Robert Southey in 1799 as he sat in The Ship Inn, and finding someone who came into contact with Porlock Vale Riding School, whether employee or trainee, who did not thoroughly enjoy the experience proves a fruitless exercise. Bertie Hill's abiding memory is typical: "Porlock had such a happy atmosphere – I've known nothing like it since." The *Horse and Hound* correspondent who came down to Somerset in 1951 was likewise smitten: "One of the things which strikes the visitor forcibly is the happy atmosphere of the place – that and the smoothness with which each part of the establishment runs. The organization of each section is planned to the n'th degree and the stable management, instruction and administration sides are all kept as separate departments, run on very business-like lines. No haphazardness here – the Army might be proud of such organization; but the Army would lack the personal touch which is so very evident at Porlock."

Free at last from the heavy burdens of war, Hern's generation seized the brief opportunity to compensate for the lost years. With its tomfoolery, beach parties, dash of romance and wanton indulgence in a whole host of hedonistic pursuits, Porlock represented paradise for any horse lover with a sense of fun; a description which, however implausible it may seem forty years later, fitted 26-year-old Dick Hern like a glove. The famous Hern temper, which would one day cause pressmen to quake in their boots, occasionally boiled over, yet there was no mistaking the fact that this consummate horseman possessed a cut to his jib which at one and the same time made him a respected and attractive figure, especially as the majority of pupils – and staff – were young women.

Hern remained at Porlock as chief instructor until 1952. In this five-year period he emulated Collings by excelling in almost every conceivable facet of equine activity. Eventing, point-to-pointing and a new craze, polo crosse, were the most prominent. Closest to his heart was point-to-pointing, to which he began to devote far more of his energies: besides riding he was Honorary Secretary of the Devon & Somerset Staghounds' Point-to-Point Committee from 1948 to 1950. During his years at Porlock, Hern partnered nine winners between the flags, nearly all of them horses owned by him (Top of the Wave, Jubilee Star) or by Tony Collings (Operatic) and his partner Captain C.D. Leyland (Shanrahan, First of June). "Dick Hern was a wonderful horseman," enthuses Bertie Hill, who as the *enfant terrible* of the West Country point-to-point circuit immediately after the war (sixty-eight winners) enjoyed many a tussle with Hern. "His strength was his great horsemanship. He could ride different horses and all would go for him. And Tony Collings backed him all the way."

Hern's classiest mount was unquestionably Shanrahan. In 1949 they won three races together: the Minehead Harriers' Members' & Farmers' at Holnicote by a distance on 6 April; the Adjacent Hunts' Moderate at the West Somerset's Nether Stowey meeting on 16 April (Mary Trinket's victory in the Morse Code Cup gave Hern a memorable double that day); and finally, on 14 May, another triumph by a distance at Holnicote in the Members' Race of the Devon & Somerset Staghounds.

Betwixt and between the point-to-pointing and the inevitable hunting Hern threw himself with considerable gusto into the new sport of polo crosse. Originating at riding schools as a cheaper indoor version of its more prestigious cousin it was, as the name implied, a mixture of polo and lacrosse. The six players per side each carried a stick with a basket on the end which they used to pick up and hurl a sorbo rubber ball. Somerset was the game's heartland. Porlock,

Taunton, Chard and Millfield were the principal exponents. At the age of fifty-six a sprightly Roy Hern expressed his lifelong zest for polo by turning out for Millfield Tutorial College, where he was building up the riding branch. His side was no match for Porlock in the Grey Sky Challenge Cup fought out during the summer of 1949, losing the final 14–1. However, father and son joined forces in the Porlock team which beat Taunton 8–6 in the Founders Cup.

Despite these competitions polo crosse was light-hearted fun compared to the rigours of Badminton and the eventing circuit. Badminton's Horse Trials sprang from the wound inflicted on national pride at the 1948 Olympics when the home team was eliminated during the cross-country phase. "With our hunting background this is a sport at which Britain should excel," argued the Duke of Beaufort. He would provide the venue. Could the competition unearth three riders to win the 1952 Olympic gold medal? The inaugural competition of 1949 was won by Golden Willow, whose rider John Sheddon hailed from the Cotswold Equitation School. Tony Collings, on Remus, had led after the dressage. With Porlock's pride at stake, the partnership returned in 1950 and made amends. Hern also competed, on King Willow, a brown gelding belonging to Millfield. Although only finishing eleventh overall they attracted plenty of attention. Having given, according to *Horse and Hound*, "one of the several outstanding displays in the dressage they completed the cross-country in an astonishing time considering that King Willow fell at the penultimate fence, pulling off his bridle." Hern remounted and, riding on with both reins flopping on one side of the horse's neck, somehow contrived to finish without time penalties.

As Badminton proved so popular, one-day events featuring shortened versions of the Badminton tests began to appear round the country. In October 1950 Hern took a promising animal called Starlight XV to a competition at Guisburn Park, the Lancashire home of Reg Hindley, one of Britain's leading eventers. Starlight was bred to be a racehorse and looked the part, but he possessed a devilishly fiery temperament: at the 1952 Helsinki Olympics, he chased the visiting Duke of Edinburgh out of his box. Nevertheless, Hern's win at Guisburn on Starlight gave the horse a firm nudge up the ladder of success which ultimately led to an individual gold medal at the 1953 European Championships in the hands of Major

31

Laurence Rook. A month before Badminton in 1951 Hern partnered Starlight at Larkhill's one-day event. After steering this volatile customer through a surprisingly good dressage which put them up with the leaders, he urged Starlight to the fastest time in cross-country. Unfortunately, they had taken a wrong turning and were automatically disqualified! Lieutenant-Colonel D.N. Stewart was given the mount at Badminton; Hern rode Tollbridge, on whom he had clocked the fastest steeplechase at Larkhill, finishing sixth overall. Neither of them troubled Vae Victis, however. Starlight was eleventh and Tollbridge did not appear for the final day's show jumping.

As professional riding instructors Hern and Collings were not eligible for Olympic selection, but it was decided that those who were shortlisted for the team should undergo six months' intensive training at Porlock during the winter and spring of 1951–2. In October eleven horses (including Starlight) and six riders (including Bertie Hill) were installed at Porlock. They concentrated on dressage, thought likely to be their toughest hurdle, culminating with two hours a day under Richard Waetjen, the German Olympic trainer, who arrived in February. Hern assisted Collings with timing and tempo over the chasing and cross-country phases. In addition, he acted as unofficial father-confessor and orchestrated the necessary light relief, entailing 'jollies' across the marshes and sing-songs in The Ship. Four months' hard work elicited sufficient progress to persuade the *Horse and Hound* correspondent that "they are all better horsemen now than when they came to Porlock." At Badminton the string gave an impressive parade and exhibition, but with the Games so close each horse competed only in those phases deemed beneficial to the development of his own individual Olympic requirements.

Dick Hern did participate, on Miss M. Roberts's Fitz. On day one they accomplished "a good test with good cadence" to put themselves in fourth place, but a fall at the fences into and out of Luckington Lane cost them dear on the cross-country and they picked up 130 penalty points. This was a great pity because Fitz jumped a clear round in the arena on the third afternoon, to come ninth overall. The duo also competed at Sherborne Park's one-day event. Again, travelling sweetly across country misfortune struck when Hern passed the wrong side of a direction flag.

By a strange coincidence Britain's chance of Olympic medals at Helsinki was thwarted by exactly the same sort of incident. With themselves in the gold medal position and the team in silver, Laurence Rook and Starlight put a foot into a small irrigation ditch towards the end of the speed and endurance phase and suffered a crashing fall. Badly concussed, Rook remounted and finished the course. However, in his confusion after briefly losing consciousness, he rode to the wrong side of some markers, thereby eliminating himself and the whole team. This was a cruel blow after so much dedicated preparation. Nonetheless, the framework for eventual success was established. At the following April's European Championships the team (with Bertie Hill on Bambi V) won the gold and the Rook-Starlight combination landed the individual title, while Hill was a member of the team which finally collected that elusive Olympic gold medal in 1956.

"Tony Collings and Dick Hern did so much that has not been printed for this country's eventing," says Bertie Hill. "They were a great team, it was always a tremendous team effort, and it was an education to have been at Porlock with them. It was very sad Tony Collings didn't live to see Dick Hern's triumphs as a trainer because he'd always supported him in his point-to-pointing. I had no idea Dick would become a major trainer, which I'm thrilled about. He was such a good instructor I thought he'd make his life out of it."

As Hill's final remarks imply, the partnership between Tony Collings and Dick Hern ended before the 1956 Olympics. That Hern should judge the 1952 Games as an apt moment to move on was understandable, but Collings's death in an air crash on 8 April 1954 was nothing short of a tragedy. Collings was aboard a BOAC Comet bound for Johannesburg, where he was to officiate at a show, when it crashed into the Mediterranean thirty minutes after taking off from Rome, killing all twenty-one passengers and crew. BOAC's fleet of Comets had only recently resumed service in the wake of a two-month investigation into their air worthiness precipitated by a crash in January in which thirty-five people perished. The horse world was grief-stricken. *Horse and Hound* printed a whole page of tributes. "His loss to British equitation is incalculable," it concluded.

Hern read the news as he anticipated his second season as assistant trainer to Michael Pope. "Towards the end of the war in Italy – over many, many grogs – we decided that when we returned to England

I should set myself up as a trainer and he could be my assistant,"
Pope later recalled. "He was a great help to me as my assistant for
five years." Having started with two tubed chasers in 1947, Pope
now handled a small string of jumpers and flat-race horses from
Steve Donoghue's old yard in Blewbury. His previous assistant, his
brother Barry, wanted to farm so, slightly later than planned, the
Italian plot came to fruition. "We didn't look on it as an industry
then, it was a sport. I had the luck to train only for personal friends.
They were sportsmen, they had plenty of money, we all got on
frantically well and we drank champagne whether we lost or won."
Naturally there was the occasional 'punt' that demanded absolute
secrecy, like the day Hern hid in a gaff-track latrine for half an hour
to stop himself from telling friends about the one they had laid out
for the seller. Pope could not teach Hern much about horses, but the
five years between 1952 and 1957 afforded the priceless opportunity
to familiarize himself with racing stable routine and to negotiate
the rudiments of entries, forfeits and the maze that is the Racing
Calendar.

Pope's horses were not top class, so there were no classic horses
on which Hern could cut his teeth. Some were decent handicappers,
however. Luxury Hotel won Epsom's Great Met in 1954 and Blason
was a useful sprinter, even though Timeform described him as "a
pansy of a horse." More importantly, Pope had a doughty chaser
called Sir John IV that Hern was able to ride under NH Rules. Hern
had plenty of point-to-point experience. Indeed, he won four more
races whilst with Pope – at Tweseldown and Lockinge in 1953,
Tweseldown again in 1954 and Mottisfort in 1955 – raising his career
total to thirteen. However, he had never actually won a 'proper'
steeplechase. Sir John IV was the perfect vehicle with which to
achieve that ambition. Owned by Edwin McAlpine, he was an
imposing bay of regal breeding, a half-brother to triple Champion
Hurdler Sir Ken. Prior to the 1954–55 season Sir John had won six
of his thirty-five races. Hern rode him for the first time in a race at
Huntingdon on 16 October 1954. Having already opened his seasonal
account at Ludlow, the six-year-old was a 4/1 second favourite to
win the Ermine Street Hunter Chase over 3 miles 200 yards and
worth all of £136. Conditions were atrocious but family rivalry
insisted he win because Sir Ken had landed the Cambridgeshire
Hurdle half an hour earlier. Arthur Freeman on Southern King tried

to make all the running and looked like doing so as he saw off Firkins, the favourite, and Mont St Michel two fences out. Then, as Tom Nickalls informed *Sporting Life* readers, "Major W.R. Hern, who had been riding a patient and well-judged race, brought Sir John IV along with a strong run and in the end was not all out to win fairly comfortably. The winner still had a summer coat and was carrying a mass of muscle while his mane and tail had been plaited by an expert." Sixteen days later the combination struck again in Stratford's three-mile Campden Handicap Chase. At Huntingdon Hern had bested one leading rider, Grand National winner Arthur Freeman; now he got the better of five times champion jockey Tim Molony. Hern partnered Sir John on four further occasions, the last (finishing second) at Taunton on 17 September 1955, his ninth and final ride under Rules. The gallant Sir John raced on till he was fourteen. For Dick Hern, on the other hand, competing in steeplechases or even point-to-points increasingly became out of the question. After all, he had a wife to consider.

Most of Sheilah Davis's family were tea planters: she was born in Assam, but came to England to be brought up by her grandparents who lived in Petersfield. During the war she drove trucks as a WASBI in Burma. "I had known her since the Porlock days," Hern told John Rickman. "She came on a course there and stayed on to do secretarial work." It is not too wide of the mark to state that in wedding Porlock's chief instructor Sheilah Davis became the envy of the school's entire female workforce. The couple were married on 9 October 1956 at Christ Church, Mayfair. A woman of some substance, Sheilah Hern was to prove a staunch ally to her husband once she became a trainer's wife. Like most of that ilk she assumed responsibility for entertaining owners and supervising staff welfare, as well as the perennial chore of chauffeuring her husband to and from race meetings.

Hern's days as an assistant were indeed numbered. "I wanted to train jumpers at that time," he has often recalled. His mind was changed by a snippet of news carried by the Racing Press in the summer of 1957. Major Lionel Holliday, one of the country's foremost owner-breeders, had parted company with the latest in an ever lengthening list of trainers to his private string. "I thought, 'Well, there's no harm in applying for the job.' I had no capital and this was the only way I could see myself setting up as a trainer except on a very small scale.'' Hern was invited up to Holliday's estate, Copgrove Hall, near Harrogate, for interview.

Chapter Five

LAGRANGE

'Heil Holliday'

MAJOR LIONEL BROOK HOLLIDAY epitomized that breed of Yorkshireman revered by his fellow Tykes yet, at best, only grudgingly respected beyond the county borders. The muck from which Holliday made his brass was the manufacture of aniline dyes. His manner tended to be just as earthy, running the entire gamut from cantankerous to downright rude. The word compromise had apparently been expunged from Holliday's lexicon at an early age, and he gloried in the social notoriety his antagonistic behaviour inevitably created. One trainer was even alleged to have muttered darkly: "When he dies, they needn't say, 'No Flowers, By Request' because there won't be any bleeding flowers." Another used to acknowledge him with a raised-arm salute of "Heil Holliday".

In such fertile humus resentment flourished. Despite his distinguished record on the Turf he was not elected to the Jockey Club until he was over eighty. "I suppose he had this very brusque manner which upset a lot of people and he wasn't a good mixer – he never liked mixing," said Humphrey Cottrill, Hern's predecessor. "It wasn't that he wanted to train them himself, it was just that he was awkward in some extraordinary way and that whatever you did it would never be right. If you won it wasn't right and if you didn't win it wasn't right. You could never satisfy him."

Employees came and went in rapid succession. Stable-jockey Stan Clayton was retained on no less than eleven separate occasions. Legend records the following exchange taking place between one of

Holliday's incoming trainers and the removal man.

Trainer: "Do you think this house is damp? I've got some nice bits of furniture and I don't want them to come to any harm."

Removal Man: "Don't worry, guv. They won't be here long enough."

Holliday was unperturbed. "They all come to me on bicycles and leave in Bentleys," he once observed sourly.

It goes without saying that there was appreciably more to Holliday than an utter disregard for life's social niceties. The wag (allegedly Bob Colling, one of his countless trainers) who said "There must be real good in a man who is such a wonderful judge of a foxhound" came close to the heart of the matter. Those subjects Holliday knew he knew inside out. Besides foxhunting – he was a MFH from 1918 to 1937 – these subjects included the breeding of thoroughbred racehorses. His activities with bloodstock commenced in 1914 with the acquisition of the Cleaboy Stud in County Westmeath, to which he later added the Sandwich Stud at Newmarket and the Copgrove Hall Stud near Harrogate.

The astute purchase which effectively triggered Holliday's fortunes came in December 1936 when he paid 4,000 guineas for a five-year-old bay mare, by Solario out of Orlass, called Lost Soul. Though she had only won a couple of minor races Lost Soul was destined to become the linch pin of his breeding empire. Her offspring won thirty-one races and, more importantly, included several daughters who themselves became influential broodmares. The most notable of these matrons was Phase. Her first foal, Netherton Maid, by the unbeaten Italian champion Nearco much admired by Holliday, was second in the 1947 Oaks. Four years later a full sister, Neasham Belle, went one better, while full brother Narrator won the Champion Stakes and Coronation Cup. Although Holliday was leading breeder in 1954 and leading owner and breeder in 1956, the 1951 Oaks was his lone classic success.

Neasham Belle was trained by Geoffrey Brooke, the first of Holliday's private trainers installed at Lagrange Stables, between Newmarket's Fordham and Snailwell roads. Built in 1880 by Tom Jennings Sr. with deep red bricks from his own kiln at Cockfield, it was named in honour of Comte Frederic de Lagrange, whose patronage resulted in the Triple Crown winner Gladiateur being handled by Jennings. Lagrange had been a private stable in the 1920s and

30s when it accommodated Lord Glanely's string. Among the good horses trained by Captain Tommy Hogg were the classic winners Rose of England (Oaks), Singapore (St Leger), Colombo (2000 Guineas) and Chumleigh (St Leger).

Brooke left Holliday's employ in the middle of the 1952 season and was immediately substituted with Humphrey Cottrill, who lasted till 1957. "I never really fell out with him," Cottrill explained, "I just got the sack. In 1956 I was third on the list of leading trainers and he was leading owner and leading breeder." This, then, was the mercurial 77-year-old potential master who awaited Dick Hern at Copgrove Hall in the summer of 1957.

"I went on my own. He did not really want to know about a trainer's wife. Much to my surprise I got the job." On 27 September the front page of the *Sporting Chronicle* declared: "Big changes at HQ". To some who reckoned they understood Holliday the appointment was less of a surprise. The old man, they chorused, believed anyone vaguely knowing their job could succeed with the horses he was breeding. What's more, he wouldn't feel constrained to pay a comparatively inexperienced man such a high salary.

Cynicism aside, Holliday and Hern were kindred spirits in some respects. An Army background and love of foxhunting yielded common ground over which two men not particularly well versed in the art of trivial conversation could develop lines of communication. If Holliday's invective became too intolerable Hern could always keep Holliday on his deaf side. "Apart from horses we used to talk about hunting, stories of when he was Master of Foxhounds, particularly of the Derwent, the Badsworth and the Grove."

Nevertheless, within the parochial waters of Newmarket's training fraternity – a brace of Jarvises, Leaders and Waughs typifying the predominance of numerous long-established families – few expected Hern's stay to be as long or as successful as it turned out to be. Ryan Jarvis's greeting to his new neighbour passed straight into Newmarket folklore. "Good morning, Dick," said Jarvis the first day they met (according to Jarvis on the Heath, not outside his yard as interminable retellings have insisted), "I suppose you have brought your toothbrush. It's all you will need."

With Holliday unwell for much of December 1957 his new trainer set about capitalizing on the unexpected freedom to acquaint himself with his new surroundings. Appreciating the various Newmarket gallops, assessing the amount of work the horses would need (more than was customary on the stiff Berkshire downland) and coming to terms with having to queue for use of the training grounds were uppermost among Hern's priorities. In achieving these ends, the assistance of stable-jockey Stan Clayton and head-lad Jim Meaney was paramount. Meaney was rumoured to possess a hot-line direct to Holliday which he frequently used. By the time *The Sporting Life*'s correspondent paid a visit to Lagrange Hern had overcome any initial hiccups. "Already giving evidence of the authentic touch in handling a 49-strong lot," wrote Warren Hill on 1 January, "he must be about the most unassuming and, delightfully, the most modest individual in racing." Three months later, on the eve of the new season, Warren Hill went further. Under the title, "Powerful Team at Lagrange – New Trainer can make a good start", he waxed lyrical:

> Britain's best cavalry regiments were founded on what is called 'esprit de cocarde', an almost untranslatable precept signifying worthiness and high bearing which exerts an intangible but potent influence in fostering pride and prestige. Always a similar spirit animates a successful racing stable. The smartness and the perky air of efficiency about the staff at Lagrange mirror the knowledge and background of a master with a capital success record in point-to-point and NH riding and first lieutenant to the late Captain Tony Collings, contributing to the building of the country's crack Olympic Three-Day Event team of 1952.

Two exceptionally cold spells in early March handicapped Hern's preparations for the coming season. However, as the Lagrange representatives – invariably first out on the exercise grounds – limbered up on Southfield, Waterhall and Warren Hill, the latter's journalistic namesake was quick to spot "a pert and fit Petition colt who has been working thoroughly and stylishly for some time" with whom Hern aimed to win the Brocklesby Stakes at Lincoln on the second day of the season. The colt in question was Plaudit, a rare bird in the Holliday coop, in that he was bought as a foal for 1,050 guineas at public auction. The policy adopted with every runner carrying the 'white, maroon hoop and cap' colours was simple: they were ridden to win and if they couldn't win, they had to do their utmost to secure a place. No exception was made for two-year-olds having their first outings.

Later in their association Hern once sent Holliday a telegrammed race report which read: "Ran well. Needed race badly." On his next visit to Copgrove Hern was politely taken aside by the butler, who said, "I should not use that expression again if I were you. The Major nearly went through the ceiling." There were no mistakes with Plaudit. On 15 March, opined Old Rowley of the *Sporting Chronicle*, "he could not have moved better and he will be very hard to beat. Practically everyone in Newmarket is bursting with enthusiasm over this colt's chances in the Brocklesby. After seeing this and several other gallops Plaudit has done I do not think their optimism is misplaced."

On a typically misty Lincoln afternoon Plaudit went to post a 13/8 favourite to repeat Holliday's Brocklesby victory of the previous year. Stan Clayton had the hard, well-muscled little bay out of the gate like a flash and they soon established a healthy lead. While the other newcomers showed their inexperience and immaturity by wandering off a true line under pressure, Plaudit ran home as straight as a gun barrel to give Hern his first winner – by three lengths – with his very first runner.

Plaudit was the forerunner of 184 winners that Hern trained for Holliday during their five seasons together. The forty successes of 1958 worth £41,265 gained Hern fifth place in the trainers' table and Holliday third place in the list of owners behind John McShain (of Ballymoss and Gladness fame) and the Queen. Holliday was also second in the list of breeders to the breeder of Ballymoss. One year later the statistics were equally impressive: forty-one victories placing Hern and Holliday seventh and fifth respectively. After a disappointing total of twenty-seven in 1960, Hern bounced back to saddle thirty-seven winners in 1961, which placed him ninth in the list and, what was more crucial, won Holliday his second owners' championship. All this paled beside the excesses of 1962, the fifth and final year of the Hern-Holliday association. Only two more races were won than the previous year. However, as one of the thirty-nine races was the St Leger, at £31,407, accounting for nearly half the stable's winning prize money of £70,206, employer and employee topped all three tables. At the age of forty-one Hern became the second youngest man to head the trainers' table since the war. (The youngest was Noel Murless, who was thirty-eight when he captured his first title in 1948.) What a way to bid farewell!

"We didn't have a row to finish up with, and in many ways I was sorry to go," Hern said of his departure. "It was just that when Jack Colling was retiring and Jakie Astor had bought the place he wanted someone to take over from Jack. I was offered the job and took it." Hern had confounded Ryan Jarvis's prophecy; he did the 'sacking' and left of his own accord. However, the debt owed the crusty old Yorkshireman was freely acknowledged. "I shall always be very grateful to Major Holliday for giving me the chance to train high class horses."

In 1958 that class revealed itself in the three-year-old filly None Nicer: "the showpiece of her sex at Lagrange, if not in all Newmarket," in Warren Hill's opinion. None Nicer's two-year-old career had been blighted by running over inadequate distances. A big, strong, attractive individual by Nearco out of the remarkable Phase – and therefore a full sister to Neasham Belle, Netherton Maid and Narrator – she cried out for longer distances. Hern kept her under wraps until mid-May when she won the Lingfield Oaks Trial. None Nicer disputed the lead for much of the Oaks, but could only plug on at one pace in the straight as the brilliant Bella Paola sprinted clear. A galloper like None Nicer required tracks such as Ascot, York and Doncaster to excel, and Hern accordingly set her sights on the Ribblesdale Stakes, Yorkshire Oaks and Park Hill Stakes. She beat Tantalizer at Ascot and Darlene on the Knavesmire to collect the first two. A further confrontation with Mother Goose and Cutter, who were second and third in the Oaks, seemingly offered None Nicer a cut and dried opportunity to demonstrate her right to be called the premier English filly of her generation over middle distances. However, None Nicer was also engaged in the St Leger, Yorkshire's very own classic, which Holliday dearly wanted to win. "She would have won the Park Hill in a canter but the old Major wanted to run her in the Leger," Hern recalls. "She had no chance of beating Alcide but she ran a marvellous race." None Nicer actually got her head in front for a few strides and might have held on in five Legers out of ten, but Alcide was no ordinary colt. Starting as the shortest priced favourite (9/4 on) since Bahram completed the Triple Crown in 1935, Alcide shot past the Holliday filly to win by eight lengths. At least Hern gained some consolation from the fact that

None Nicer got the better of a prolonged dog-fight with the 2000 Guineas and Derby third Nagami to win second prize. At the end of the year she was the top-weighted English filly in the three-year-old Free Handicap, albeit 10lb below Bella Paola.

Thus, in his first season, Hern had trained a champion of sorts. In 1959 he was to develop another. In January 1958 Warren Hill had neglected to mention a brown colt by Golden Cloud called Galivanter. As the season progressed his omission seemed justified because Galivanter failed to win any of his five races and eventually gave sufficient impression that he was no longer in love with the sport to be awarded one of Timeform's notorious squiggles. Galivanter was a different horse in 1959. After winning a Warwick maiden he prevailed in four competitive handicaps (recording Timeform's fastest time figure of the season in the BRA Sprint at Sandown) and finished half a length second to the champion sprinter Right Boy in the Nunthorpe Stakes at York to earn a Timeform rating of 131 – with no squiggle in sight.

The 1960 campaign introduced Hern to racing's down side. Galivanter threw a splint and was pin-fired, only to suffer persistent lameness in his hip. For three months he never left his box. Hern's classic filly No Saint could not win in ten attempts, despite being good enough to finish second in the Ribblesdale and Yorkshire Oaks. Equally frustrating was Proud Chieftain, a tall, handsome son of Bride Elect, a daughter of Netherton Maid. He could not run as a two-year-old because he had been badly infected with red worm as a foal. This left him terribly weak as a yearling and persistently loose droppings told Hern that his insides were still not working properly. When Hern finally got him on the racecourse he won Newmarket's Column Produce Stakes on 6 April 1960, but thereafter he failed to progress as his trainer had hoped. He was beaten in his Derby trial and in two warm-up races for the St Leger. Although he had run on to finish fifth to St Paddy in the Derby, Proud Chieftain's pretensions to classic standard had taken such a series of knocks by the autumn that he was demoted to handicap company at Brighton on 15 September instead of lining up at Doncaster. Carrying top weight he finished fourth. Hern's seasonal tally of twenty-seven winners relegated him to a depressing twenty-eighth position in the trainers' table. If the past was any sort of guide Hern might as well have started packing his 'toothbrush'.

43

Galivanter's reappearance at Ripon in late April 1961, after an absence of nineteen months, provided Lagrange with just the fillip to commence the new season. Conceding all of $1\frac{1}{2}$ stones to eleven of his sixteen opponents, Galivanter simply left them for dead and won the City Handicap by two lengths. Four days later he added the Palace House Stakes at Newmarket and, after honourable reverses at Redcar and Ascot, Galivanter returned to Headquarters for the July Cup. The outsider of three, the rivals backed to beat him were Tin Whistle (three lengths behind, conceding 7lb, in the Palace House) and Noel Murless's grey filly Favorita, beaten only once in nine races. Hern's sprinter saw off the filly in the Dip, and Tin Whistle, despite meeting Galivanter at levels, never threatened. "Galivanter is now the sprint champion," stated *The Sporting Life* "and Dick Hern is to be congratulated on bringing him back." Galivanter wound up his rejuvenated career with another fine performance at Ripon to win the Great St Wilfrid Handicap, giving the placed horses 21lb and 35lb, although he found the three-year-olds Floribunda, Cynara and Silver Tor too speedy in the Nunthorpe. Nevertheless, Galivanter retained his Timeform rating of 131 and, more significantly, acted as Hern's talisman throughout a potentially trying season. Twenty-nine years would pass before Hern trained a better sprinter in the shape of Dayjur, who cut a brilliant swathe through the King's Stand, Nunthorpe, Ladbroke Sprint Cup and Prix de l'Abbaye de Longchamp of 1990.

For his part Proud Chieftain improved half a stone with another year on his back. Placed in the Coronation Cup, Eclipse and Champion Stakes, his successes in two sponsored handicaps at Kempton and York netted over £6,000. "I don't think people realize what a good horse Proud Chieftain was although he was not quite the tops," was Hern's verdict. "He died young and would have made a marvellous stallion."

As the 1961 season drew to a close Hern struck with another game handicapper. Avon's Pride, who had been involved in the finishes of the Great Met, Northumberland Plate, Vaux Gold Tankard and Ebor without winning any of them, finally got his reward in the Cesarewitch. Autumn, however, is the time when two-year-olds bred for the classics catch the eye: Hern unveiled his candidate for the 1962 Derby in the Duke of Edinburgh Stakes at Ascot in early October. Hethersett was a bonny bay, half-brother to Proud Chieftain. After a decisive five-length victory his jockey Harry Carr reported authoritatively, "This will be your Derby horse." Captain Cecil Boyd-Rochfort's retained jockey since 1947, Carr had partnered classic horses such as Meld, Alcide and, in the 1959 Derby, Parthia. His opinion was never proffered lightly and merited respect. Hern gave Hethersett one more race later that month in the newly inaugurated Timeform Gold Cup over Doncaster's round mile. In a slowly-run race Hethersett was struck into, sustaining a bad cut above the hock and making his fifth place (beaten three lengths) behind Miralgo disappointing rather than catastrophic.

Hethersett began his classic campaign in Brighton's Derby Trial on 14 May, thereby gaining valuable experience of an undulating, switchback, left-handed track. "The colt came down the hill like a ball," said Hern after watching his horse romp home by five lengths. The time of the race was over a second faster than the meeting's other $1\frac{1}{2}$ mile race, which belied the minority view that Hethersett's victory was bloodless (he faced just two opponents) and the form meaningless. His Derby odds were halved to 7/1 favourite and Holliday was the recipient of a £100,000 offer for the colt from an American, which needless to say he rejected out of hand. Hethersett did not run again before Epsom. Hern considered the ground unsuitable in the Lingfield Derby Trial. On 5 June Holliday rode his cob off the Heath, having seen Hethersett complete his preparation, with every hope of his life's ambition being realized twenty-four hours later.

Subsequent events strongly suggest that Hethersett would have justified 9/2 favouritism (backed down from 6s) for the 1962 Derby had truly sensational circumstances not intervened. Seven of the twenty-six runners crashed to the turf as the field began the descent to Tattenham Corner: Hethersett was among them. Hern was tracking Hethersett and soon knew the worst. "If you are a spectator on the grandstand you lose sight of the runners here because of the crowd along the rails on the inside of the course. It is just possible to follow the horses by watching for the jockey's cap. I was 'on' Harry's cap with my binoculars and then suddenly I lost him. A few seconds later the field was round Tattenham Corner and into the straight followed by several loose horses. With that I realized he had gone."

Epsom's notoriously tricky mixture of inclines, bends and cambers

45

had wrought carnage before. In 1909 the American-bred favourite Sir Martin fell rounding Tattenham Corner and in 1920 Abbot's Trace and Steve Donoghue were brought down in virtually the same spot when bumped by a tiring rival. Four years later another renowned Derby jockey, Charlie Smirke, came to grief on his very first Derby mount, Buck's Yeoman, who slipped on the terribly wet Hill. In 1929 Kopi, who later was compensated in the Irish Derby, likewise fell hereabouts after clipping the heels of a horse in front of him. However, only Anmer's fall of 1913, brought about by the actions of suffragette Emily Davison, could be spoken of in the same breath as the spill of 1962. Even the 1962 Grand National saw Aintree's merciless fences claim only nine fallers from thirty-two competitors.

Harry Carr was convinced Hethersett had been robbed of victory.

> My horse was moving so well approaching the halfway mark that I felt pretty sure I would beat those in front of me and that I would win... Then it happened. The French colt King Canute II suddenly stumbled but did not come down, and Romulus could not avoid him. He galloped straight into him, fell, and all I could do was to pray that Hethersett would jump over him. But we had no such luck, and down Hethersett came and my last recollection before I was knocked out was Hethersett stretched out on the ground with one of his forelegs over the back of Romulus.

Thankfully none of the jockeys was killed and only one horse, King Canute II. Although he went head over heels, breaking the tree of his saddle, Hethersett survived unscathed but for some nasty cuts on his near fore. Harry Carr, who rode a treble on the first day, which included Avon's Pride, smashed his right shoulder so comprehensively that a silver pin was inserted to piece it all back together again. The extent of Major Holliday's Epsom injuries was harder to fathom. In addition to Hethersett's disaster, Proud Chieftain lost the Coronation Cup by less than a length and Nortia, winner of the Lingfield Oaks Trial, could not finish better than sixth in the fillies' classic. Once satisfied of Hethersett's well-being Holliday headed for Copgrove, uttering not a syllable until his car reached Doncaster whereupon he said to his chauffeur: "We'll win the Leger with that horse."

Following a lengthy investigation, the stewards, led by the Duke of

Norfolk, blamed the crash on the quality of some of the participants
rather than any shortcomings of the track. They concluded: "There
was no evidence of rough riding. The general opinion of the jockeys
was that too many horses were falling back after six furlongs and
the remainder closed up and in the general scrimmage some horse
was brought down, the rest falling over that horse. The Stewards
accepted that view and regret that such a large number of horses
not up to classic standard were allowed by their owners and trainers
to start." With customary tabloid aplomb the *Daily Mirror* informed
its readership more succinctly: "Derby 'Duds' get the blame."

Holliday's intention was for Hethersett to contest the Eclipse
Stakes on 7 July but by that date the invalid's exercise had not
progressed beyond a walk. Hern got him fit enough to run in the
Gordon Stakes at the beginning of August. Firm ground and lack of
condition told: Hethersett looked uncomfortable and beat only two.
Three weeks later in the Great Voltigeur it was a different tale.
Hethersett took the lead over a furlong out and, in soft going, repelled
Miralgo's determined late flourish by a short head. At Goodwood
Hethersett had been $8\frac{1}{2}$ lengths behind Miralgo. Conditions at Doncaster once again suited Hethersett, the officially good ground had
been drenched by steady rain throughout the day. The Italian Derby
winner Antelami was the heavily backed favourite at 7/2 followed
by his Epsom counterpart Larkspur and Monterrico, who was third
in the Great Voltigeur, on 8s. Opening at 10/1, Hethersett drifted
out to 100/8. From the outset one or two sceptics had thought
him unlikely to stay even $1\frac{1}{2}$ miles on breeding and pointed to his
scrambled York victory as evidence of his inability to last another
quarter mile.

Several St Legers have been secured by greater margins but few
more impressively than Hethersett's. After some ugly overcrowding
at the turn which, with the Derby still fresh in mind, set hearts
aflutter, the outcome was never in doubt. Harry Carr was sitting up
like a policeman and as soon as he gave the office passing the
two furlong marker Hethersett quickly strode clear to win by four
lengths. This was a moment for Holliday and Hern to treasure,
bitter-sweet in terms of what-might-have-been in the Derby but in
every other respect unsurpassable. To an out-and-out Yorkshireman
like Holliday victory in Yorkshire's classic took some beating. Now,
four years after None Nicer's valiant attempt, Dick Hern had

accomplished it for him. After Hethersett's Derby mishap the Queen Mother wrote Holliday a characteristically thoughtful letter of commiseration; her equally characteristic letter of congratulation was framed and mounted at Copgrove.

Hethersett turned out for the Champion Stakes. The shorter distance and faster ground were against him, and though running on bravely he could not peg back Arctic Storm, winner of the Irish 2000 Guineas. However, Hethersett had won a special place in Hern's affections. "He was a lovely little horse with a marvellous temperament. After the Derby when he was on the easy list he never got fresh. He used to stand quietly out in the yard when we put the hosepipe on him. He didn't mind the cars coming in and out. He took it all as a matter of course. He was a real gentleman."

Thanks to Hethersett Hern vacated Lagrange in the best possible style. His first classic victory guaranteed the trainers' championship for himself and the title of leading owner and breeder for his patron. "He has had great success for one so young and so recently introduced to the profession," commented *The Times*. Jack Jarvis, the senior Newmarket trainer, organized a farewell party in Hern's honour. Then the 41-year-old Hern decamped for West Ilsley and the Berkshire Downs, where an even more illustrious phase of his career would unfold.

Chapter Six

THE DOWNS

'A lovely way of conditioning horses'

HERN'S IMPENDING DEPARTURE from Lagrange had been public knowledge throughout most of 1962. His friend John (later Sir John) Astor had purchased West Ilsley Stables, and the incumbent, R.J. Colling, was retiring from training to join the BBA. The youngest child of the 2nd Viscount Astor, the Eton and Oxford educated 'Jakie' served with the Household Cavalry and with 'Phantom' during the war, winning the Croix de Guerre. As a young man he had ridden under both codes, experience he put to good use after the war as a steward, and as member of the Turf Board, Racecourse Betting Control Board, Horserace Totalizator Board and the Thoroughbred Breeders' Association. Somehow he also found time for a parliamentary career as member for the Sutton division of Plymouth between 1951–59. Two years before his father's death in 1952, he and his brother William inherited the Astor racing interests, which dated back to the turn of the century and the acquisition of the broodmares Conjure, Popinjay and Maid of the Mist for a combined total of 5,600 guineas. From these three foundation mares at the Cliveden Stud descended a stream of top class animals that would carry the 'light blue, pink sash' Astor jacket to victory in twelve classics, including the 1953 Oaks on Ambiguity, a descendent of Conjure. Although Jakie Astor had bred such useful horses as Rosalba and Indian Twilight at his Warren and Hatley Studs (not to mention the great stayer Trelawny whom he sold on as a three-year-old), he had not tasted success in a classic. Rosalba understandably found Petite Etoile too hot in the 1,000 Guineas, while Escort finished fourth in Hethersett's Derby. With the classic objective in mind Astor set about developing and modernizing West Ilsley for his new trainer.

The Ilsleys, midway between Oxford and Newbury on the north facing scarp of the Berkshire Downs, possessed a lengthy history as a centre for training racehorses. From his yard in East Ilsley James Dover sent out full brother and sister Lord Lyon and Achievement to land the Triple Crown and the 1000 Guineas–St Leger double in 1866 and 1867 respectively. West Ilsley's Hodcott House was converted into a racing stable by Frank Barling just before the outbreak of World War I, but in 1919 he moved to Newmarket and the legacy passed to Captain Richard Gooch, an adroit trainer of stayers. Using the testing gallops to fine effect, Gooch won three Goodwood Stakes, two Goodwood Cups, a Chester Cup, Jockey Club Cup and an Ascot Stakes between 1925 and 1934, despite breaking his back while hunting with the Quorn in 1928. After World War II Major Eric Stedall won the 1946 Stewards' Cup with Commissar.

Jack Colling moved into Hodcott House for the 1950 season. The eldest son of Bob Colling, who had trained Netherton Maid for Major Holliday, he nursed a penchant for geldings, of whom he once said: "Give me a stable full of geldings and I will have the bookmakers crying for mercy." This he did with the likes of High Stakes and Alcimedes. Colling was allowed to stay at Hodcott House and the Herns occupied the Old Rectory (appropriately once the home of Maitland Wilson, a Jockey Club handicapper) half a mile away in West Ilsley village.

West Ilsley's pride and joy were, and are, its gallops, which are so good that in Colling's words, "If I'd come here sooner I would have had fewer grey hairs. There are 15 different gallops and the going is always perfect." Indeed, it proves almost impossible to wear out any one strip. Standing high up on the Downs so that it is an overcoat colder than in the valley below, horses trained here tend not to come to hand as early as those prepared in less exposed conditions. The summer gallops run from above the village to a dip below the clump of trees on Scotchamer Knob, near The Ridgeway; the winter gallops, which are closer to the yard on Hodcott Down, run up against the collar toward The Ridgeway and would be the envy of many a trainer in summer.

However, when it comes to identifying West Ilsley's principal asset these gallops, in Hern's opinion, assume second place to his staff, many of whom came with the yard. "Having a good team is the most important thing," he said in 1980. "I am extremely lucky – many of my lads have been with me for years. It's continuity and loyalty that count. It's teamwork that makes the operation a success and everyone has played their part."

In the yard Hern could draw upon the vast experience of Buster Haslam and Geordie Campbell. Haslam had been apprenticed to Jack Colling in 1937 when still in Newmarket, but failing to make the grade as a jockey he rose to second head-lad and, eventually in 1957, to travelling head-lad. At the time of his death in 1990 Haslam was one of the best-known faces on British racecourses, and one of the shrewdest and most respected. For nearly half a century he had been the nonpareil of travelling head-lads. "He was one of the outstanding figures on the English Turf," said Hern in his address during Haslam's memorial service. "When I took over from Jack Colling he said to me: 'You never need worry as long as Buster is there'. We never said much because there was no need. We understood each other so well. But Buster could always tell you exactly how a race had gone and he nearly always turned out to be right. He had spent his whole life with horses and seemed to know what one was likely to do before they did it. With him in charge, however far away he was, you felt every bit as confident as if you'd been there yourself." No one's kit and tack were ever more spick and span and the standards he imposed on himself stood muster with those of his guv'nor. "Only once do I remember him making a mistake," said Willie Carson. "He forgot to bring blinkers and it took him two weeks to get over it. He was a great man, part of the team, and the last of the good old travelling head-lads."

Campbell was also a Colling apprentice. In his case National Service saw him gain too much weight and Colling appointed him second travelling head-lad, a position he filled for nine years. In 1968 Hern promoted him to head-lad. Other key backroom personnel to play influential roles in the years to come were blacksmith David Blythe, feeder Tom Barnes, gallop man Terry Barnes, box driver Peter West, secretaries Harrap and Holmes, and Hern's assistants Stan Clayton, David Murray-Smith, Ian Cocks, Alex Scott and Neil Graham.

On the gallops Hern was equally blessed with talent in the saddle. Harry Grant, Reg Cartwright and, after 1970, Brian Procter made a magnificent trio of work-riders, augmented at various times by Bobby Elliott, Jimmy Lindley and Alan Bond. As stable-jockey Hern inherited Joe Mercer, many peoples' idea of the quintessential English jockey. Mercer began his riding career in 1947 as a 13-year-old, half-crown-a-week (12½p) apprentice with the fearsome Major E.B. Sneyd at Eastmanton House on the fringe of Sparsholt, near Wantage. His father Emmanuel was a coach painter and a frustrated jockey. Although there was no racing blood in the family Mercer slowly but surely graduated from Phoebe (a toy horse on wheels) via the neighbourhood milk horse to the local riding school where he received the odd ride on a pony in return for mucking out. Meanwhile, elder brother Manny had joined George Colling at Newmarket and was prospering. He did so well that Sneyd, who had tutored the brothers Eph and Doug Smith, asked Manny if he had any younger brothers who would like to be jockeys. Joe Mercer the jockey was first seen in public at Brighton in 1949 on a horse of Sneyd's called Flare Up and a year later he rode his first winner on Eldoret at Bath. In 1951 Mercer rode work for Jack Colling (alongside Harry Grant) and in 1953 on the recommendation of Gordon Richards, Colling's first jockey, the trainer offered the eighteen-year-old a retainer to ride as stable-jockey. By the end of his apprenticeship in 1955 Mercer had ridden 200 winners, including the Oaks on Ambiguity, and been champion apprentice three years in a row, sharing the title with Lester Piggot in 1954. Mercer and Hern knew each other through their association with Michael Pope and Hern had put Mercer up on a number of Holliday horses, such as Nortia in the Lingfield Oaks Trial and Nassau Stakes of 1962. "So we really understood each other," said the jockey, "and got on well from the start." Within two years this understanding resulted in Mercer breaking new ground by topping the century mark and winning a second classic after a hiatus of twelve years.

These were the leading lights in a community centred on Hodcott House. Its duck pond, brick-built stable block, cedarwood bungalows, covered ride and various outbuildings creating the impression, and atmosphere, of a tiny, self-contained hamlet. Set aside as it is from the village of West Ilsley itself, one can appreciate why Lord Wigg addressed Dick Hern as 'the Mayor'. Explains David Murray-

Smith: "The place lends itself to the development of a community. There are plenty of houses for married lads and therefore they tend to stay." Joe Mercer agrees: "It's a community of married lads and they do have all the amenities. The village almost belonged to the owners. They've thirty odd houses in the village." Nevertheless, however much credit Hern gives to his loyal band of workers, such loyalty and devotion to duty only tends to develop if there is something, or someone, worthy of those selfless qualities.

In the first instance, Dick Hern fit to a tee Clarence Randall's notion of the executive most likely to succeed in management: "The leader must know, must know that he knows, and must be able to make it abundantly clear to those about him that he knows." Hern's staff were well aware that their boss knew as much about every job in the yard as each individual specialist and, furthermore, could probably do each of those jobs as well as they could. Graft on to self-confidence some God-given gifts, accumulated experience and the equally sought attribute of being able to command wisely, and one ends up with a leader who will be obeyed cheerfully and without question.

"If we did have a grouse we'd send someone in to state our case to the guv'nor and he always listened and did his best to iron things out," says Rodney Boult, who, like Mercer, began his racing life in the autocratic environment of the Sneyd regime and thus had every reason to value Hern's concession to democracy. Says Joe Mercer: "We never had a cross word – a difference of opinion, that's all. Once work was finished he didn't take it home with him."

Yet there was never any doubt who ran the show. Hern was a perfectionist who set himself a strict daily routine. Up every morning at 5.45 am, schedules meticulously prepared and written out for his work-riders, he entered the yard on the dot of 7 am. "If I am on time there is no excuse for anyone else to be late. When you work to a timetable everyone knows what they have got to do. If it is done in dribs and drabs it's a shambles."

In the spring of 1963 West Ilsley housed sixty-two horses with whom Hern could weave his particular brand of magic on behalf of owners who included Lord Rotherwick, Viscount Hambledon, the Earl of Durham, Lady Ashcombe and Charles Clore, besides Jakie Astor and Lord Astor. The secret of Hern's success with this first batch of horses – and all that were to follow in their hoofprints across

53

Hodcott Down – is virtually impossible to pinpoint. How does one begin to analyse the greenness of a gardener's fingers? Like a gardener the trainer applies his skills to certain raw materials, some more malleable than others. For plants and soil read horses and gallops; good husbandry equates to sound stable and man management. Patience, dedication, energy, a sense of priorities – and a sense of humour – are crucial to both practitioners. Although not a formula promising to uncover the very core of Hern's ability to train racehorses more successfully than his contemporaries, at least it provides an acceptable analogy for those who have worked with Hern to ponder his methods.

"In stable management he is second to none," states Joe Mercer unhesitatingly. "And he can produce a horse first time 100% fit. He's not one that grills his horses but he gets them fit. They may look big but he builds them up on those Downs and they're fit. There's no need for a breastplate or things like that on his horses. One great asset is that because of his owner-breeders he has been able to train generations of horses. He knows the dams and families, and that's a great help."

Alan Bond was Hern's second jockey in 1977. Twice champion apprentice during his time with Ted Smyth at Epsom, Bond was then retained by Henry Cecil. "He leaves no stone unturned and is devoted to his horses twenty-four hours a day. On the gallops he likes to get on with his job. The horses knew when he was around – if one dawdled he'd chase up behind on his hack with the long-tom cracking. He'd fire something at you if you did something wrong but five minutes later it would be forgotten."

Bobby Elliott, another former champion apprentice, concurs. He partnered Major Holliday's lightweights for Hern and rode a lot of work at West Ilsley, notably aboard Brigadier Gerard and Bustino. "He runs a very efficient establishment and all the lads work well together. He's not that much of an introvert as people think. He's always pally with the staff and quite jovial at breakfast when all the work is done."

Old Harrovian David Murray-Smith joined Hern in February 1974 at the age of nineteen having spent a year with a leading stable in Ontario. He 'did his two' for four years and then served as pupil-assistant in 1978 and 1979 before taking up a similar position with Vincent O'Brien. Armed with that calibre of yardstick he is in a unique position to assess the Hern technique. "His gift is hard to describe in a few words. The hallmark, I suppose, is patience, attention to detail and his ability to get a horse right on the day. He is a true horsemaster. 80% of his horses are home-bred from well established families and he always trained them in the classic mould, not over exposing them as two-year-olds, a style which is now returning. He is a very dedicated man with no other interests apart from horses."

Murray-Smith's shoes were filled by Ian Cocks, who likewise possesses the rare experience of having worked with another giant of the training profession, in his case Fulke Walwyn. Cocks spent the first half of the 1960s at Saxon House as an unpaid lad and amateur rider, partnering a dozen winners before turning pro and accepting a job with Colonel G. Gibson. However, he soon returned to Upper Lambourn, renewing his links with Walwyn and Richard Head, until a broken thigh precipitated the end of his riding days. He assisted a former Saxon House colleague Gay Kindersley for a while and then, in the summer of 1979, spotted Hern's advertisement for an assistant trainer, occasioned by the illness of Stan Clayton and the departure of Murray-Smith. "Horsemastership is Dick Hern's great thing. Today a lot of trainers are not horsemasters. He can spot a lame horse at half a mile and he misses nothing. He is very organized on the gallops but still manages to reveal a sense of humour. Some trainers are far more awkward. Everything is done to precision, however, or you are in a lot of trouble because he is an absolute perfectionist."

References to Hern's powers of concentration and overwhelming professionalism crop up time and again. One of the later Hern protégés to branch out successfully on his own account was Alex Scott. "During working hours he isn't a man for talking too much. But if I had to describe briefly what I've learnt and what makes him such a great trainer I would say, thoroughness, attention to detail and 'never settle for second best'. I've also learnt the importance of consistent decisions and of establishing a system of training in which everyone who's involved in making the wheels turn knows and understands why they must turn like that in order to make the system work. That's why, in spite of the Major's injuries and illnesses, the yard has still been able to turn out Group winner after Group winner."

Yet again the same themes vigorously declare themselves. And, just as one begins to suspect one in particular has failed to make an impact on Scott he adds: "The Major spends much more time with his horses than most trainers. He works very, very hard on his horses and gives them all his time." Always the horses. The old cavalry maxim of "Horses first, men second, officers last" was the basis of Hern's credo, though perhaps he modified it a little: horses first, second and last might be a more accurate definition of Hern's version. "The secret of this man is he's dedicated to his horses," says Brian Procter. "You can go out there some mornings and you think he's looking straight through you but his mind is on the horses. He knows every ounce of flesh on them. He likes to hear the truth and if a horse isn't working as well as I think it should be then I'll tell him, even if he disagrees. Perhaps you get a horse that's making a whistle and he'll say, 'Well, I can't hear it'. I might be wrong, he might be wrong, but if I'm right he'll always say so."

Lord Carnarvon has watched Hern at close quarters for over twenty years. "He's an incredible horseman who understands the shape and the handling of a horse better than anyone I can think of. He is absolutely meticulous in stable management and inspires incredible loyalty and admiration from the members of his staff – although he can be just as snappy with them at times as he can with the Press."

So, are we any nearer to unravelling the mystery of Hern's genius? Should 'genius' be the correct label to apply in this instance? Few, if any, would dispute its application; but if applied then we may never discover the secret of Hern's 'green fingers', because genius, by definition, defies reasoned explanation.

Occasionally, Hern has attempted to put his philosophy into words: "I try not to be hard. I like to put myself in the position of the animal. Obviously, they can only go on winning and running if they are enjoying it. I have to live with the horses. I see them every day and I like to keep them contented and fit. A horse must always feel like doing it. You must never overdo the homework. Once they get sick of it they are finished. Let them go at their own pace, never push them. Training on the Downs here is a lovely way of conditioning horses because you have not got to be too hard on them. They are often on the 'collar' climbing. That's why here you can keep an animal fresher and sweeter than they can at Newmarket,

Above: Wick House as it is today. (*Michael Tanner*)
Left: The equestrian prowess of the Hern boys is evident from the rosettes which still adorn the tackroom wall. (*Michael Tanner*)

Like father, like son: *Above left*: Roy Hern (standing, centre), 2nd Battalion Glamorganshire Yeomanry (*Bryn Owen*); *Above right*: Dick Hern (second row, second right), North Irish Horse.
Below: Aboard Tollbridge at the 1951 Badminton Horse Trials. (*Peter A. Harding*)

Above: Michael Pope's assistant trainer riding out on Grey Leg. (*S & G Press Agency*)
Below left: One successful partnership: Dick and Sheilah Hern arrive at the Savoy Hotel for the dinner at which Brigadier Gerard was honoured as Racehorse of the Year for 1972. (*Desmond O'Neill*)
Below right: Another successful partnership: Major Holliday talks, Major Hern listens. (*S & G Press Agency*)

Above: Hethersett proves how unlucky he was at Epsom by winning the 1962 St Leger to present his trainer with a first classic victory. (*S & G Press Agency*)
Below: Provoke's rain-sodden St Leger of 1965: the expression of horse, lad and owner say it all. (*S & G Press Agency*)

Above: The 'Major of West Ilsley' surrounded by some of his team circa 1974. (*Syndication International*)
Below left: An early morning council of war with jockeys Mercer and Elliott. (*Syndication International*)
Below right: Dressed to combat the chill of a downland morning. The hack is Hardbake, whom John Dunlop trained to win the Bessborough Stakes at Royal Ascot in 1971. (*Ed Byrne*)

Above: The passage of time confirms the view that the 1971 2000 Guineas is indeed a candidate for "Race of the Century". Brigadier Gerard routs Mill Reef and My Swallow (far left). Minsky trails. (*Hulton-Deutsch*)
Below: Bidding farewell to a champion, October 1972. (*W. W. Rouch & Co.*)

Above: 1974 1000 Guineas: Highclere prevails by a fraction to give the Queen her first classic success for sixteen years. (*S & G Press Agency*)
Left: Lady Beaverbrook and her trainer appear to be facing a firing squad instead of Gerry Cranham's camera. (*Gerry Cranham*)
Below: It's now Willie Carson's job to explain to Lord Weinstock (centre) and his son Simon (right). (*George Selwyn*)

Above: At long last success in an Epsom classic: Dunfirmline takes the Jubilee Oaks of 1977. (*Gerry Cranham*)
Below: Derby, 1979: "There's only one way to ride a Derby" – Troy wins by 7 lengths. (*Gerry Cranham*)

where of course there are marvellous facilities but you have to be that much harder on horses."

However, when all is said and done, that philosophy could belong to any one of a hundred trainers. Making it work constitutes a different matter altogether and that's a genius bestowed on Hern and precious few others. It would, for instance, be very easy to overwork a horse on the stiff downland gallops. "The first morning I led the yearlings up the canter," says Alex Scott, "the Major barked at me when I pulled up, 'You're all the same from Newmarket, you all go too blanking fast'." Flushed by constant success it would also, for instance, be very easy to get carried away on the wave of adulation brought with it and for the heart to overrule the head. That is flawed genius; the kind that brings the whole edifice tumbling down round one's ears. Neither horses nor ego can be pandered to. "One of the great qualities of Dick Hern as a trainer is that he never loses his sense of proportion over horses," wrote John Hislop, rider, assistant trainer, author, journalist and, more specifically, owner-breeder of one horse, Brigadier Gerard, about whom one could be excused for becoming swept away. "They are treated according to their individual requirements, regardless of status. Some trainers think that because they have a classic horse he must be given twice as much work as an ordinary horse, whether he requires it or not; with the result that by the time they have finished with him he is no longer a classic horse. The Brigadier was always a completely normal horse in his requirements as regards being prepared for a race; consequently, his training was strictly orthodox. When he became famous, the Press were always asking Dick what special treatment he received in the way of training and feeding, and it was difficult to convince them that he had none."

Unfortunately for Hern there was no Brigadier Gerard hiding in West Ilsley's boxes during 1963. Having taken over from a trainer of Jack Colling's inclinations it was no surprise for Hern to find that one of his best animals was a gelding, Grey of Falloden. However, the classiest inmate of West Ilsley that initial summer was Darling Boy. A five-year-old entire with eight wins so far in a twenty-four race career, he improved so much under Hern's care that after winning the Jockey Club Stakes (from Hethersett) and the £4,539 La Coupe at Longchamp – Hern's and Mercer's first win in France

57

and his biggest prize of the season – he was sold as a stallion for around £40,000.

Lord Astor's Grey of Falloden was a four-year-old chestnut by the great stayer Alycidon out of a mare who traced to Maid of the Mist, a daughter of the mighty Sceptre. "He was a tremendous handicapper and a wonderful horse to ride," says Mercer. In 1963 the gelding won the Queen's Prize on his reappearance and was never out of the first four in six subsequent races, which included the Chester Cup, Queen Alexandra Stakes, Doncaster Cup and Jockey Club Cup, though he failed to win any of them. The following year saw Grey of Falloden at his peak, his four wins highlighted by the Doncaster Cup and the Cesarewitch. The Newmarket marathon was his ninth outing of the season and he carried 9st 6lb, but taking up the running three furlongs out he made light of this burden to withstand the fast-finishing Magic Court by three-quarters of a length and to break a weight-carrying record for the race that had stood since 1911. The handicapper had not exactly shown Grey of Falloden much leniency to date, and he surely would not start now. Hern could not win a handicap with him in 1965. The gelding shouldered 10st into third place in the Queen's Prize, was runner up in the Northumberland Plate with 9st 8lb and finished sixth in the Cesarewitch, again with 9st 6lb. The highest weight carried by the five that beat him was 7st 11lb! As a gelding Grey of Falloden was barred from the Ascot Gold Cup, so it was especially galling for Hern to see the coveted race won by Fighting Charlie, a horse his gelding had given 7lb and beaten 1½ lengths in the Henry II Stakes at Sandown, while Grey of Falloden had to be content with a facile win in the Queen Alexandra worth five times less. "If he was in training today," Hern insisted in 1988, "he'd be running in the Gold Cup and he'd win it." The old warrior continued for a further four seasons until the age of ten, but he only won once more. "He was a great character and used to get postcards sent to him," remembers Sheilah Hern. "He took the fancy of racing people because he was genuine and brave and there weren't many older horses around in those days."

Hern had other smart handicappers in Red Tears, winner of the 1964 Zetland Gold Cup, Gurkha, who beat his half-brother Trelawny in the 1964 Brown Jack Stakes and Mahbub Aly, a smallish colt of Lord Astor's who tenaciously won the 1967 Chester Cup by six

lengths. In the early months of 1965 it appeared that he had un-
earthed another in a three-year-old colt belonging to Jakie Astor
called Provoke. By July Provoke had only managed five runs in his
entire life and had won two 1½ mile maidens. He had been plagued
with little splints and rather soft bones as a two-year-old and showed
scant promise until some work on Newbury racecourse toward the
backend impressed Joe Mercer. "The moment I said that the lad
changed his attitude to the horse, the horse changed his, and everything went the right way."

As a late May foal out of a half-sister to Trelawny, Provoke needed
time and longer distances: at York's August meeting he got both.
In the Melrose Handicap over 1¾ miles he handed Santa Vimy her
first defeat of the season and upon being withdrawn accidentally
from the Newbury Autumn Cup it was decided to let him take his
chance in the St Leger. The hot favourite for the race at 11/4 on
was the Paddy Prendergast-trained, Lester Piggott-ridden Meadow
Court, second to Sea Bird in the Derby and winner of the Irish Derby
and King George. So confident was the Meadow Court entourage
that a celebration party had already been fixed at their hotel. Hern
and Mercer, staying in the same hotel (Punch's on the old A1 south
of Doncaster) were undismayed, however, because for three days it
had done nothing but rain from morning till night – just the conditions to give a dour stayer like Provoke a sporting chance of
causing an upset.

It was still pelting down as the tape rose on what would be the
slowest St Leger run at Doncaster since 1897. "There was so much
mud on all the colours that when the racecourse commentator saw
a horse winning by a street he thought it must be Meadow Court,"
Hern later recalled. "Most people were shouting Meadow Court home
but I knew the horse in front was mine." Provoke, backed from 40/1
down to 28/1, won by a ridiculously easy ten lengths giving Mercer
ne'er an anxious moment. "I knew I was going to win half a mile
out, mine was going so well. I took the lead from Solstice and As
Before three out and was never in danger after, although Meadow
Court stayed with me for 100 yards," he informed the Press.
"Provoke was always going well and I have had to drive him much
harder in most of his other races." Certainly the colt had plenty of
fire left in him. Returning through the murk to the winner's circle a
flashbulb popped and he threw Mercer. Astor was quick to praise

Provoke's lad, Tom Gunner: "If Provoke had not had the careful handling Gunner gave him he might have gone the wrong way." Meadow Court's owners went through with their party and took the gracious step of inviting Astor and Hern. "I always hope I could have behaved as well if the position had been reversed," Hern remarked.

Provoke's triumph against all odds had two repercussions. First, it initiated a rare St Leger double, for a week later Craighouse (owned by Lord Astor) won the Irish equivalent on only his fourth racecourse appearance. In the previous sixty-five years just Dick Dawson (1929) and Paddy Prendergast (1963) had achieved such a feat of training. Secondly, Provoke's earnings lifted Hern to third place in the trainers' standings – and Astor likewise in the owners' list – the highest position he had occupied since moving to West Ilsley.

Little did Hern suspect that an epidemic was brewing which would test his resolve to breaking point over the next three years. "We had an absolutely terrible time," he told John Rickman. "The flu completely crucified my string. It was so bad we even took the tan out of the covered ride and replaced it with sand just in case there were any bugs in the tan. That's how desperate we had become. It was nearly driving me mad but I realized there was little to be done except sweat it out."

The 1960s witnessed the first visitation to Britain of what came to be known as 'the virus', a blanket term to describe at least five different strains. Its cause remains almost as baffling as it was in 1966. Stables like West Ilsley, in isolated spots surrounded by farmland, seem more prone to outbreaks, leading to suggestions that the virus is in some way a product of environmental pollution resulting from the increased use of pesticides by farmers. The virus and widespread crop spraying did start at about the same time. Occasionally horses cough or have runny noses, but more often than not they betray no symptoms except unaccountably poor performances on the track. In the 1960s there were no vaccines on the market and rest was the only cure. Moreover, horses frequently gave the impression of having recovered fitness, merely to perform abysmally yet again.

Once entrenched in a yard the virus is extremely difficult to eradicate. In 1966 Hern sent out just twenty-four winners for less than £10,000 in stakes to finish a miserable 56th in the trainers' list.

Both of his Leger winners were afflicted. "Neither was worth a carrot as a racehorse afterwards," he lamented. Provoke never ran again and Craighouse ran once, finishing last. At one stage things got so depressing, remembers Joe Mercer, that Hern even threatened to shoot his hack when it too started coughing. By the close of 1967 West Ilsley seemed to have weathered the storm. Hern's sixty winners was his best ever. Among the juveniles was a very useful colt in Remand, victorious in all three of his races, which had culminated in the Royal Lodge Stakes. By Alcide out of a half-sister to Persian War (Hern won two races with the triple Champion Hurdler in 1966 before Astor sold him) he represented one of the stoutest Astor bloodlines. Since the two horses above him in the Free Handicap were either not engaged in the Derby (Vaguely Noble) or unlikely to stay (Petingo), Remand looked a distinctly live prospect to compensate Hern for the unfortunate downfall of Hethersett.

Hern's string attacked the new season as if the virus was a thing of the past. In the Chester Vase Remand gave 4lb to the much vaunted Connaught and beat him by half a length. Then all the old danger signs began to surface. The horses coughed, had bloodshot eyes and were listless. In the Epsom paddock Remand (the 4/1 second favourite) was not recognisable as the horse who had won at Chester. "He had just fallen apart," says Mercer. Only a tiptop Remand could have troubled Sir Ivor, who was undeniably one of the very best post-war classic horses. In the circumstances Remand ran respectably, there or thereabouts at the three furlong pole before weakening near the finish. Two places and $3\frac{1}{2}$ lengths ahead of him was Connaught, which represented a 12lb turn-around of their Chester form. The big, burly Connaught might have been dis-advantaged by Chester's tight bends and had probably improved a bit since, but on formbook evidence his Derby display stated that a healthy Remand would have challenged Sir Ivor. Ten months passed before Remand appeared – and won – again, but any thoughts of a highly profitable comeback were illusory. The virus had done its work far too thoroughly. Hern's 1968 tally of twenty-one winners would be the lowest of his career and his horses were so stricken that one-time classic candidates were reduced to competing in maiden races at minor tracks.

A truly wretched time was capped by the death of Roy Hern on

1 September, aged seventy-five, as a result of complications arising from cancer of the gall bladder. Much of his later years were devoted to nurturing young polo players at Millfield School. "The man behind Millfield's polo success," was the bold title above his obituary notice in *Horse and Hound*, a fitting tribute from which Roy Hern would have derived considerable satisfaction. Winifred survived her husband by eighteen years (they had long gone their separate ways). She died on 18 June 1986 at the ripe old age of ninety-three and is buried in Chedzoy churchyard beside her parents and her first-born son.

The 1969 season offered Hern hardly more cheer than the previous one. For the third time in four years he had no classic representatives – 1963 is the only other such year in his entire career – and he failed to make the top twenty trainers for the second season in succession. The one ray of sunshine came in September with the successful debut of a bay filly by one of his former favourites, Hethersett (who had died after siring only three crops) out of Verdura, the dam of another, Avon's Pride. She possessed the optimistic name of Highest Hopes and belonged to Brook Holliday, the son of Hern's ornery old Yorkshire employer. The Major had died in December 1965 aged eighty-five. Unbeknownst to him, he had bred another colt capable of winning the Derby and plenty more besides: Vaguely Noble was out of Noble Lassie, whom Hern had trained to win the Lancashire Oaks of 1959, but with Major Holliday dead he was not entered for the classics.

Highest Hopes proved a troublesome filly. She was very 'shouldery', scarcely able to walk when she came out of her box in the morning and she lived on phenylbutazone. Hern's problems were immense. He needed to find soft ground on which she could exercise safely and then had to prepare her gently, alert not only to the vagaries of the weather, but also to the danger of running the filly with traces of drugs in her system. In Joe Mercer's opinion Hern's handling of Highest Hopes during 1970 marked his finest piece of training. "Highest Hopes was a cripple. Dick made a little gallop on Summer Down just for her. About four furlongs of thick grass, chopped and cut." Highest Hopes responded by winning both of her prep races for the 1000 Guineas. Sensationally, the 3/1 co-favourite finished tailed off behind Humble Duty, whom she had earlier beaten at Newbury. Hern was nonplussed. The ground was good, she looked a picture and a dope test proved negative. "I just cannot understand it," said Jimmy Lindley who rode her at Newmarket. "She was never going well and we were beaten at half way."

Whatever ailed Highest Hopes in the Guineas was conspicuously absent between 14 June and 20 September, when she proceeded to stamp herself the best staying filly in Europe as a consequence of three forays across the English Channel. She began by running Sweet Mimosa to two lengths in the Prix de Diane (the French Oaks) over $10\frac{1}{2}$ furlongs at Chantilly. Five weeks later she won the Prix Eugene Adam at Saint-Cloud from the French 2000 Guineas winner Caro and six other colts. After looking the winner of the Yorkshire Oaks at the distance Highest Hopes succumbed to a late rally from the Oaks' winner, Lupe, but on her third French raid she settled that score and a few others for good measure. The Prix Vermeille, run at Longchamp in September, is the European championship for three-year-old staying fillies. The 1970 field included all three principal European Oaks' winners – Lupe, Sweet Mimosa and Santa Tina (Irish) – but none of them stood an earthly against the enterprisingly ridden Highest Hopes. Mercer shot her into the lead on the final turn and poached a two length advantage which ultimately proved to be the margin of victory. "Highest Hopes the champion," declared *The Sporting Life*'s front page report of a Vermeille won in race record time. "We had decided not to challenge until $1\frac{1}{2}$ furlongs out," explained Mercer, "but Highest Hopes ran so easily that when I saw Parmelia accelerating $2\frac{1}{2}$ furlongs out I did not hesitate to go after her."

The £47,640 won in the Vermeille raised Highest Hopes' French earnings to over £84,000, a phenomenal sum when one considers Lupe's three English successes earned £39,003 and Humble Duty's five only £48,450. She wound up her career in the Champion Stakes. A training setback made her participation doubtful up until the last minute and she ran as miserably as she had in the Guineas, beating only one. On her day there was no mistaking Highest Hope's ability. Timeform awarded her a rating of 129 – 8lb ahead of Lupe and 2lb ahead of Humble Duty. Only two Hern fillies would receive higher marks.

West Ilsley had come out of the doldrums. Of course Highest Hope's francs were irrelevant to Hern's placing in the trainers' table, yet he still reached fifth spot with fifty races won. The most eye-catching of Hern's twenty-five individual winners was the strapping bay colt who bolted home in the Middle Park Stakes at Newmarket on 1 October. Hern's training novitiate set in motion by one Holliday had concluded with success for another. The arrival of Brigadier Gerard heralded the dawn of a fresh era in which Hern would securely establish himself at the very peak of his profession.

Chapter Seven

THE BRIGADIER

'He's the best horse that stumbles least'

FROM THE DAY HE WAS FOALED Brigadier Gerard was destined for greatness. A beautiful mahogany bay with black points and a small white star, he was impossible to fault on conformation and in name, for he was christened in honour of Conan Doyle's dashing hussar hero. However, enviable looks and a fine name come to nought if the racehorse lacks courage, soundness and the will-to-win. Suffice it to say Brigadier Gerard retired with a career record of one defeat in eighteen, ten victories in races of Group I calibre, two track records, a host of other historical 'firsts' and a Timeform rating of 144 eclipsed in forty-five years of publication only by Sea Bird's 145. "I felt very proud of Brigadier Gerard," says Hern. "He was the sort of horse every trainer dreams of having because he seemed to be head and shoulders above his contemporaries."

Although Brigadier Gerard raced in the colours of Mrs Jean Hislop he was the brainchild of her husband John. The dapper, elfin-faced Hislop is one of the English Turf's greatest all-rounders. A prominent amateur rider either side of the war he also turned his hand to writing and journalism, paying particular attention to the art of jockeyship and the science of bloodstock breeding. Brigadier Gerard was the consummation of a lifelong love affair with the family of the legendary Edwardian racemare Pretty Polly. As a young man Hislop nurtured ambitions of becoming a trainer and spent several years as a learner-assistant with Victor Gilpin at Clarehaven Stables in Newmarket where Gilpin's father had trained the peerless mare to win twenty-two of her twenty-four races, which included the 1000 Guineas, Oaks and St Leger of 1904. At first hand Hislop saw the regular flow of top class animals who traced to Pretty Polly and determined to acquire for himself a mare belonging to her female line. The chance presented itself at the Newmarket December Sales of 1945 and, for 400 guineas, he bought Brazen Molly, young, unbroken, unraced and barren, but a granddaughter of Pretty Polly.

Brazen Molly's first foal had died, but she eventually produced four winners, of whom Stokes was second in the 1951 2000 Guineas. Her last foal, a highly-strung filly by the French Derby winner Prince Chevalier, failed to win a race. This was La Paiva, yet it was she who, on 4 March 1968, delivered the colt of Hislop's dreams. La Paiva's first three offspring were already winners and her 1967 foal, Town Major, had made it four by the time he and elder brother General Wolfe were joined at West Ilsley by Brigadier Gerard in November 1969. The Brigadier's sire, Queen's Hussar, added to the romance. A decent miler in his day with successes in the Lockinge and Sussex Stakes as a three-year-old, his unfashionable pedigree and disappointing four-year-old career caused him to stand at a lowly £250, the kind of sum, however, that Hislop could afford. Hislop had served with Astor during the war and initially patronized his trainer with the grey filly Bell Crofts in 1966. Hern won two minor races with her. Hislop's new contribution to West Ilsley's firepower would provide far more explosive ammunition.

The Brigadier was amenable and docile, perturbed only by thunderstorms and the proximity of a pony, which he would associate with a playmate of his youth. "He always does everything one asks of him, in the nicest possible way," said Hern. His policy with youngsters who are likely to be campaigned seriously as two-year-olds, is to educate them and bring them to three parts fitness in the spring before any dry weather begins to put a dangerous jar into the ground. The Brigadier's first test of racing ability came on 4 April 1970, a lovely morning, clear and fresh, when in company with six other colts he took part in a four furlong gallop on the Trial Ground, a special strip on top of The Ridgeway that Hern keeps chained off and locked, for special occasions such as this. The Brigadier was primed and ready. On the way to the start he whipped round and dropped Jimmy Lindley. Having told his rider who was boss the Brigadier stood still waiting to be remounted. He tended to victimize fully-fledged jockeys only, sparing Bob Turner, his regular partner at exercise: both Bobby Elliott and Joe Mercer also were forced to undergo this initiation ceremony. From a level start Brigadier Gerard took the lead and was comfortably ahead passing Hern, who stood with the Hislops at the finish. Either the chasing bunch was moderate, they concluded, or the Brigadier was pretty smart.

A slight temperature meant the colt missed his intended debut at Sandown and a spell of dry weather further delayed his appearance until the Berkshire Stakes at Newbury on 24 June. Hern's early conditioning work was advertised as soon as the Brigadier stripped for action. He travelled to post so impressively that Lord Porchester, the son of Queen's Hussar's owner, and thus an extremely interested party, rushed off to back the 100/7 outsider of five. The others all had winning form, but once Mercer let him go the Brigadier catapulted eight to ten lengths clear prior to easing down near the line. The next day Colum, one of the Brigadier's victims in Hern's gallop of 4 April, took his debut race by three lengths. Hern now knew he had a very decent horse on his hands.

The Brigadier's racecourse education continued without hitch in Salisbury's Champagne Stakes eight days later and the Washington Singer Stakes at Newbury on 15 August. He won them both in a canter. "I don't know what this horse is," said Mercer on dismounting at Newbury, "all I know is that when I ask him he just goes 'ping' and he's there." Brigadier Gerard's programme had been mapped out by his sagacious owner long before he had ever seen a starting stall. If the horse proved good enough Hislop wanted to run him in the Middle Park Stakes at Newmarket's first October meeting. He considered it unwise to run a prospective Guineas horse beyond six furlongs at this juncture in case a hard race took the edge off its speed. In addition, the Brigadier could only benefit from an outing on the Rowley Mile and an overnight stay in the racecourse stables.

Up until now the Brigadier had risen to every challenge with the minimum of fuss, but the form of his three wins could not be argued to be top drawer. The Middle Park would reveal his true colours. Ranged against him were the thrice unbeaten Mummy's Pet; Swing Easy, winner of the New Stakes, July Stakes and Richmond Stakes, but no match for the invincible My Swallow in the Prix de la Salamandre; Fireside Chat, behind Mummy's Pet at Doncaster and beaten four lengths by Mill Reef (who received 7lb) in the Salisbury Stakes; and the filly Renoir Picture. At home the Brigadier was outstripping his galloping companions with awesome monotony. One of them, Fine Blade, had just won his first two races. When Fireside Chat set only a moderate pace through the opening half-mile, certain to favour a pure sprinter like Mummy's Pet (the 6/5 on favourite), Joe Mercer kicked the Brigadier (9/2) into life and that was that. The favourite was beaten by three lengths.

Brigadier Gerard received 9st 5lb in the Free Handicap, 2lb below My Swallow and 1lb below Mill Reef. Some judges were critical of the Middle Park form, but lines through Fireside Chat and Swing Easy did not require excessively liberal interpretation for Brigadier Gerard to be regarded at least as the equal of the two horses rated above him. Someone, apart from Hern and Hislop, certainly thought so; Hislop received an offer of £250,000 for his colt, which was politely refused.

With three outstanding colts in the field (not to mention Nijinsky's brother Minsky) the build-up to the 1971 2000 Guineas was the subject of unprecedented media attention. Comparisons with the Guineas of 1886 won by the future Triple Crown winner Ormonde from another hitherto unbeaten colt, Minting, in a select field of six were commonplace when it became known that a similar sextet of quality would contest the 1971 race. Mill Reef, My Swallow and Minsky each won their respective prep races.

Confident in Hern's ability to get the Brigadier fit, Hislop elected to go for the Guineas without a previous outing. "You get very little time to learn about your classic three-year-olds before their testing time materializes," argues Hern, "and you want them, above all, to enjoy their work. They have it hard enough on the course." Instead, the Brigadier, who had grown an inch over the winter, was worked at Newbury racecourse on 18 April, and six days later given a final five furlong gallop on the Trial Ground. A few gallops have written themselves into Turf history, such as the famous day Fred Archer put the spur to St Simon and was run away with, or that spring morning in 1879 when Mat Dawson sent four past and future classic winners – Silvio, Jannette, Charibert and Wheel of Fortune – down the full Rowley Mile at level weights for the enlightenment of their owner Lord Falmouth with the words: "There's a sight, my Lord, the like of which you may never see again." Brigadier Gerard's final gallop, a week before the Guineas, was soon to be spoken of in the same category.

His companions were the four-year-old Duration, a recent winner at Warwick, who received 15lb rather than concede the stone weight-for-age allowance applicable at this time of year, and the three-year-old Magnate. The Ridgeway was no place to be at 7 am on Saturday, 24 April. The elements raged at their most foul. Dick Hern and his anxious owners crouched in their Land Rover at the finish mark as the windows rattled to the sound of teeming rain – conditions the Brigadier detested. Duration 'won' the gallop by about half a length. However, he had pinched four or five lengths at the start, according to Mercer, who, in addition, later discovered the suede jacket he'd been wearing had absorbed so much rainwater that he had carried 8lb more weight than arranged. Thus, the Brigadier had been attempting to give Duration one year and 23lb, i.e. 37lb in all. By a strange quirk of fate Duration's next race came thirty-five minutes before the 2000 Guineas in an apprentice handicap over the Rowley Mile. He won easily. Seven and a half lengths away in third, receiving 6lb, was National Park, Mill Reef's lead horse. "Absolutely bloody marvellous," said a smiling Hern to his jockey.

With the exception of My Swallow, the Brigadier dwarfed his rivals in the paddock. A magnificent specimen of highly-tuned horse-flesh quietly waiting to be unleashed, he reflected immense credit on his trainer. Hern knew this phlegmatic attitude to be the sign of a horse primed for action. "Unless they are temperamental by nature, the fit ones do not play the fool. They don't mess about." The message was not lost on Hislop. "Win, lose or draw," he told Hern, "I've never seen a horse better trained in my life." Despite a nod and a wink in their direction from Hislop regarding the Brigadier's homework, few gentlemen of the Press bar Clive Graham (whose nap he was in the *Daily Express*) took any notice and, like Ormonde, Brigadier Gerard was only third best in a six-horse market. They bet 6/4 Mill Reef, 2/1 My Swallow, 11/2 Brigadier Gerard.

Hern and Hislop climbed the steps to the grandstand roof from where, on a warm sunny afternoon, they could obtain an uninterrupted view right down the course. My Swallow, tracked closely by Mill Reef, bowled along in front towards the centre of the track, much as Minting and Ormonde had done in 1886. Fred Archer, aboard Saraband that day, explained Minting's ultimately dramatic capitulation thus: "When you get two smashing good horses trying to cut each other down over the Rowley Mile the pressure is so great that one or the other is sure to crack some way from home; it may be just a toss up which gives way first, but the one who does has no struggle left." It is impossible to state with any degree of conviction whether Mill Reef and My Swallow ruined their chances of with-standing Brigadier Gerard's challenge by taking each other on from the gate in the way they did. There were only six runners and neither of them wanted to be held up. "I wouldn't say they jumped off and cut each other's throats," says Mercer, "but they went a hell of a lick and played beautifully into my hands." Coming down into the Dip, Mercer gave the Brigadier one slap and in three strides the outcome was settled. Exhibiting the *élan* of the hussar whose name he bore, Brigadier Gerard elegantly put three lengths between himself and Mill Reef before the post was reached. My Swallow was a further three-quarters of a length adrift. "Not a moment's trouble. I thought we were going to win as soon as we went under the five furlong gate."

Hern had executed a tremendous feat of arms, for seldom in the increasingly competitive post-war era has the 2000 Guineas gone to a colt having his first run of the season. Happy Knight (1946) and Ki Ming (1951) won for Henri Jelliss and Michael Beary, while in Hern's training lifetime only Noel Murless, with Crepello (1957) and Royal Palace (1967) had engineered such a coup.

Brigadier Gerard side-stepped the Derby. Before even reaching the Newmarket winner's enclosure, Hislop had decided against making any attempt on a second classic. He believed neither track nor distance were right for his horse at this stage. Hislop's strategy entailed an assault on the principal races over a mile, finishing up with an initial attempt over $1\frac{1}{4}$ miles in the Champion Stakes on 16 October, the result of which would help determine likely targets for the four-year-old career he had always intended his horse should undertake. The Brigadier swept majestically through this pro-gramme of St James's Palace Stakes, Sussex Stakes, Goodwood Mile, Queen Elizabeth II Stakes and Champion Stakes collecting three of them by an aggregate of twenty-three lengths, but in the first and last he came perilously close to losing his undefeated record. Although the 2000 Guineas must have taken something out of him, Brigadier Gerard's weight loss was a negligible 7lb. (Nijinsky lost 29lb after his St Leger – sometimes a really severe race will cost a horse all of 40lb.) His narrow squeak at Ascot was due more to the soft ground (disliked by most of Queen's Hussar's progeny) than to any lack of fitness. Lester Piggott sent Sparkler straight into the lead, a sound tactic in heavy going since pursuers will experience difficulty accelerating to order. Two furlongs out precisely that occurred as Mercer started his run. The Brigadier floundered on a patch of exceptionally false ground, losing half a dozen lengths. Mercer sat still. The Brigadier recovered his equilibrium. Then, that rhythmic, hissing-swishing symphony denoting the perfect unison between Mercer's breathing and whip action gradually began to assume significance. Twenty-five yards from the post the Brigadier drew level with Sparkler and in the dying moments he thrust his head in front for the first and only time in the race.

Hern soon discovered the extent of the Brigadier's struggle: the horse had lost 24lb. Hislop's notion to run him in the July Cup was abandoned and the Brigadier waited for the Sussex Stakes on 28 July. The ground was officially declared soft, but it was nowhere near the quagmire of Ascot, and Brigadier Gerard proceeded to gallop his four rivals silly. He led from the stalls to trounce Faraway Son, the recent conqueror of My Swallow at Longchamp and the disqualified winner of the 1970 French 2000 Guineas, by five handsome lengths. Exactly a month later the Brigadier revisited Goodwood for another bloodless victory, beating Gold Rod by ten lengths in the Goodwood Mile, and in Britain's all-aged autumn mile championship, the Queen Elizabeth II Stakes at Ascot, only the French-trained Dictus, who had beaten Sparkler at Deauville, got to within eight lengths of him. "If Joe Mercer did not push him along a bit," his admiring trainer told reporters, "he would pull himself up, he's so lazy."

All that remained was to see how the Brigadier coped with the extra quarter mile of the Champion Stakes. Despite his long season the horse seemed better than ever and he had matured into an even stronger, more imposing individual. However, on the Saturday of the race it began to rain, a thin drizzle which by midday had developed into a downpour. The Brigadier instantly showed his distaste for the wind and rain. Only reluctantly did he negotiate the long trek across the Heath into the teeth of the gale to reach the starting gate. From their eyrie on the grandstand roof Hern and

Hislop watched the Brigadier cruise past Welsh Pageant into the lead with barely a furlong to run. "It's all over," ventured Hern. It wasn't. Bogged down by the sucking ground the Brigadier's stride shortened, while the diminutive 20/1 Irish outsider Rarity, a soft ground specialist, scuttled across the sodden turf, gaining hand over fist. The pair were inseparable passing the post, but the Brigadier had held on by a cat's whisker.

Paul Mellon's decision to keep Mill Reef in training with an eye to winning another Eclipse, King George and Prix de l'Arc de Triomphe caused much salivation in racing circles since this meant the possibility of a return match with Brigadier Gerard over a distance more conducive to the Guineas' runner-up. Before the 'Race of the Century', as the Press were already touting the Eclipse, it was hoped to give the Brigadier experience of Sandown in the Coronation Stakes on 21 April, but the onset of wet weather prompted his withdrawal. Instead he made his seasonal bow in the Lockinge. The expected victory took little out of him and nine days later he went to Sandown for his Eclipse dress rehearsal in the Westbury Stakes, where a second workmanlike, rather than spectacular, performance carried the day. However, with this season's principal objectives coming later in the year Hern had left plenty to work on.

The Brigadier's win in the Prince of Wales's Stakes at Royal Ascot was a foregone conclusion but there was drama nonetheless. Three days before the race Joe Mercer was involved in a plane crash. The light aircraft carrying him to a riding engagement in Brussels struck an overhead cable after taking off from Newbury. The pilot lost his life, as would have trainer Bill Marshall, his wife and the other passenger had not Mercer pulled them from the wreckage before it exploded. Though physically intact, Mercer was badly shaken by the experience. The Hislops were loath to sever the successful association between horse and jockey and insisted that Mercer should ride the Brigadier if he felt able. Under Hern's watchful gaze the jockey rode work on the Tuesday morning and pronounced himself ready for the fray. It is never wise to attach human qualities to equines but almost unbelievably Brigadier Gerard seemed to sense Mercer was not at his strongest. "The Brigadier knew I wasn't right; he did it all for me and never pulled at all." Despite ambling out of the stalls and losing several lengths, the partnership beat the subsequent Irish Derby winner Steel Pulse by five lengths in a new course record time and returned to a tumultuous ovation. Mercer was out on his feet and did not ride again for nine days.

Like many a contest hailed as the 'Race of the Century' since the 1903 original, when Derby winners Ard Patrick and Rock Sand took on the quadruple classic heroine Sceptre in the Eclipse, the 1972 version also went up in a puff of smoke. After winning the Prix Ganay and Coronation Cup Mill Reef fell sick and dropped out of the Eclipse with a temperature of 102°, probably the result of a mouth abcess. In fact, as rain began to fall, Brigadier Gerard's own involvement became doubtful. But, minus Mill Reef, the opposition was mediocre and, having walked the course, Hislop found the going reasonably sound up the centre of the straight. The Brigadier would run. He didn't relish the prospect of battling through yet more rain and mud but with his tongue lolling out he kept going up the hill to beat his old foe Gold Rod, though only by a length on this occasion. The race time of 2.20.20 was the slowest in Eclipse history, some fifteen seconds outside Mill Reef's record of the previous year.

In Mill Reef's continued absence because of a virus infection, Brigadier Gerard's participation in the King George VI & Queen Elizabeth II Stakes became a distinct likelihood. His pedigree insisted he would not stay $1\frac{1}{2}$ miles, but his generally relaxed style of running and the way he saw out the stiff Sandown $1\frac{1}{4}$ miles in atrocious conditions both suggested he could. Hern resisted the temptation to work him over the distance to find out. He kept him to seven furlongs. The Brigadier's forte was speed and it must not be blunted. At last the weather was on the Brigadier's side and a bright day greeted his sternest examination. Besides the extra distance he was also confronted by four other classic winners. From Italy came their unbeaten Derby winner Gay Lussac; representing France was Riverman, winner of the 2000 Guineas, the Prix Jean-Prat and Prix d'Ispahan over nine furlongs; Parnell and Steel Pulse had won an Irish St Leger and Irish Derby respectively. The classic horses, befitting the occasion, would fill the first five places.

Brigadier Gerard was an odds on favourite at 8/13; he was never anything else after the 2000 Guineas. Mercer's instructions were to "ride him on the assumption he stays". He desperately needed every ounce of stamina because the other jockeys were determined to make the pace hot in the hope of finding a chink in the Brigadier's armour. First Selhurst and then, after five furlongs, Parnell tugged the field

73

along. Mercer restrained the Brigadier until approaching the bend whereupon they smoothly began to make up ground on the leader. Parnell resolutely maintained his gallop – he had, after all, finished a close second in the $2\frac{1}{2}$ miles Prix du Cadran – but the Brigadier collared him at the quarter-mile pole and seemed set for a comfortable victory. However, he was now in unknown territory and, perhaps feeling the strain, he rolled towards the rails, causing Parnell's rider, Willie Carson, to stand up dramatically in his irons. Pulling his mount to the outside, Carson renewed his challenge but the gap was still $1\frac{1}{2}$ lengths at the line. At the inevitable stewards' enquiry the head-on patrol film, although confirming the Brigadier's erratic course, also showed that Parnell had made the incident look worse by hanging slightly left himself. After thirteen minutes the loudspeakers announced the places remained unaltered.

The Brigadier had now earned £203,218 from a perfect sequence of fifteen victories from fifteen starts. Among English classic winners Ormonde retired with an unbeaten record of sixteen, while Bayardo (1909 St Leger) won fifteen in a row after running unplaced in the 2000 Guineas and Derby. Two great fillies also matched Brigadier Gerard's score: Thebais's fifteen races included the 1000 Guineas and Oaks (1881), as did the Brigadier's ancestress Pretty Polly's in 1903–4. Then, in Paris, Pretty Polly forfeited her proud record to a totally obscure outsider in circumstances everyone was at a loss to explain satisfactorily. Sixty-eight years afterwards her kinsman would meet the same fate on his sixteenth racecourse appearance.

The Brigadier's downfall came not in Paris in the Arc (for which he had been entered) but at York in the newly-instituted Benson & Hedges Gold Cup over $10\frac{1}{2}$ furlongs. Apparently none the worse for his hard race at Ascot, he had regained his weight and was giving no indication of running the temperature that one or two of Hern's horses were. The 'Race of the Century' again evaporated when Mill Reef's training failed to please Ian Balding (and once and for all on 30 August when Mill Reef fractured a leg at exercise) leaving the Brigadier with most to fear from the two three-year-olds Roberto and Rheingold, first and second in the Derby. Trained by Vincent O'Brien, Roberto had been second in the 2000 Guineas prior to his short head Epsom victory, which largely resulted from the machine-gunned twelve stroke tattoo applied to his rear end by Lester

Piggott's whip during the final furlong. Piggott got the mount on Roberto after the horse's intended jockey Bill Williamson, injured in a fall ten days beforehand, was deemed unfit to take the ride. Continuing to play his customary game of musical chairs, Piggott now abandoned Roberto, who – quite understandably considering the race he had at Epsom – ran appallingly in the Irish Derby, and switched to Rheingold, winner of the Grand Prix de Saint-Cloud in the interim. As Williamson was diplomatically "unavailable", Roberto's owner John Galbreath, forthright boss of the Pittsburgh Pirates baseball team, took the unusual step of flying over Panamanian-born Braulio Baeza specially to ride Roberto (named after the Pirates' ace player Roberto Clemente) in this one race. Hindsight shows Roberto to have been an in-and-out performer (much like his dam), but 15 August 1972 was most definitely one of his good days. The level, left-handed track, the fast ground and the extended $1\frac{1}{4}$ miles were just his cup of tea and, galvanized by the different style and strategy of his new jockey, Roberto ran out of his skin.

In the United States every track is left-handed and in order to avoid the unpleasant kick-back from the dirt the predominant tactic is to start fast, get to the lead and stay there. When the York gates clanged open Baeza gunned Roberto six lengths clear. Crouching low into his horse he kicked again turning into the long half mile straight, leaving his pursuers, with the notable exception of the Brigadier, toiling in his slipstream. "A lot of people said Baeza stole the race but to my mind he didn't," says Mercer. "I thought I would be able to go and pick him off whenever I wanted to. Sadly, I couldn't." Two furlongs out the Brigadier got to Roberto's quarters and the record York crowd, who had applauded his entry to the paddock and turned out in their thousands for this moment, began to roar their approval. In a trice, the cheers subsided to groans at the sight of Mercer's whip rising and falling to no effect. Roberto kept on like a machine and Mercer, accepting this first defeat as graciously as he had celebrated fifteen consecutive victories, dropped his hands to spare the Brigadier any unnecessary punishment. The winning margin was three lengths and Roberto's time knocked a staggering 1.9 seconds off the course record which had stood since May 1959.

Roberto had excelled himself and run up to his very best form. The question for Hern to ponder was whether Brigadier Gerard had run up to his. The fact that he too finished inside the old track record and, according to an examination of the photo finish strip, had beaten his reliable yardstick Gold Rod by seventeen lengths (the judge gave it as ten) compared to one in the Eclipse and $10\frac{1}{2}$ in the Lockinge, suggested he had. However, when the horse was being led back to the stables he lowered his head and Buster Haslam noticed a large clot of mucus come out of a nostril. This could have obstructed his breathing during the race and prevented him from receiving sufficient oxygen to increase his speed when he needed to. Hern was convinced the seeds of Brigadier Gerard's defeat were sown in the very moment of victory at Ascot. "You could say he didn't stay $1\frac{1}{2}$ miles. I know he won over that distance at Ascot and beat some very good horses but the effort of doing so – of running out of his distance – just took the edge off him." It seems fair to conclude that a third tough race inside five weeks, after an enervating rain-sodden Eclipse and a stamina-sapping King George, was a shade too much even for the Brigadier. What with the journey and the race he was found to have lost 22lb.

Subsequently, Roberto ran tamely in two races at right-handed Longchamp, whereas, given a seven week rest and put back to a mile, Brigadier Gerard came out and, by design, smashed Ascot's track record in winning a second Queen Elizabeth II Stakes by six lengths from Sparkler. His swansong was to be another repeat, in the Champion Stakes, and the Brigadier duly vacated the stage he had graced for three seasons on a high note. "The Brigadier got 18,000 cheers," reported *The Sporting Life* after he had boosted his first prize-money to £243,924, a record for stakes won entirely in Britain.

"I had tears in my eyes and knew other people did," confesses Mercer. "It was the end of a wonderful partnership. He was a freak horse with tremendous enthusiasm and great speed and the class to win beyond his distance. He was a horse you never thought about getting beat on." Neither could the normally inscrutable Hern avoid the emotion of the afternoon as a call for three cheers rang out across the Heath. "I will be sorry to lose him," he said. "He has been a marvellous horse to train. After a time I could never see him getting beaten as long as we kept him well."

Hern had maintained the Brigadier's ability and enthusiasm through three seasons of intense competition at the highest level against his contemporaries, his seniors and, lastly, his juniors. "Dick's handling of the Brigadier's training was a copy-book example of how a racehorse should be prepared for his engagements," acknowledged John Hislop. As a result the horse had won races of Group I status at six furlongs, a mile, $1\frac{1}{4}$ miles and $1\frac{1}{2}$ miles, accomplishments beyond any other English classic winner of the post-war era. He was, and still is, the solitary English classic winner of the twentieth century to win as many as seven races as a four-year-old and deservedly captured the Horse of the Year award. The Brigadier returned the compliment by assisting Hern to his second trainers' championship and Hislop to the owners' and breeders'.

Sadly, by the time Brigadier Gerard died of a heart attack on 29 October 1989, the triumvirate of owner, trainer and jockey had split up and gone their separate ways. "Brigadier Gerard was a great racehorse," said Hern. "I was very sad to learn of his death. When I trained him I can never remember not being able to do with him what I wanted. Day to day, at exercise, he was never sick or sorry." Mercer added: "It's like losing one of the family. He was a great character and a lovely horse to be associated with." John Hislop contributed a touching, yet completely objective, appreciation to *The Sporting Life* which ended: "None has any just pretensions to greater honour and acclaim."

Although the Brigadier was not an unqualified success as a stallion, the passing of those seventeen years had done nothing to diminish his aura as a racer. Since the inception of the Pattern in 1971 no horse has won more than the Brigadier's thirteen (which excludes his Middle Park) and, in a way, it was fitting that none of his progeny inherited his unique talent. Defeated once he may have been, but as Timeform reminded its readers in their 1971 appreciation of him, there is an old proverb which goes: "The greatest beauty hath its blemishes and he's the best horse that stumbles least." It was impossible to believe Hern would ever train his like again, however long he remained in the profession.

Chapter Eight

NEW PATRONS & NEW LANDLORDS

'The main thing is to give your owners a good season'

OF THE COUNTLESS THINGS Hern absorbed at Porlock with
regard to the running of a happy and successful establishment, one
of the most profound was the Collings' credo that owners must
always come first. It was they who were special; they provided the
horses, they paid the bills. And in the guise of Lionel Holliday and
Jakie Astor they also paid Dick Hern's salary. Few owners are
rewarded with a classic winner, yet the training fees must still be
paid and, as Hern knew to his recent cost, there are times when
runners, let alone winners, are few and far between. "Before you
start thinking about next year's Derby and Oaks you must take
every precaution to keep the horses free from disease. The main
thing is to give your owners a good season. Their expenses are so
high, especially the owner-breeders."

To the list of owner-breeders already with horses at West Ilsley
when Hern assumed control would be added by 1972, the names of
Her Majesty the Queen, Sir Michael Sobell and Dick Hollingsworth.
All three favoured the low profile adopted by Hern himself. His
business was their business and nobody else's, a view not calculated
to endear any trainer to members of the Press hungry for information. Of Hern's new owners only Lady Beaverbrook enjoyed a
higher profile, which resulted from her compulsion, since she was
not an owner-breeder, to outlay vast sums of money at the yearling
sales.

The honour of training for the Queen was bestowed upon Hern in

1966 with the announcement that West Ilsley would receive six yearlings – Bristol Fashion, Forestry, Guiding Light, North Queensferry, Penal Code and St Patrick's Blue – in preparation for the following season. Captain Cecil Boyd-Rochfort was retiring at the end of 1968 after twenty-five years as a royal trainer, and West Ilsley – like Ian Balding's Kingsclere – was within sufficient hailing distance of Windsor Castle and Buckingham Palace for the Queen to visit at her convenience. Hern's inaugural intake was not particularly distinguished. They mustered nothing from seven outings in 1967, and St Patrick's Blue, who ultimately turned out to be the best of them, never even got to the track. Forestry opened Hern's royal account in a poor maiden race at Bath on 17 July 1968 but was soon upstaged by St Patrick's Blue who won the Cranbourn Chase Stakes at Ascot nine days later.

The first royal horse of any genuine ability that Hern trained was Charlton, a colt by Charlottsville out of Ibrox (home of Glasgow Rangers) and named after the footballing brothers. Charlton only ran once as a juvenile owing to sore shins, but Hern had him out early in 1970 to win his maiden. However, after winning the Predominate Stakes he was sore once again and missed the Derby, running in the King Edward VII Stakes at Royal Ascot instead. The hard ground nearly prompted his withdrawal and, in retrospect, he ought not to have run: for the third time in his life Charlton was jarred up. As the colt had been *hors de combat* for two months Hern aimed him at York's Eglinton Stakes rather than the fixture's accepted St Leger trial, the Great Voltigeur. All things considered Charlton won cosily and made the journey to Doncaster for the final classic. He finished fourth. Clearly Charlton was some way below the best of his generation over middle-distances but on breeding he might develop into a Cup horse (Ibrox was a half-sister to the Queen's dual Doncaster Cup winner Agreement). A crack at the Ascot Gold Cup seemed less far-fetched after Charlton won Sandown's Henry II Stakes, and with the advantage of soft ground he started second favourite for the stayers' blue riband, but was comprehensively drubbed by Rock Roi. He was a difficult horse to keep sound (Hern worked him uphill, seldom risking his joints with downhill exercise) and his limitations had been exposed. He won the William Hill Gold Trophy over the St Leger course in July and on his final appearance bravely carried top weight into fourth place in the Ebor, beaten by two necks and a head, in spite of a tendon going inside the final furlong.

Hern enjoyed better luck with the filly Albany, though not before resorting to sleight of hand. Albany was by the Queen's 2000 Guineas' winner Pall Mall out of her equally fine racemare Almeria, who won the Ribblesdale Stakes and Park Hill Stakes of 1957. She was a small filly with thinly soled feet and did not win in her first season. As a three-year-old she was coming into season every fortnight, which made her an erratic performer. Back in 1961 Hern encountered a similar problem with the Holliday filly No Saint and solved it by having her covered. Within three weeks No Saint's attitude began to change, her form improved accordingly and she won her first race for two years. Hern, and the Queen's racing manager Lord Porchester, therefore suggested to Her Majesty that Albany be covered by Queen's Hussar, who belonged to Porchester's father and stood at the Highclere Stud a stone's throw from West Ilsley. Safely in foal, Albany went to Newbury and won the Sandleford Priory Stakes. Then, after running fifth in the Oaks she travelled to Chantilly and was beaten only a neck by Cambrizzia in the Prix de Minerve. A month later Albany gained due recompense, signing off with an easy success in the Prix de Psyche at Deauville.

In the batch of royal yearlings delivered to West Ilsley toward the end of 1972 was a filly by Queen's Hussar out of Highlight, whose dam Hypericum won the 1000 Guineas of 1946. Named Highclere, the new arrival represented one of the Queen's most productive families – that of Feola – which numbered Aureole, Doutelle and Above Suspicion among its luminaries. Well-grown and feisty, she took some looking after and none of Hern's lads were keen to pick up the gauntlet. "There was a lot of fire inside Highclere," Hern reported. "A lot of credit must go to Betty Brister who did her. If she had an indifferent groom it might have ruined her." Brister, the solitary 'lass' in Hern's employ at the time, volunteered for the job. She alone fancied the challenge.

"She was a lanky filly and rather immature at two," recalls Joe Mercer. Moreover, Highclere had two distinct sides to her character. "In season she was dead but out of season she was really aggressive." Although Highclere ran three times as a two-year-old Hern realized that her potential would not be tapped until she was three. Nevertheless he did not envisage her developing into a classic filly to compare with None Nicer or Highest Hopes.

Highclere wintered well on a regime of trotting and cantering but failed to impress everyone in her early work. Rodney Boult regarded one gallop as the grimmest he has ever seen by a top class horse. "Joe Mercer rode Highclere and I was on an old maiden. We went a good gallop but she never got near us and I was never off the bit." Queen's Hussar had improved out of all recognition when fitted with blinkers so Hern tried them on Highclere. "About mid-April I worked Highclere a couple of times in blinkers which definitely helped her to concentrate and to run on better and so we decided to run her in blinkers in the Guineas." Due to her tardy progress Highclere missed all the trials and, following the pattern established by Brigadier Gerard, went to Newbury for a seven furlong gallop a week before the 1000.

Hern viewed the race with the Queen in the Jockey Club's Ladies' Box. The 4/1 favourite was Polygamy, winner of the Ascot trial, whom Highclere had met twice in 1973 with honours even. The royal filly was easy to back at 12/1. Hern knew she would stay every inch of the Rowley Mile and told Mercer to make the most of this stamina by riding her up with the pace. Mercer obeyed his instructions to the letter, striking the front on the descent into the Dip so as to accumulate every bit of momentum for the climb to the winning post. "Up the final hill Polygamy came at me and it was touch and go all the way to the line, but my mare just stuck her head out and would not give in. I went on riding till well past the post because the finish at Newmarket is so difficult to judge exactly." The royal party believed Highclere had been caught, but the camera showed she had hung on by a fraction.

Joining Noel Murless (Carozza) and Cecil Boyd-Rochfort (Pall Mall) as the trainer of a classic winner for the Queen made Hern's fourth classic success in his own right an occasion to be doubly cherished. To win a second Guineas with an offspring of Queen's Hussar – the only two classic winners he ever sired – making its seasonal debut was, furthermore, quite extraordinary. In fact, Highclere was the first since Fleet (1967) to win the 1000 Guineas first time out. From the unsaddling enclosure the Queen informed reporters that Highclere's next race was likely to be the French Oaks, the Prix de Diane, on Sunday 16 June, rather than the English Oaks because Chantilly was a more suitable track for the gangly, 16.3 hh filly. The slightly shorter distance (one mile $2\frac{1}{2}$ furlongs) also carried more appeal. After Polygamy had upheld Guineas form by winning at Epsom from a field which included three French challengers, the likelihood of Highclere lifting a first French classic for Hern and his royal patron increased by leaps and bounds. Comtesse de Loir and Hippodamia were considered the pair she had to beat, although her own stable companion Gaily, Sir Michael Sobell's winner of the Irish 1000 Guineas, had her supporters. The Hern fillies were flown over two days before the race. Highclere travelled contentedly and was full of herself – a sure sign that she was raring to go.

The race went like a dream. Hippodamia led into the straight with Highclere lying close up in third. "Then the miracle happened," said Joe Mercer afterwards. "Hippodamia came off the fence as she began to tire and I just shot through the narrow gap on the inside and that was it." Highclere won by two lengths and achieved something previously found impossible by the great French filly Hula Dancer, namely the 1000 Guineas–Diane double. Indeed, she was the first to win both.

Pandemonium ensued as Highclere returned to unsaddle. Hern, for one, took an age to penetrate the cordon of gendarmes. "There were so many patting her on the backside," said Mercer, "that it was a wonder she didn't kick out and kill the lot of them." Within thirty minutes of receiving the glittering gold trophy the Queen was on her way back to Windsor. The Herns and Mercers took a mite longer. However, as their light aircraft was crossing the Channel toward Shoreham, and customs clearance, a message crackled over the radio from the Queen's private secretary, Sir Martin Charteris, inviting them to dine at the Castle. The plane diverted to Heathrow where a car awaited them. At Windsor the Queen welcomed her "weary warriors" and escorted them through to meet their fellow diners, Prince Philip, the Queen Mother, Princess Anne, Lord Mountbatten, Lord and Lady Porchester and Michael Oswald, manager of the Royal Studs. "Dick was panic-stricken when the pilot had told him," says Mercer. "He had no tuxedo, needed a shave and was worried sick. It didn't matter, we smartened up when we got there. Winning the Diane gave me the greatest thrill of my career and the party was the loveliest thing on the greatest day of our lives."

Highclere soon recovered the 22lb lost during her Gallic expedition and, Hern felt, deserved a crack at the colts in the King George VI & Queen Elizabeth II Stakes. As it happened she would have most to fear from her own sex. She coped admirably with all of the colts, who included the Derby winner Snow Knight, but could not catch Dahlia, heroine of the race for the second year running. Undergoing a severe race over a distance beyond her optimum probably affected Highclere as much as it had Brigadier Gerard for she, too, ran below par in the Benson & Hedges Gold Cup. Dahlia virtually trebled her superiority while Snow Knight reversed Ascot form to the tune of nine lengths. Similarly, Highclere's final race, the Arc, in which she was the Queen's first representative and beat only two opponents, is also best forgotten. This was the first occasion Highclere had been asked to run in soft ground and on race day itself Hern found that she had come into season. He very nearly withdrew her. One of her Diane victims, Comtesse de Loir, ran Allez France to a head, which demonstrated how a top form Highclere might have fared. Still, Highclere went to the paddocks with an enviable record and her name would soon be heard of again.

One of the colts with egg on his face at Ascot was Buoy, with whom Dick Hern had won the Coronation Cup for Dick Hollingsworth. The addition, in 1972, of the tall, bespectacled and reserved Old Etonian owner of the Arches Hall Stud in Hertfordshire to Hern's growing coterie of owner-breeders introduced to West Ilsley members of the marvellous Felucca family that had been providing stockbroker Hollingsworth with top class winners for the best part of twenty years. Felucca was by the unbeaten Italian champion Nearco out of Felsetta, whom Hollingsworth's father Sydney purchased as a foal for 860 guineas in 1933. Of little account on the track, she became a veritable goldmine at stud, breeding eight winners. In 1955 her daughter Ark Royal won the Lingfield Oaks Trial, Ribblesdale Stakes, Yorkshire Oaks and Park Hill Stakes and lost just once, in the Oaks to Meld. The following year another daughter, Kyak, repeated the Park Hill victory and in 1958 Cutter, a frequent adversary of None Nicer, completed the Doncaster hat-trick after finishing third in the Oaks. At four Cutter won the Yorkshire Cup.

Buoy's dam, Ripeck, was a daughter of Kyak. Like nearly all the breed, he was big and backward as a baby and did not run as a two-year-old. He put himself in the Derby picture by winning the Predominate Stakes, but not being an Epsom type he went for the

Irish equivalent, finishing third. The St Leger seemed his ticket, especially after he won the Great Voltigeur from the Gordon Stakes' winner Duke of Ragusa. Buoy confirmed the placings at Doncaster but had no answer to the finishing speed of Peleid. Hern was at a lost to explain Buoy's defeat. "He was a great horse with a superb action. He wasted absolutely no time in the air. You hardly ever get a horse his size – he was at least 16.3 – with so much quality."

Any accusations that Buoy was merely a one-paced plodder were dispelled in 1974. He sprinted away from his field in the Yorkshire Cup over $1\frac{3}{4}$ miles and then made every yard of the running to win the Coronation Cup. With only a handful of competitors, Hern warned Mercer that the pace might resemble a crawl and to act positively. It was and he did. Stealthily increasing the tempo he and Buoy seized the initiative at the top of the hill and were ten lengths clear rounding Tattenham Corner. Although the Grand Prix de Paris winner Tennyson was gaining fast at the death, Buoy had enough in reserve. "It's not often you work out a plan in a race and find everything goes right," said a satisfied Hern. A concession of 4lb to Relay Race undid Buoy in the Hardwicke Stakes, but he easily added the Princess of Wales's Stakes to his tally before finishing fourth in the King George, the highest placed four-year-old colt. A sprained tendon in the Grand Prix de Deauville brought his career to an end.

In 1975 Buoy's close relative Sea Anchor carried the crimson Hollingsworth jacket in the classics. Despite winning the King Edward VII Stakes he unfortunately fared no better, finishing fourth in the Irish Derby and ninth in the St Leger. Staying was his game, however, and at four he won the Henry II Stakes, Goodwood Stakes (under a record ten stone) and the Doncaster Cup. In the Ascot Gold Cup only Sagaro and Crash Course were his masters.

In 1960 Dick Hollingsworth and Jakie Astor had agreed to an exchange of mares for a period of three years. Astor's Indian Twilight, winner of the Yorkshire Oaks and a half-sister to Trelawny, passed in one direction and Cutter in the other. Indian Twilight produced one winner for Hollingsworth before dying in 1961; Cutter, barren in her first year for Astor, produced a poor colt in 1962 and then a filly, Cutle, whom Hern trained to win twice over middle distances as a three-year-old. Cutle's second foal was a grey colt whom Astor christened Sharp Edge, and in 1972 he proved himself a useful two-year-old. His single defeat in four outings came in the Royal Lodge Stakes when he suffered anything but a clear run. Previously he had won at Newbury, Nottingham and Goodwood. Sharp Edge was almost as 'shouldery' as Highest Hopes and it was a devil of a job for Hern to keep him sound. Most of the time he worked on sawdust. He immediately stumped himself up during the Craven Stakes and only participated in the 2000 Guineas thanks to overnight rain. Much happier on the softer ground, Sharp Edge ran on strongly to snatch third place behind Mon Fils. With the going again to his advantage at the Curragh on 19 May he comfortably won the Irish 2000 Guineas by three lengths. An equally authoritative victory followed in Chantilly's Prix Jean Prat over nine furlongs in heavy ground, elevating the colt's reputation to such heights that he started a heavily-backed favourite for the Eclipse Stakes. Restrained in order to get the $1\frac{1}{4}$ mile trip, Sharp Edge was baulked as he tried to launch his challenge and trailed in last. Hern could only manage one more race with him – the Champion Stakes, after an absence of three months – in which he was the first male to finish behind Hurry Harriet and Allez France.

The most powerful figures among Hern's owner-breeders as the 1970s wore on were Michael Sobell and his son-in-law Arnold Weinstock. Born of Jewish parents in Austria on 1 November 1892, Sobell came to England when he was twelve and developed into a brilliant industrialist, a pioneer in the mass production of television sets. He eventually sold out to EMI but bought back a factory in South Wales and set up a new company, Radio Allied Industries.

In 1949 Arnold Weinstock married Sobell's daughter Netta, whom he met at a charity ball (Sobell was knighted in 1972 in recognition of his philanthropy), and was introduced to the family business in 1954. Weinstock's father, a Polish tailor, died when he was five and his mother shortly afterwards, leaving him to be raised by his brother. He was both clever and ambitious. After obtaining a degree in statistics at the London School of Economics, he took a post at the Admiralty, but by 1949 he had left the Civil Service and was working with Lewis Scott, the Mayfair property developer.

In 1961 Radio Allied Industries was taken over by GEC. Although he was only thirty-seven, Weinstock's managerial skills were already so highly regarded that it was rumoured in the City that GEC had paid £8.5 million for the company purely to secure his services and commitment. He was quickly installed on the main board and in 1963 became chief executive. Within four years the group's profits had increased by 375% and, at a cost of £160 million, GEC acquired Associated Electrical Industries, the biggest successful takeover bid in Britain. Weinstock was only just beginning. The following year he added English Electric to his collection, making GEC one of the world's largest electrical groups, with a market value of £900 million and a workforce of 250,000. Frequently described as a tough and sometimes ruthless manager of men, he was a businessman with but one aim in life, to earn a fair return on shareholders' capital. "Where he goes," one City journalist observed, "lesser mortals try to follow."

When asked once to explain his motivation Weinstock replied: "There are people who are committed to doing a thorough job, not only for reward but for its own sake." Such words might easily have been spoken by Dick Hern. Owner and trainer obviously spoke the same language, which was just as well. Hern was welcoming aboard an immensely forceful and dynamic character.

Although Weinstock (knighted in 1970 and made a life peer in 1980) had always been interested in the Turf it was his father-in-law who initiated their entry into the world of ownership when he paid 3,500 guineas for London Cry in December 1957. Sobell took two-thirds and Weinstock one-third and they sent him to be trained by Sir Gordon Richards. The partnership did not have to wait long for a substantial return on its investment because London Cry proceeded to win six of his nine races in 1958, culminating with the Cambridgeshire at odds of 22/1. The racing bug had bitten; interests were expanded, but buying at the sales proved too unpredictable. The answer was simple: breed your own. So, on the death of Dorothy Paget in 1960, Sobell and Weinstock bought her entire bloodstock empire – the 300-acre Ballymacoll Stud Farm in County Meath plus 120 thoroughbreds – lock, stock and barrel for £250,000. Among the countless broodmares they acquired in the deal were Interval, Desert Girl, Country House, Darlene (another old rival of None Nicer's) and Shrubswood, while their ready-made winner of the 1960 Park Hill Stakes, Sunny Cove, would also make her mark. Desert Girl's son Tiger won the 1963 Gordon Stakes after finishing third in the Irish Derby, a position filled four years later by Dart Board (out of Shrubswood), who was also third at Epsom and fourth in the St Leger. Undoubtedly the best animal to sport the 'pale blue, yellow

and white checked cap' colours was Reform (by Pall Mall out of
Country House), whose eleven victories from fourteen starts included
the St James's Palace Stakes, Sussex Stakes, Queen Elizabeth II
Stakes and Champion Stakes.

On Sir Gordon Richards' retirement from training at the end of
1970 the Sobell-Weinstock horses came to West Ilsley for the start
of the new season. Such a move constituted yet another massive seal
of approval for Hern the man and Hern the trainer. Only the best
would do for Sobell and Weinstock. Among their horses were Darlene's three-year-old colt Homeric and a pair of chestnut two-year-
olds, Sallust (out of Bandarilla, a daughter of Interval) and Sun
Prince (out of Sunny Cove's daughter Costa Sola), who would all
contrive to pay their way. But Sobell and Weinstock had bigger fish
to fry. "I knew Jakie Astor well and I said to him that if he ever
decided to sell West Ilsley that we would be interested," Weinstock
said after he and Sobell had become Hern's new landlords in 1973.
The Astor regime had the beneficial safety net of friendship. This
one was strictly business and smacked of the Holliday era. Hern
would need to be on his mettle. The profit and loss columns would
have to bear scrutiny.

Homeric turned out to be Hern's classic colt in 1971. He survived
a bad bump to win the Lingfield Derby Trial by two necks from
Spoiled Lad and Athens Wood but finished behind the latter in the
Derby itself. Athens Wood maintained the upper hand throughout
the remainder of the season, beating Homeric in the Gordon Stakes,
Great Voltigeur and St Leger. At Doncaster the margin was a neck.
Nine months later a neck was all that separated Homeric from
causing a real upset, for that was all Mill Reef had to spare at the
end of a pulsating race for the Coronation Cup. Homeric's proximity
to Mill Reef may have flattered somewhat, since Mill Reef, who was
found to have lost 33lb after the race, soon went down with a viral
infection. Even so, Homeric did go on to win the Prix Maurice de
Nieuil at Saint-Cloud in July and, staying in France to be trained
by John Cunnington, later won the Prix Kergorlay and was third,
finishing lame and beaten by only two lengths, in the Arc.

Successful juvenile campaigns were enjoyed by both of Sobell's
chestnut colts, though neither Sun Prince nor Sallust began aus-
piciously. "The first time Sallust ran he finished last and was a big
disappointment," remembers Mercer. "So we worked him in blinkers

and he went so fast that he sustained sore shins and couldn't run again for weeks." Wearing the blinds, Sallust broke his maiden at Salisbury and then ran the exceptionally speedy filly Stilvi to half a length in the National Stakes before winding up his season (minus blinkers) with a victory in the Richmond Stakes at Goodwood.

Sallust displayed a marked tendency to sweat up before his races. His compatriot Sun Prince was just as keen at home, where he was invariably ridden by Rodney Boult. "He was a very hard puller and very hard to beat on the gallops." By contrast, on his debut at Newbury, Sun Prince revealed no such vigour and finished a remote third. His odds of 20/1 for the Coventry Stakes, Royal Ascot's premier event for two-year-old colts, therefore looked about right, that is, until he came bursting up the stands rail to win going away. Sun Prince had made light of Ascot's desperate ground and at Maisons-Laffitte a month later he again used his stamina to excellent purpose, outstaying the future champion sprinter Deep Diver to win the Prix Robert Papin. Unfortunately, Sun Prince was struck into during a second French Group I race, the Prix de la Salamandre, causing him to finish last, but in the Middle Park he ran as though six furlongs was becoming too short for him. In the Free Handicap, topped by Crowned Prince on 9st 7lb, Sallust received 8st 11lb and Sun Prince a pound less.

In 1972 Sallust proved himself indisputably the best three-year-old miler in Europe. He sweated away his chance in Kempton's Guineas trial, and plans for Sallust to compete in the French 2000 (Sun Prince was earmarked for the English 2000 Guineas) were shelved. Thereafter his conduct and performance were beyond reproach. He won all of his five remaining races, starting with the Diomed Stakes on Derby day and concluding with the Group I Prix du Moulin de Longchamp, the mile championship of Europe, on 8 October. In between he collected the Prix de la Porte Maillot, the Sussex Stakes (Group I) and the Goodwood Mile. He twice inflicted defeat on the 2000 Guineas' winner High Top to fully justify his Timeform rating of 134, 5lb superior. Interestingly, Sallust's victims also included Brigadier Gerard's perennial rivals Sparkler and Gold Rod, beaten out of sight in the Sussex and Moulin respectively.

The responsibility of carrying West Ilsley's banner in the 2000 Guineas had fallen to Sun Prince. In the Greenham Stakes he raised no more expectations of classic glory than Sallust had at Kempton a fortnight earlier, for he only beat two home. He was a lot fitter at Newmarket and ran considerably better without ever appearing likely to trouble either High Top or Roberto. However, on his third and final appearance of 1972 (a chipped bone brought about this premature curtailment), Sun Prince accounted for Home Guard and Grey Mirage in the St James's Palace Stakes. Sallust's retirement to the Irish National Stud gave Sun Prince the opportunity of supplanting his erstwhile stablemate at the top of the milers' tree. He needed a couple of races to recover battle hardiness but Hern had him in peak condition for the Queen Anne Stakes. After a rare battle with Sparkler he completed a notable Royal Ascot hat-trick of Pattern races at two, three and four years of age. Races became tougher to win thereafter and the Queen Anne was his last. Sun Prince was some way short of Sallust's class. Even so, Hern would never again have three milers of the quality of Brigadier Gerard, Sallust and Sun Prince in his yard simultaneously as he did in 1972.

In Joe Mercer's view Hern had possessed a two-year-old superior to both Sallust and Sun Prince in 1971. The animal in question was Rampage. First time out this 16,500 guineas colt won the Salisbury Stakes; next time he collapsed and died during the New Stakes at Royal Ascot. He belonged to Marcia, Lady Beaverbrook, another former patron of Sir Gordon Richards who had sent horses to Dick Hern.

Once she entered the world of racehorse ownership in 1966, upon the death of her second husband, Lady Beaverbrook spent a small fortune on yearlings ($£1\frac{1}{2}$ million within ten years) to carry her 'beaver brown and maple leaf crossbelts'. Her infrequent visits to the racecourse, her frail build, white hair and dark sunglasses created the impression of a Miss Havisham figure with nothing better to do with her money than spend it on racehorses which seldom repaid their purchase price. However, this could not disguise the fact that Lady Beaverbrook had been a shrewd businesswoman who became wealthy in her own right before either of her marriages.

Born Marcia Anastasia Christoforidi, the daughter of a tobacco merchant of Cypriot extraction, she grew up in the suburban atmosphere of Sutton, in Surrey, far from the giddy whirl of the upper-class roundabout. A burgeoning interest in politics led her to write a letter to the *Sunday Express* which so impressed the editor that he obtained for her a secretarial post with Sir James Dunne, a friend of Lord Beaverbrook and another successful Canadian businessman. She earned £1.50 per week. Acting on Dunne's advice the young secretary invaded the stock market. That June she realized all her assets and plunged the lot on Maid of Essex in a hot sprint at Royal Ascot. The filly was a certainty, she had been reliably informed. The Maid won by a short head at 8/1!

After acting as Dunne's personal assistant throughout the 1930s, and nursing him through an illness that almost proved fatal, she became his second wife on 7 June 1942. When Dunne died in 1956 he left a conservative £6 million. Soon afterwards his widow sold her own personal holdings in his Algoma Steel Corporation for $7.2 million. Consequently, Lady Dunne was not short of funds when, at the age of fifty-three she married Lord Beaverbrook on 7 June 1963, and she insisted that he make no provision for her in his will. Beaverbrook died of cancer in 1964. He had flirted with racing in the 1920s, breeding the useful colt Miracle which, sold to Lord Rosebery, won the Eclipse. Lord Rosebery now returned the compliment, as it were. "He thought I should not sit around and mope but have a go with racehorses." Accordingly, his lordship bid 4,800 guineas for a filly which Lady Beaverbrook appropriately dubbed Rosebid – seven letters in the name, the number associated with both her wedding days and, coincidentally, the same number as in *Express*. Sent to Walter Nightingall, Rosebid won first time of asking in Epsom's Banstead Stakes on 26 April 1967. Later that year Hametus landed the valuable and prestigious double of the Imperial Stakes (at Kempton) and the Dewhurst.

Hametus failed to train on, unlike Royalty, a 21,000 guineas half-brother to the Gimcrack and Papin winner Double Jump whom Hern inherited from Sir Gordon Richards. A brown colt by Relko, he finished second on his only start as a juvenile, but he began 1971 by reeling-off six wins on the trot. Despite these victories being achieved in relatively quiet waters (the sixth was in a three runner race at Redcar), such was Royalty's progress that he was allowed a shot at the Prix de l'Arc de Triomphe. Royalty acquitted himself wonderfully well. Shrugging off the effects of some early interference he came storming up the straight to pass horse after horse and finish sixth, about six lengths behind Mill Reef. Left trailing were Bourbon (French St Leger), Irish Ball (Irish Derby) and Ortis (Italian Derby). Royalty's display looked even better once Mercer divulged that he had broken down half a mile from the finish. Although the intention was to keep him in training Royalty never ran again.

Not far behind Royalty in the Arc was Michael Sobell's French-based Oarsman, who earlier in the year had been trained by Hern. He was the first foal of the Doutelle mare Ship Yard. Her fourth foal, a bay colt by the Eclipse and King George winner Busted, came up for sale at Newmarket in October 1972. Hern and Sir Gordon (now acting as racing manager to Lady Beaverbrook and Sobell) put the colt on their shopping list and bought him for 21,000 guineas. Lady Beaverbrook called him Bustino. He managed one run as a two-year-old before a runny nose and flu symptons persuaded Hern to put him away for the winter with the Derby his prime objective. However, for a raw colt like Bustino to enter calculations for the Derby, which comes so early in the racing calendar, he urgently needed plenty of efficient tuition at home and racing experience on the track. Besides inheriting horses and owners from Sir Gordon, Dick Hern also gained some of his staff. Chief among them was Brian Procter, who became West Ilsley's principal work-rider. It was his responsibility to educate Bustino.

A native of Greatham, near West Hartlepool, Procter joined Sir Gordon in 1958 and rode his first winner two years later on Olmedo, at Bath, getting the better of stable-jockey Scobie Breasley on Beaudeer. By the end of his apprenticeship Procter had partnered fourteen winners but during his last six years with Sir Gordon he added only two more, the last being Dart Board on 10 September 1966. "It's been a struggle ever since I finished my apprenticeship – I should have pushed myself more – and everything seemed to be going downhill until things levelled out when I came to West Ilsley. Bustino was the toughest horse I've ever ridden here, tough as old boots; the more you'd dig, the more he'd keep giving you. Brigadier Gerard was the first good horse I sat on here. The good ones never frighten you, but when you think how much they're worth, you keep thinking to yourself, don't fall off whatever you do." By April Bustino was in steady work and learning fast. In one six furlong gallop, says Procter, "I got hold of him, cracked him down the shoulder and he shot through to get the better of the others." Within a fortnight 'the others' all won races.

Bustino's seasonal debut was set for the Sandown Classic Trial. As a maiden Bustino received 5lb from most of his eight rivals, of whom Snow Knight was made favourite. Bustino won, all out, by half a length from Snow Knight, a pretty satisfactory performance from Hern's viewpoint since this was only Bustino's second race and Snow Knight's sixth. The Lingfield Derby Trial came next on Bustino's agenda. Now he met Snow Knight at level weights but, given normal improvement, Hern believed this to be a comparatively straightforward task. This time Bustino put $2\frac{1}{2}$ lengths between himself and Snow Knight, which represented an improvement of 9lb on their Sandown running.

Therefore, it ranked as a bitter disappointment when Bustino, the 8/1 third favourite, finished fourth at Epsom, particularly as the race went to Snow Knight, at 50/1 the second longest-priced winner since the war. Snow Knight blazed a trail from the top of Tattenham Hill at which point Bustino had only three behind him. Mercer realized he was too far off the pace. "But I was stuck and couldn't get out. All of a sudden the tempo quickened and I didn't get a clear run until far too late. We came from nowhere and were flying at the finish."

Apart from offering tantalizing evidence that Bustino may have been an unlucky loser, the Derby confirmed the colt to be an out-and-out stayer. Consequently, Bustino went to France for the Grand Prix de Paris run over a distance just short of two miles, as rigorous a test of stamina for a three-year-old in June as could be imagined (so much so that the distance was reduced to $1\frac{1}{4}$ miles in 1986). The ground was very soft, worse than anything Bustino had encountered, and he ran a grand race to get within two lengths of the future triple Ascot Gold Cup winner Sagaro. Bustino lost 34lb in this gruelling trip to Paris, which capped a taxing early season campaign for the colt. Hern rested him until it was time to limber up for the Great Voltigeur, his stepping stone to the St Leger. The York race was no formality, however, because it was also the 'trial' selected by Peter Walwyn for his Leger candidate, the Irish Derby winner English Prince. Bustino passed English Prince with two furlongs to run and galloped on relentlessly to win by four lengths.

English Prince was subsequently withdrawn from the classic on account of soreness in his off fore, but Bustino continued to burn up the gallops. Eleven days before the final classic Bobby Elliott rode Bustino in a $1\frac{1}{4}$ mile gallop prior to his departure for Hong Kong and his winter job. He pronounced it the best piece of work he had seen at West Ilsley. Brian Procter replaced him for Bustino's last bit of sharp work, five furlongs up the all-weather two days before the race.

"The gallop lad had put the cutter by the side of some trees, just off the gallop. It hadn't been put there before and as Bustino spotted it he whipped round and put me flat on my back. Knowing the Leger was so close, I hung on for dear life." Just as well he did, for Bustino seemed certain to atone for the disappointment of Epsom. Neither Imperial Prince nor Giacometti, who finished ahead of him in the Derby, were sure to stay the extra quarter mile and the rest of the field were decidedly second-rate. Hern chose to run Riboson as a pacemaker to ensure there was no dawdling. Riboson and Jimmy Lindley accomplished their task to perfection, leading Bustino to the three furlong marker, whereupon he strode away to win by three lengths from the dogged but outclassed Giacometti.

At long last Lady Beaverbrook had won a classic. "I must admit that the build-up to today has been rather like facing a major operation," she told pressmen, "but it was worth it. I love Bustino. He's so gallant, kind and lion-hearted." Hern, too, praised Bustino's courage. "He's a grand racehorse, very tough and genuine and he got the trip well. What he wanted was a good pace. I always thought he was unlucky in the Derby – Joe Mercer could never get where he wanted."

1974 had been a fine year for Hern. He had won four classics in three different countries via Highclere, Gaily and Bustino, and just lost out to Peter Walwyn in the race for the trainers' championship. Gaily's Irish victory brought another £19,401, while Highclere's Diane yielded £93,550 and Bold Pirate's success in the Prix Saint-Roman £9,533.

Bustino's final season will forever be remembered for the race he lost in record time – the King George VI & Queen Elizabeth II Stakes – rather than the race he won in record time – the Coronation Cup. When he reappeared at Epsom it could be seen that he had matured into a tremendously powerful individual who, to be accurate, now stood 16.1 hh and weighed 9½ cwt. With the faithful Riboson once more handling the pacemaking chore Bustino clocked 2.33.31, over two seconds faster than Grundy had won the Derby. "Because he won the St Leger people believe he is purely a stayer but that's a lot of cock," declared Sir Gordon Richards defiantly. "To say he just plods along does not make sense when he has beaten the course record. He may be a staying sort but he still has a remarkably good turn of foot.''

Hern's schemes for Bustino's Ascot clash with Grundy were positively machiavellian. The loss of Riboson through a cracked cannon bone had deprived him of the one horse who could be relied upon to force an early gallop which would extract the venom from Grundy's finish. Peter Walwyn's chestnut had won the Irish 2000 Guineas and could be expected to outsprint Bustino in a slowly run race. However, Hern had not played all his cards. He'd had the good sense to leave three others in the race as potential pacemakers. Irritatingly, none of the three, Kinglet, Highest and Bigribo, was individually good enough to replace the inestimable Riboson. Hern realized that there was only one thing to do. He decided to adopt the audacious ploy conceived by Walter Earl for the Ascot Gold Cup of 1949. Earl inserted two pacemakers to run the finish out of Black Tarquin so that Alycidon's stamina won the day. Highest was the fastest horse at Hern's disposal, so he would lead over the initial six furlongs. Then, Kinglet would take over. All the while, Bustino would lie handy, ready to strike the instant he entered the short $2\frac{1}{2}$ furlong Ascot straight.

Hern's plan almost worked. Despite watering, the track, with the country in the grip of a heatwave, was lightning quick and conducive to a flat-out assault on the clock. There were, of course, other contenders besides Grundy and Bustino: the Irish Oaks heroine Dibidale; Star Appeal, recently triumphant in the Eclipse and later to win the Arc in sensational style; not to mention the irrepressible Dahlia bidding to win the event for the third successive year. Dahlia was a mare in a million but she was not the animal of 1974 and everyone suspected that the King George really boiled down to a shootout between Grundy (5/4 favourite) and Bustino (4/1). Nevertheless, it was the two 500/1 also-rans who stole the show to begin with.

The distinguishing black cap atop Frankie Durr immediately bobbed to the head of affairs. In what seemed the blink of an eye the field was strung out in Indian file like a band of pony trekkers. The gallop down into Swinley Bottom was murderous. Highest was clocked at 24.17 and 21.13 over the opening two quarters, which constitutes sprinting speed. Meeting the rising ground Highest predictably dropped away completely spent, leaving Kinglet to pick up the tempo with no discernible slackening. The order of pursuit now read Star Appeal, Bustino, Grundy, Dahlia and stayed that way until four furlongs from home. Having run a mile in 1.35.39 Kinglet was exhausted. If this white-hot pace was to be maintained round the turn and into the straight Bustino would have to dictate it himself. Mercer gave him a kick and smoothly, decisively, they opened a gap of maybe four lengths.

Pat Eddery, momentarily caught napping on Grundy, gave chase. All eyes were riveted on the big bay answering every hiss of Mercer's rhythmic demands and the flaxen-maned chestnut responding gamely to Eddery's whip. Grundy got his nose in front at the furlong pole. Bustino fought back heroically. The gap closed again. Then, Bustino's tongue flopped out, his strength ebbed away and he rolled toward the rail, finally, like the submission of some leviathan of the deep, conceding honourable defeat to a younger and stronger opponent.

It was all over. "Only those with iced water for blood could remain aloof from the excitement that flooded through the stands," wrote Hugh McIlvanney in the *Observer*. "The last two furlongs turned out to be perhaps the best two-horse race any of us can hope to see." In *The Sunday Telegraph*, John Oaksey also assured his readers that this race "will never be forgotten by anyone fortunate enough to see it ...Grundy and Bustino combined to do British racing a signal honour." Needless to say the track record had fallen – by 2.36 seconds – the time of 2.26.98 stating quite categorically that the 1975 King George had actually been the second fastest electrically-timed $1\frac{1}{2}$ miles ever run in this country.

"I'm as proud of Bustino as if he had won," said Hern, whose sole regret was the absence of Bustino's usual pacemaker. "I think he might just have done it if Riboson had been there to lead him into the straight. Bustino was in front a long time and it proved just too much for him in the end." Joe Mercer's immediate reaction was to concur: "There cannot be a horse alive who could give Grundy a stone and hope to live with him. The pace was red hot and my horse just faltered in the last 100 yards. He was so brave. He broke the track record giving away a stone." Some years on, however, he was to reflect: "Bustino got beaten because he broke down half a furlong from home. He only cantered once after that. His tendon had gone.

If you watch the race, he's winning, winning, winning. Then all of a sudden he changes his legs."

This epic duel effectively polished off both protagonists. Grundy was humbled in the Benson & Hedges Gold Cup not only by Dahlia but also by Card King and Star Appeal, all three of whom he had thrashed at Ascot. Bustino developed a tendon strain when doing his first sharp canter a week afterwards. He remained on course for the Arc until 31 August. Then, as painter Peter Biegel was posing Bustino for a portrait, Hern ran a hand down his off fore and detected tell-tale signs of heat. Turning on his heel, he marched to the phone and rang the Press Association to announce Bustino's retirement. Although Brigadier Gerard won a King George ("He was whacked at the end"), Joe Mercer insists Bustino was the best horse over $1\frac{1}{2}$ miles he ever rode.

If any horse surpassed Bustino in Lady Beaverbrook's affections it was Boldboy. He alone is provided for in her will; he alone enjoyed a tenth birthday party attended by Dick Hern, Joe Mercer, Willie Carson, Sir Gordon Richards and his doting owner. Boldboy cost Lady Beaverbrook a mere 13,000 guineas and as a gelding could neither repay her with prestigious Group 1 victories nor a lucrative income from his activities at stud. Yet it is Boldboy she loves above all others. "Boldboy gave me so much pleasure in his racing days that he will always be well cared for. He means a great deal to me and I always visit him when I'm in Newmarket." Boldboy's accommodation at the Warren Stud befits a lady's favourite. He has a shelter shed separating two paddocks (one winter, one summer) and a pair of spanking new boxes have been modified by the insertion of a linking grill so that Boldboy can stand muzzle to muzzle with his companion, his owner's Ebor and Northumberland Plate winner Totowah. He possesses a head collar embossed with his name and a board on the wall tabulates his victories as if he were a stallion.

Boldboy's transformation from wayward youngster to a lady's favourite is one of the most remarkable episodes in Dick Hern's entire training career. Boldboy competed for eight seasons, winning fourteen of forty-seven races and was out of the first four on just five occasions. He won eight Pattern races and was considered by many to be the classiest gelding to have run in Britain since the war. But Boldboy was no saint. Indeed, in deference to the cinematic hero of the day Jonathan Powell of the *Sunday Mirror* called him

Jaws. "He's put four stablelads in hospital and spends most of his life on a running-lead attached to a metal bar across the width of his box. He's tough, obstinate, pig-headed, bad-tempered ..." Boldboy certainly had a hell of a temper. "He bit my arm once and sent me to hospital," admitted his lad Allan Thimbleby, "and picked up one lad by his shoulders and carried him right out of the box."

Boldboy was a one-sided rig and this defect doubtless conspired to lower his purchase price. His volatile temperament was inherited from his paternal grandsire Nasrullah and, as if that were not sufficient, Boldboy was subjected to a disturbing psychological experience as a yearling. "He had an accident on the plane bringing him over from Ireland, smacking his jaw, and was confined to his box for a fortnight," relates Thimbleby. "Well, he lashed out one day, kicked-in the side and then got some of the splintered wood stuck in his backside which left a three-inch wound about a quarter of an inch deep. He carried this scar for the rest of his life. After that we built this special box for him with the walls made up of vertical railway sleepers covered with rubber and a net under the ceiling to stop him rearing."

Hern's ordeal was only just beginning. "Boldboy was not easy to train, and was very difficult in the starting stalls. In fact he became positively dangerous. When you persuaded him to go in, he would lay down on his side and stick his legs right through the other side. I was always afraid that the jockey would get hurt because the colt would throw himself violently about when he went in." Boldboy's pathological hatred of confinement in the stalls, possibly derived from the traumas of that plane journey, had to be cured if he was to fulfil his potential. Hern had special attachments fitted to the West Ilsley practice stalls so that the sides went right down to the ground, eliminating any chance of Boldboy thrusting his feet underneath.

Boldboy was the most arduous task Hern ever entrusted to Brian Procter. "He was a bit of a lad. We had to do an awful lot of work with him, went out twice a day, three canters – anything to get him to stand in there and realize things weren't as bad as they looked. You mustn't let them think you're afraid of them in any way. The minute you do, they'll have you forever more, turn your back and one way or another they'll try to do you." Somehow Boldboy was installed for his debut race at Ascot, though he showed no inclination

97

to vacate them and finished fourth. At Newbury, two months later, he threw Mercer two or three times in the paddock and refused to go near the dreaded apparatus.

Having eventually got Boldboy through a stalls test, Hern decided on the outrageous policy of bypassing maiden races, in which large fields spelt potential mayhem at the gate, in favour of a tilt at the Middle Park Stakes. Not wishing to risk his stable-jockey, the mount went to Procter. "Of course, Boldboy was quite up to Middle Park standard," says Hern. "When I gave Procter a leg up on him I said, 'Now then, Brian. This is your chance to win the Middle Park' and I really meant it. Brian did wonderfully well. He got him in the stalls, got him out and rode a good race. He looked like winning for a long way and finished fourth. The trouble was that I could not give Boldboy the right preparation because to get him in the frame of mind for the race I had to work him very hard beforehand." Procter deserved the plaudits. Down at the start Boldboy's head-band rose over the horse's ears and when Hern went to pull it back Boldboy cocked his head and clouted the hapless jockey full in the face.

Despite Boldboy's promising performance it had to be admitted that his career was in the balance. "I knew he had fair ability and did not want to castrate such an animal. But I also knew that, with a winter over his head and, being that much older, his chances of success were not good. In fact, if he had remained entire, I doubt if I could have trained him. He would have been no use." Or, as Mercer puts it, "Had he been a colt he wouldn't have been worth a two-bob bit."

The vet's knife almost certainly rescued Boldboy's racing career since, although tricky on occasions, he never again refused to enter the stalls. He could not now run in the Guineas but in defeating Mon Fils, the eventual winner, and Lunchtime, the top two-year-old of his generation, in the Group III Greenham Stakes, he emphasized the fact that it would have been within his compass. Whether one judges Boldboy's subsequent career to be that of a miler or a sprinter it remains safe to assert that he never competed in anything other than the highest possible class in either category. Throughout his seven campaigns as a gelding, totalling forty-five races, Boldboy only twice competed in handicaps. On his first visit to France, he broke the seven furlong track record at Longchamp in winning the

Prix de la Porte Maillot, another Group III event. In September he showed his versatility by adding a third, the Diadem Stakes over six furlongs, before reverting to seven and taking the Challenge Stakes. His quartet of Group III successes had netted £22,274.

During the next six years Boldboy added the Lockinge (Group II) over a mile, the Duke of York Stakes (Group III) and Vernons Sprint Cup (Group II) over six furlongs, a second Challenge Stakes and a four-timer in his customary debut race, the Abernant Stakes at the Newmarket Craven meeting. Of these, the Duke of York on 12 May 1977 remains the most vivid to Dick Hern. Heavy rain had threatened his participation and only after Hern and Sir Gordon Richards had walked the course was the decision taken to run. The last thing Lady Beaverbrook wanted was for Boldboy to be pulled about in the mud. She need not have worried, for as Hern recalls, "He came up that far rail with the others only just in sight. A most impressive performance." That season his earnings of £44,271 put him ninth in the list of leading horses with only Group I winners above him.

Boldboy ran his forty-seventh and last race at Haydock on 21 May 1979, finishing third. He narrowly failed to crack the £100,000 barrier in first prize-money, retiring with £95,392 from his fourteen victories. If place money were added the figure rose to £131,073 (plus £482 won as a colt in the Middle Park), more than double the existing record for a gelding on the Flat in this country. And despite the march of inflation this sum was not exceeded until the inter-continental exploits of Hern's Bedtime and the northern hero Tele-prompter in the mid 1980s. "A very sound, brave horse and so consistent," Hern says by way of a summary. "A grand horse to train. He hardly ever ran a bad race, was effective from six furlongs to a mile and kept his form right through the season."

Boldboy's final race at Haydock was in the hands of Willie Carson, who had replaced Joe Mercer as West Ilsley's stable-jockey in 1977. The furore surrounding that decision placed Hern in an invidious position, which was both awkward and compromising. Though not of his making, the decision nevertheless sucked him into the eye of the storm. He was bound by it and therefore figured extensively in the attendant speculation inevitably whipped up by the media.

Chapter Nine

EXIT MERCER

'The pound will be knocked off the front page ...'

ALBEIT RESPECTED AND ADMIRED by his peers, Dick
Hern was not, in 1976, a man with whom the racing world at large
could identify. Joe Mercer was. Everybody liked Mercer – owners,
trainers, stable-lads, punters, journalists – everybody. Consequently, when the jockey, accompanied his boss and Lord Porchester
into the Epsom Pressroom on Thursday, 3 June 1976 and said, "Will
you tell them, Dick or shall I?" he stirred up a hornet's nest. After
twenty-four seasons as West Ilsley stable-jockey – fourteen of them
with Hern – he had been sacked at the instigation of Sir Michael
Sobell and Sir Arnold Weinstock in favour of Willie Carson.

The racing community was stunned and shocked by the sheer
timing of this announcement let alone its content. Only twenty-four
hours earlier Mercer had ridden the Hern-trained Relkino into second
place in the Derby. Clive Brittain, who retained Carson, was unaware
he was losing his jockey until he went out to give Carson the leg-up
on to Hunnylyn in the second race of the afternoon. Nor was his
principal owner, Captain Marcus Lemos, amused: "It was the way
the whole wretched business was announced. I first heard the news
on television. I still maintain I should have been told first."

Needless to say, none of the West Ilsley backroom staff had any
inkling that a change was in the offing. "It came as a shock to us all
but it was not something we would know about," says David Murray-
Smith. However, Joe Mercer knew of his impending dismissal the
previous October. Now, having learnt that his worst fears would be

realized, he asked for an announcement to clear the air. Taken aside in the Epsom car park by Lord Porchester, he was shown the prepared statement. It read: "The owners of the stable have made an irrevocable decision to make a change. It was not in the other owners' interests to employ two jockeys in the same stable. I know Her Majesty will be pleased for Joe to continue to ride her horses at Kingsclere."

So, after riding over five hundred winners for Dick Hern, Mercer was out of a job that had seemed his until he no longer wished to don boots. The sudden and chilling dispatch of a man widely regarded as the supreme exponent of the skills associated with the traditional, classical, school of English jockeyship was bound to ignite furious speculation about the circumstances leading up to such a decision. It did. Within minutes of the news being made public John Oaksey was telling ITV viewers, "The mind boggles if you are not satisfied with Joe Mercer."

Oaksey's candid response typified immediate reaction. According to Lord Porchester even the Queen was "very distressed that Joe was going. But she said that the owners had a majority of the horses and also owned the yard and there was nothing that we could do. We discussed the possibility of having two jockeys. Joe might still have been able to ride the royal horses. But that would not have worked. You can't have two number one jockeys in one stable."

One could argue endlessly about the relative merits of the two jockeys, it was agreed, without ever reaching any cast iron judgements. Carson had twice been champion jockey; Mercer had never finished better than third. On the other hand, Mercer was the big-race jockey, with five classics to his name whereas Carson had only one . . .and so it went on. Leaving aside the contentious question of ability, the most obvious advantage of the switch was Carson's age. At thirty-three he was eight years younger than Mercer. He could also ride at 7st 10lb, some 8lb lighter than Mercer, a considerable asset in a yard like Hern's where blue-blooded horseflesh warranted nothing but the best assistance from the saddle at all times. West Ilsley has never produced a leading apprentice rider, which is somewhat surprising in view of Dick Hern's Porlock reputation as an instructor of rare talent. Quite simply, the kind of horses Hern trained for the Sobells, Weinstocks, Beaverbrooks *et al* were too valuable to be entrusted to apprentices. This sort of owner wanted to see the stable-jockey guiding their investment, not Joe Bloggs. It was essential that the stable-jockey partnered as many of West Ilsley's runners as possible and in that respect Carson's 8lb advantage would prove invaluable.

"I accept that in my position I will attract publicity," Weinstock once admitted. "But that does not mean that I enjoy it." As soon as this story broke, he was assured by Lord Porchester, "The pound will be knocked off the front page of the *Evening Standard*" – no gross exaggeration as it transpired. Profiting from three days in which to prepare their arguments, the Sunday papers fired the most damaging salvos, none more penetrating than those loosed by John Oaksey in *The Sunday Telegraph*.

In his piece entitled "The day Joe had to go" Oaksey began by pointing the finger of responsibility directly at Weinstock. "There is not much dispute about who decided that, after 24 years at West Ilsley, Joe Mercer should be replaced by Willie Carson. Nor, of course, is there any dispute whatever that the man who effectively owns and controls a stable, in this case Sir Arnold Weinstock, has every right to do the hiring and firing just as he pleases. But whatever part other members of Sir Arnold's family may have played, the buck stops on his desk. It was not Dick Hern, Joe Mercer's friend and colleague for 14 years, who wanted a change and I have as yet been unable to find a single other owner with horses in the yard who does not deeply regret it." Then Oaksey turned his attentions to the reasons why these owners did not

band together to fight for the man who has served them so faithfully and so well. The answer lies partly in what I suppose could be called the 'power structure' at West Ilsley – and partly in the way the change was engineered. First of all, Dick Hern himself is a salaried 'private' trainer employed by the Sobell-Weinstock family. Of course, in theory he could have refused to carry on without Joe Mercer but a trainer's position is entirely different from a jockey's, and no one in their senses, least of all Joe himself, would have expected Dick quixotically to ruin the career he has worked so long and hard to build. As for the other owners ... two things have inhibited their will and ability to resist. One is that most of them were never consulted or asked to give an opinion – but merely presented with a *fait accompli*. Mr Astor, for instance, who built up West Ilsley into the superbly equipped establishment it is today ...had not even been told of the intention to change jockeys when he first heard it via the racecourse grapevine. But lack of consultation was only one reason for the owners' lack of resistance, and it is the other, to my mind, that puts the whole concept of a large stable controlled by one man who is not the trainer under what ought to be a highly critical microscope. Because, of course, the owners at West Ilsley feel at least as much loyalty to Dick Hern as they do to Joe Mercer. So, since an owner's only effective ultimate weapon is the withdrawal of his horses they were on the horns of an impossible dilemma. It is not much use kicking one good man in the teeth to protect another.

If Oaksey's sterling defence had not already demonstrated the expertise born of an Oxford law degree, a masterly closing address, which was guaranteed, if not designed, to catch the ear of judge and jury, most certainly provided ample proof of his advocacy. Businessmen should not impose their mercantile attitudes on racing, argued Oaksey.

I have no doubt that Sir Arnold Weinstock considers his decision the responsible and business-like precaution of a man in charge of a top class 80-horse concern. When a vital, highly paid executive comes within sight of retirement your efficient tycoon does not let personal feelings stop him engaging a younger replacement. And there is admittedly no certainty that when Joe Mercer eventually decides to retire a substitute of Willie Carson's calibre will necessarily be available. But a far more common business reaction – which may or may not have an application in this case – is that when things are bad, when the graph is sloping down and costs are exceeding profits, someone has to be to blame. So you sack him and (maybe) things get better. What such an attitude ignores is that the raw materials can also fail, and in racing the raw material is the horse. But for some unknown reason most people would far rather blame a jockey or a trainer than admit that they could conceivably have bought or bred the thoroughbred equivalent of an arthritic tortoise.

The allegation that Weinstock had resorted to ruthless business stratagems in a sphere totally alien to them was echoed by Richard Baerlein in *The Guardian*. "Businessmen never seem satisfied for long in racing. When things go wrong in business they can put their fingers on it and put things right. The same cannot be done with horses who are totally unpredictable and governed by nature. Someone has to take the blame for their failures. It is never the horse."

Whilst West Ilsley had won fifty-six races in 1975 only Bustino's Coronation Cup was of Group I status, and for the third successive season the Sobell-Weinstock partnership did not loom large in the list of leading owners. Since the purchase of West Ilsley, the Sobell horses had won thirteen races worth £19,920 in 1974 (twenty-first position) and twelve worth £10,407 in 1975, relegating Sobell's name to fiftieth in the table. It had not been all misery. In 1974 Gaily won the Irish 1000 Guineas (without Mercer, who chose to ride Boldboy in the Lockinge), Bold Pirate won the Prix Saint-Roman (Group III) and Auction Ring, in the colours of Weinstock's son Simon, the July Stakes (Group III). As a three-year-old Auction Ring added the King George Stakes (Group III). However, unlike earlier Sobell representatives, these three came from the sales ring instead of Ballymacoll. Gaily cost $120,000, Bold Pirate $52,000 and Auction Ring $35,000, money that had to be recouped or accounted for. Minor Pattern races were insufficient to balance the books. That the stable-jockey was solely to blame and that a replacement would spark a change of fortune were notions that hardly bore inspection. "It is time for the uncluttered truth," demanded Tom Forrest in the *Sunday Express*, otherwise "rumour was left to do its dirty work." In actuality, Forrest had scooped his fellow newshounds by gaining interviews with both Weinstock and Mercer, "the two men who know the facts."

Weinstock justified coolly and analytically what was generally held to have been his decision (Sobell, after all, was now eighty-three).

> I do not want to say anything uncomplimentary about Joe Mercer. Or to mislead anybody. The two decisive factors were Mercer's age and the possibility of engaging Willie Carson. Mercer is now forty-one and he does have other business interests besides riding. It could be only perhaps three years or so before he would retire and at that point it would be vital for the stable to find a top-class rider to replace him. There is a real scarcity of young jockeys with the ability to hold down a job of such responsibility. And suddenly Carson became available

because of the death of his employer, Bernard van Cutsem last year. The chance of signing him up could not possibly last for long. Already he'd had a large offer from another stable. If he had taken it the opportunity would have gone. When any long-standing arrangement breaks up there is always some hostility in the reaction of the British public. But it is not only the past which must be considered, but how well all the people concerned come out of it. Joe Mercer has not been injured, he is not sick, his powers are not declining. If it were otherwise things might be changed. He is at the top of his profession still. Already, it is reported that he has offers of two other retainers. He will get plenty of rides, perhaps make more money and be better off than if he had stayed. All relationships are complicated and it would be wrong to say that everything has always been light and happiness between Mercer and myself. Minor differences must arise in any stables...it should not be suggested that this affected our decision.

What had Mercer to say in reply?

We had not been getting on together, not seeing eye to eye. I am a plain fellow, always talk straight about horses, speak of them as I find them. Some owners just feel hurt if you do not think their horses are the best. With Dick Hern it was different. We always understood each other as regards horses. Any of our differences were settled as friends. And over a period of years it worked bloody well. I can tell you that since the news broke I now have four offers...from Ian Balding and three other trainers. But money is not everything. I have had marvellous offers before and always turned them down because loyalty meant more. That is what hurts when I remember.

Forrest concluded his piece by asking readers: "Has cold business come first? Has loyalty been outraged?" Jack Logan (alias Sir David Llewellyn) of *The Sporting Life*, for one, was in no doubt and said so in his Friday Commentary of 11 June which was provocatively headed: "Why the Knights of West Ilsley deserve praise." Logan informed his devotees: "As an example of much ado about nothing, false priorities and infectious folly, the Joe Mercer affair is already a classic of its kind." Journalists had got carried away and had overreacted, maintained Logan; the very timing of the announcement, far from being callous, actually reflected the clear consciences possessed by the "Knights of West Ilsley" in reaching their decision.

With blinding vision that perhaps verged on pomposity, Logan continued:

> Its real cause should be obvious to anyone familiar with the day to day running of a modern business. It is simply that industry needs to secure a succession of skills. Joe is 41. If that is not exactly the conventional age for admission to the jockey's geriatric ward, it is at least knocking on the door of retirement. It was therefore the merest prudence for the stable owners to look around for a successor and, once found, to sign him up. When Willie Carson became available these wise businessmen moved quickly to protect their investment and with it the future livelihood of all the workers employed at West Ilsley and all ancillary businesses which depend upon the stables prosperity. What alternative did they have? What is their critics' idea of a proper age of consent when it becomes respectable to replace a jockey? Far from being pilloried this distinguished member of the Jockey Club and his son-in-law deserve the highest praise for their foresight, humanity and realism – three qualities of which the Turf is much in need.

It is not inconceivable that some of Logan's readership thought his vehement defence of Sobell and Weinstock lacked one or two qualities of its own.

Time, as usual, healed most of the wounds but a few scars always tend to remain. In 1976 Mercer confided to the *News of the World*'s Robin Gray, "If I'd been the stable owners, perhaps I'd have done the same." Perhaps. Three years later, after the sadness of his departure had been assuaged by the acquisition of his one and only jockey's championship, he told Claude Duval: "At the time it was a very unpleasant thing. Very bad. But I accept that the owners of the stable were going for somebody who would be around for a long time and Willie was available." However, in Richard Baerlein's biography of 1987, Mercer pointedly refers to the differences of opinion he had with the Weinstocks regarding the ability and performances of their horses. "In those days young Simon thought he knew everything and even questioned my riding one day at Newbury ...I more or less said to Dick that if the boy wanted to tell me how to ride them, then he'd better ride them himself. I think that was the start of it all."

Sir Arnold Weinstock was equally unrepentant. In 1979 he said:

Quite frankly, I don't have to explain myself. We own the majority of the horses in the yard – and indeed the yard itself. It's got to be the owners' choice who rides for them. But I will admit that it was a painful thing and in some quarters we have never been quite forgiven. Some people wrote some stupid things at the time about the incident. We were accused of being the only owners in the yard who held the opinion that a change was needed. We weren't. I said nothing at the time. I will say that sometimes you hit it off with people and sometimes you don't. With Willie I get on much better than I did with Joe.

Throughout the turmoil of June 1976 Dick Hern was tight-lipped and the fact that his friendship with Joe Mercer survived unharmed probably says more about his private views on the matter than any of the bland, non-committal statements he made to the Press at the time. Inwardly he must have been squirming and close to being torn asunder by the emotional conflict generated by two qualities he prized so highly – loyalty and obedience. The Army had drummed these two into his heart and soul. His owners were his superiors; they called the shots. He must be obedient and, therefore, loyal to their cause. And yet, what of his obligation to a loyal friend and sub-ordinate? In 1986 he would ask Khalid Abdulla to remove his horses from West Ilsley rather than see Willie Carson replaced on them by their owner's retained jockey (Pat Eddery) in all their races. "It is unfortunate but you have to have some principles in life," Hern said at the time. But in this instance the owners in question were also his landlords. They held the whip hand not he.

Was his own resignation not the only honourable course of action? Generations of soldiers have testified to the fact that the Army does not teach its men to think but to respond. The honourable response, not necessarily the most sensible, logical or beneficial, but the most honourable response in the circumstances as they were known, was surely Hern's resignation. Baerlein and Logan had openly debated the pros and cons of this eventuality. Wrote Baerlein: "One can never tell anyone how to react to a sudden situation but there must have been a temptation for Dick Hern to resign his position over this episode and the same applies to the racing manager, Sir Gordon Richards. It is one of the most amazing decisions in my racing career and one from which no one can come away with honours bar Joe Mercer." Logan retaliated, "Resignation rarely ruffles the smooth surface of the Turf no matter how deeply consciences are troubled."

Whatever the rights and wrongs of the 'affair' there was widespread disappointment when it became apparent Hern had chosen to sit tight and say nothing. Such passive acquiescence did not square with the image of a forthright, no-nonsense decision-maker which Hern had projected ever since Hunt's Gap. Possibly it was a matter of Hobson's Choice. A fresh start away from West Ilsley meant capital, lots of it, and trainers have never been noted for their financial perspicacity. "Eat, drink and be merry – tomorrow we're bankrupt" is their oft heard motto. As John Oaksey had pointed out, Hern, like Mercer, was only a salaried employee and had been throughout his training career. Where could he hope to find an establishment like West Ilsley? However, ran the counter-argument, surely Hern, as the trainer of over eight hundred winners including five English classics, must have accumulated enough financial resources to strike out on his own should he ever so desire. If funds were lacking his name alone represented gilt-edged bankability for potential patrons and/or investors. Sufficient questions remained unanswered for several parties to be left wondering whether there was more going on than met the eye. Guesswork and rumour were allowed, invited even, to do their usual "dirty work". The solitary sad thing that could be said without fear of contradiction was that Joe Mercer had neglected to heed one of the oldest English proverbs: "Never fall out with your bread and butter." The extent to which the equally venerable Yiddish proverb – "Make sure to be in with your equals if you're going to fall out with your superiors" – applied in this instance is impossible to evaluate.

So, West Ilsley began 1977 with a new jockey, William Fisher Hunter Carson. "At least we've got both a nice man and a proper jockey in Joe's place," John Oaksey was told by one of the stable's owners (almost certainly Jakie Astor, an old friend). "If it had been almost anyone else there really would have been a revolution." Carson had had his first ride for Hern – a winning one – on Kinglet, in the David Dixon Gold Cup at York on 14 May 1974. Whereas Mercer always appeared sinuous and languid in the saddle, the Carson style was more overtly energetic, a bubbling kettle on the hob which would come to the boil and steam its way to the finish. The hallmark of a Carson ride is the indomitable will to win, a characteristic noted and applauded by Sir Gordon Richards, Lord

Porchester, Sir Arnold Weinstock and Dick Hern. "I continually see Willie win races from positions where there was every justification for him to drop his hands – he simply never gives up," says Hern.

On Sir Gordon's recommendation Carson was booked for whichever of Bustino and Appleby Fair Mercer rejected for the 1974 Derby. As it happened Appleby Fair never made it to Epsom but Carson's turn came sooner than anyone could have envisaged. In 1975 his guv'nor Bernard van Cutsem, for whom he had ridden his only classic winner, High Top, died from cancer. "We were very close, he treated me like a son", said Carson. His second retainer with Clive Brittain therefore became his first for 1976 by default. Suspecting he might be available, the "Knights of West Ilsley" made an approach.

Carson's ambitions to be a jockey were fired by an afternoon spent in Stirling's cinema watching "The Rainbow Jacket", the story of a ragamuffin's metamorphosis from tearaway to top jockey. Carson was a slow developer and did not ride his first winner till the age of nineteen. "I'm not a natural rider. It has taken very hard work to learn the business. I've come late on the scene, but that's not a bad thing. Jockeys who get success early sometimes blow it." That first winner, Pinkers Pond in a six furlong apprentice handicap at Catterick on 19 July 1962, was trained at Middleham by Gerald Armstrong to whom Carson had been indentured since 1959. "I'd had twenty-two rides on screws and rubbishy horses. Pinkers Pond had been a disappointing horse, not doing his best, and it was blinkers first time. Charlie Brown, the travelling head-lad, had stirred the little horse up the day before with the blinkers on him. They'd told me I could ride him if I could hold him, and put me on. Charlie chased him round the dung hill in the yard with the Long Tom, he was whizzing round so fast that sparks were coming off his hooves. Then we went out to work with two others horses and he went brilliantly and I just about managed to hang onto him. It was a close thing but I was determined not to get carted because here at last was a chance of riding a winner. The hardest part of the race was getting to the start because he remembered the day before and was taking a bit of a tug going down. In those days it was a barrier start and that was a worry because you could easily lose it there, not like today. But with twenty-two rides I had a bit of experience compared with some of the others. I just kicked him in the belly and sent him on his way. He made every yard and won by six lengths."

There were no frills at Middleham for 'Scottie' Carson, as he was known round the yard. "When I got married at the age of twenty, I was still earning 10/6 a week – 52½p – and we lived in a caravan." On Gerald Armstrong's retirement in 1962 Carson's papers were transferred to brother Sam in Newmarket and there were periods of gloom. "During that time I'd been thinking of giving up racing and maybe becoming a chef or a carpenter or something. But I can remember saying to Robert Armstrong one day, after I'd ridden a double, that I thought I just might make a jockey after all. From then on I took it a bit more seriously. I look back on those days with pride. It was tough with both Armstrongs but it was a good sort of toughness." Carson lost his allowance in August 1965 and the following season he rode thirty-five winners.

Influential people began to sit up and take notice. "Sam Armstrong would always tell us to watch and copy a senior jockey who was our build and I was told to watch Doug Smith, Lord Derby's retained jockey. One day Sam called me into the house. I assumed I was going to get a rollocking but he told me Bernard van Cutsem wanted me to join him as understudy to Doug, who was going to retire in a year or so. I was shaking like a leaf when I went to Stanley House to see Lord Derby. I had never ridden a horse for him and had never spoken to a lord before in my life."

Carson fitted in perfectly at Stanley House and was soon christened 'Prince William' by the stable lads, but before he could capitalize on this fresh impetus he very nearly came to a sticky end on the Great North Road. "The week after the 1967 season finished I drove my new Jag straight under the back of a lorry in the fog. I don't remember what happened, I might even have fallen asleep. I broke my femur, jaw, wrist and had to have 27 stitches in my face. I was a wee bit mangled. The front wheel of the car was in the radio, the windscreen was gone, my broken leg was touching my chin and my head was out in the open. I kept going in and out of consciousness, but I could hear one of the ambulance-men say, 'Have a look at the driver, he looks a goner'. I couldn't move or say anything but I remember thinking, 'I'm not gone yet . . .I'm still here'."

The unquenchable Carson spirit prevailed. When the new Flat season commenced he was still unable to walk without the aid of callipers, yet somehow he was back in the saddle to partner Laureate in the Derby. Nor could a crashing fall at York in May 1972, which left him nursing a fractured cheekbone and a cracked wrist, foil his surge toward a first jockeys' title. Informed he would be out for six weeks he rode again in four and eventually landed the championship with 132 winners.

"I don't know of a better jockey than Willie Carson," Weinstock said of his new rider. "His courage is tremendous. He simply loves the horses and he laughs and smiles a lot, but for all his laughing and joking he is deadly serious under it all." It seemed Carson would suit West Ilsley as comfortably as he had Stanley House; he definitely appeared to have taken Weinstock's measure. "He always takes the piss and even tells me how to ride his horses. I answer him back and we get on well. He digs and digs to try to get you annoyed. Anyone who is annoyed always tells the truth – but I don't fall for his style."

Carson was not about to fall into the same trap as Joe Mercer.

Chapter Ten

AT LAST, THE BLUE RIBAND

'It's every trainer's dream to win this classic'

IN THE SPRING OF 1977 Dick Hern bestrode the peak of his profession. On the retirement of Noel Murless at the end of 1976 none of Hern's contemporaries could match his tally of two trainers' titles and five classics. In fact, of those contemporaries, only three – Ian Balding, Peter Walwyn and Henry Cecil – had registered their presence in both respects. This enviable record was sullied only by lack of success in the two Epsom classics. In 1976 Relkino, Smuggler and Riboboy had been Hern's eleventh, twelfth and thirteenth representatives in the Derby (Admiral's Launch made it fourteen in 1978), while in 1975 Harmonise, his most recent Oaks runner, constituted his tenth attempt on the fillies' classic. Relkino's second spot proved the best (and only) placing for a Hern runner since Trimmer had set the ball rolling in 1958: Remand and Bustino ran fourth, Proud Chieftain fifth and Homeric seventh. The Oaks picture was even bleaker. The only filly with a superior placing to Harmonise's fifth was None Nicer, another trailblazer from 1958, who finished fourth.

However, after nineteen barren seasons the tide was about to turn. Over the next seven Hern would collect two Derbys and three Oaks which helped push his overall total of English classics to thirteen. Furthermore, he also won a French St Leger, Irish Derby, Irish St Leger and the Irish Oaks twice, and Shoot A Line's victory in the 1980 Irish Oaks made Hern the only man other than Vincent O'Brien to have trained the winner of each English and Irish classic. That same year Hern's third trainers' championship established a new record for first prize money of £831,964. Obviously inflation had a lot to do with that large an amount but one cannot belittle the fact that a third of the sixty-five victories which yielded that total came in Pattern races. Hern's position in the trainers' table never dropped below fifth, he achieved a career-high total of seventy-four winners in both 1977 and 1978, and he concluded this purple patch on a triumphant note with a fourth trainers' title in 1983. Carson bene-fitted accordingly, thrice winning the jockeys' championship – in 1978 with his highest career total (182) until the excesses of 1990. Hern's status as the role model for aspiring English trainers was undisputed. He was truly master of all he surveyed.

The experiences of Hethersett and Remand were stark reminders if Hern needed any, which is doubtful, that luck plays a not incon-siderable part when it comes to winning a Derby. Though Hern had never saddled a filly for the Oaks with any realistic confidence, there had been many worse Derby winners than Hethersett and Remand. Hethersett's subsequent St Leger victory with the Derby winner Larkspur back in sixth was evidence enough of his misfortune, while Remand had been regarded by Piggott, who rode the horse as a two-year-old, as the only danger to Sir Ivor. West Ilsley's summer gallops are left-handed, downhill and uphill just like Epsom, so all Hern's Derby and Oaks candidates were well prepared to cope with the eccentricities of the course. The raw material to win an Epsom classic would surely resurface. All Hern craved was a slice of good fortune to come with it.

"I loved her the moment I saw her and Dick always liked her very much. She was always a marvellous mover." The subject of Lord Porchester's adulation was Dunfermline. She was by Royal Palace out of Strathcona, a disappointing filly with whom Hern had managed to win one race in 1970. Strathcona was the last foal of Stroma, who was bought on a whim by the Queen for 1,150 guineas at the Doncaster Sales in 1956 and whose second foal, Canisbay, won the 1964 Eclipse. Hern's first portion of luck lay in the death of Stroma, for Strathcona, instead of being culled as her racing re-cord warranted, replaced her dam in the royal studs. Neither of Strathcona's first two offspring (both colts) were of any account. Dunfermline was the third.

She made her debut at Sandown in July 1976, over seven furlongs, finishing third, and was then put by for the St Leger meeting which the Queen would be attending. Dunfermline worked impressively before setting off for Doncaster. Thereafter little went her way. She fretted on the journey, sweated up and, to cap it all, was struck into shortly after leaving the stalls. In a maiden race she might have recovered, but Porchester and Hern had chosen to run her in the May Hill Stakes against fillies with excellent winning form. Even so, Dunfermline was only beaten half a length by Triple First, winner of the Waterford Candelabra Stakes at Goodwood. There was, however, just the slightest suggestion that Dunfermline had hung fire when asked to go and win her race, a feeling which persisted after she was outfought by Miss Pinkie in the closing stages of Ascot's Argos Star Fillies Mile. She had carried her head high. Joe Mercer attributed it to greenness rather than any lack of generosity and argued against blinkers. She had, on only a pound better terms, turned the tables on Triple First, for example. Hern could thus afford a degree of optimism. "I knew she was one of the best staying two-year-old fillies and it was reasonable to suppose there was improvement in her when she learned more about racing. Well, as a three-year-old she was a different filly."

Dunfermline wintered satisfactorily and was usually ridden by Stan Clayton, Hern's former stable-jockey at Lagrange, who had joined him as assistant trainer. Though meek and mild in her box, Dunfermline, a tall, rangy, full-quartered individual, was inclined to pull like stink in her slower paces and she sorely needed a man of Clayton's experience. Hern also fitted her with an Australian nose-band to counteract her tendency to hang. Willie Carson returned from Hong Kong to sit on her for the first time on 12 March and recalls that he was not bowled over. He preferred the Queen's other filly Circlet and, indeed, considered Lady Beaverbrook's Topbird superior to the pair of them. As fate would have it, Circlet went in her wind and Topbird was winning a handicap while Dunfermline won the Oaks for the Queen in her Silver Jubilee year.

Dunfermline had one race prior to Epsom. The Queen was present at Newmarket to see her win the Pretty Polly Stakes over $1\frac{1}{4}$ miles (from the future Irish Oaks' winner Olwyn) but commitments conspired to keep her away from the scenes of her filly's finest hours. Any remaining fears that Dunfermline's high, rounded action might be inconvenienced by the firm ground and Epsom's gradients were promptly pushed to the back of Hern's mind when he arrived at the course. Carson had been involved in a car accident and would be delayed. He immediately engaged Joe Mercer but Carson duly arrived, perfectly intact (unlike his new Ferrari), to partner Lady Mason in the second race of the afternoon.

Since Dunfermline was apt to get nervous at the stalls, Hern detailed David Murray-Smith to lead her across the Downs in the belief that a familiar voice would give her assurance. Her thirteen intended opponents were headed by Durtal, bidding to complete the Epsom double for owner Robert Sangster and jockey Lester Piggott after The Minstrel's thrilling neck victory over Hot Grove (and Carson) in Wednesday's Derby. However, the longer the preliminaries continued the more on-edge the favourite became, and as Piggott tried to restrain her approaching the road crossing *en route* to the $1\frac{1}{2}$ mile start his left stirrup iron clipped a concrete post and broke. Durtal's saddle began to slip and the petrified filly suddenly took off, initially dragging but, fortunately, soon dislodging Piggott in the process. A delay of ten minutes ensued as she was caught and withdrawn.

With the favourite sensationally out of the reckoning, Dunfermline's principal dangers appeared to be old adversary Triple First, winner of the Musidora Stakes, and Mrs McArdy, winner of the 1000 Guineas, neither of whom was guaranteed to see out the $1\frac{1}{2}$ miles in a strongly run race. Thanks to Vaguely Deb, the pacemaker for Freeze The Secret, the early gallop was testing: too testing for either of them but absolutely ideal for Dunfermline. Overcoming a bump at the top of the hill, she made up her ground on the descent and gradually wore down Freeze The Secret in the straight to win by three-quarters of a length. Despite wearing a huge grin as he passed the post, Carson had endured a few anxious moments. When Brightly had interfered with his mount they only had two horses behind them. "To be honest I began to panic just a little. Dunfermline had to be put in the race somehow. I pulled her out, gave her two back-handers and to my amazement she took off like a rocket. I knew I had them beaten but about $1\frac{1}{2}$ furlongs from home my filly started to hang to the left, partly because of the firm ground and partly because the course slopes inwards in the straight. I was desperately worried about a possible Stewards' Enquiry if I did not keep straight and I could not really ride her out to the full. She won by guts. The Oaks was a fairytale and my proudest moment in racing. My only regret on the day was that I didn't have a little Union Jack to carry as I rode into the winner's enclosure. I'd planned to get one off someone in the crowd if I won but nobody had one. It would have been a bit unorthodox but I wouldn't have cared. I'm a great Royalist."

Shortly afterwards Carson received a pair of gold cuff links engraved with the 'E II R' of a grateful monarch.

Dunfermline's Oaks victory can be credited to her dour courage and infinite stamina, for she proceeded to lose the Yorkshire Oaks when neither quality could be brought into play. No one was prepared to set a legitimate pace and Carson was more or less obliged to sit and suffer. He and Dunfermline were beaten for pure speed in the last quarter mile and finished a six lengths' third to Busaca. Hern was now in a quandary. The Park Hill Stakes would provide Dunfermline with the right sort of opposition, but it usually cut up into a small field and the possibility of a muddling gallop, and he had no filly suitable as a pacemaker. Fortunately, the Queen owned a useful staying colt in Gregarious who could fit the bill if Dunfermline challenged for the St Leger. She would need all available assistance because Alleged, the O'Brien-trained favourite, had literally waltzed off with the Great Voltigeur Stakes making all to win by seven lengths. However, like many of her kind, Dunfermline began to flourish as autumn approached and she worked spectacularly before travelling north. The onset of rain forty-eight hours before the race caused Dunfermline's odds to tumble from 16/1 to 10s. Carson "fancied her chance very much." Besides Gregarious (Alan Bond) she was accompanied by another stablemate, Bustino's half-brother Tobique (Joe Mercer). Alleged was the hottest favourite since Nijinsky.

For the opening two minutes of the St Leger Dunfermline's fate lay in the capable hands of Alan Bond. "Riding the pacemaker is just as difficult as riding a winner. You've got to get the pace exactly right, not half right. I led them into the straight and expected Willie to go by me but it was Lester. Dunfermline stayed for ever and the longer you gave her a lead the better. So, Lester became the pacemaker, all to Dunfermline's benefit. He should have sat behind and beaten her for speed. I was pleased to have done my job correctly.

The Major rang me that evening – and so did Lord Porchester – to congratulate me and that was very satisfying.''

Alleged and Dunfermline drew right away inside the final two furlongs with the filly gradually asserting herself to win by a length or so. This day there was a Stewards' Enquiry (the two tired horses had drifted toward each other) but after twenty minutes a mighty roar signified the places remained unaltered. ''I did not think there was any question of losing the race,'' said Carson. ''I asked Lester if everything was all right and he said straight away that there was nothing to worry about and he had no intention of objecting.'' Dunfermline thus became the fourteenth filly in 197 years to achieve the Oaks–St Leger double, and only the second since the war.

In view of the fact that Hern was adamant that Dunfermline owed her victory to the rattling good gallop set by Gregarious, it was a trifle surprising to see her sent to the Arc without a pacemaker. Gregarious had broken down and as the Arc is traditionally run at breakneck speed thanks to any number of pacemakers, Hern and Porchester declined to nominate a substitute, a decision they were to rue. Alleged handsomely gained his revenge. Happier on the faster ground and over a shorter distance, he dictated the pace (a sluggish one to begin with) and when the royal filly should have been launching her challenge at the top of the straight she ran into a pocket on the rails. In the resultant scrimmage Dunfermline lost a hind shoe. Nevertheless, staying on in her characteristic fashion, she was the first filly to cross the line, a short neck from gaining third place and four lengths behind Alleged.

Dunfermline recrossed the Channel for the French St Leger (the Prix Royal Oak) four weeks later. She and her new pacemaker, Sea Boat, suffered a terrible journey. Their aircraft was delayed by fog and air traffic control problems and Dunfermline arrived at Longchamp in a very agitated state. Not surprisingly the Arc consolation failed to materialize. Dunfermline was kept in training for a third season but she never recaptured the vital spark that had made her such an outstanding filly on St Leger day. That is, until the decision was taken to retire her. ''But then suddenly,'' Hern remembers, ''for the first time that year Dunfermline began to thrive. By the time they took her off to stud she was better than I'd ever seen her. But by then, of course, it was all too late.'' Her 1978 form was not within 10lb of the 133 rating Timeform gave her in

1977, which remains the highest attained by a Hern-trained filly.

As a result of Dunfermline's efforts the Queen finished the 1977 season third in the owners' list and second in the breeders', her best placings since 1959. One rung above Her Majesty in the table was Lady Beaverbrook, who owed her position to the exemplary work of Boldboy (five wins for £44,271) and Relkino (two for £69,123). Although never in the same league as one-time delinquent Boldboy, Relkino still posed Hern a few problems. He was woefully hard to settle in a race. Hern equipped him with a Citation bit for the 1976 Derby. "He ran a smashing race and the bit worked well," observed the trainer, "but he didn't quite last it out." Disaster followed disaster in the second half of the season. Relkino finished behind his own pacemaker in the Eclipse, three horses he had beaten in the Derby finished ahead of him in the Great Voltigeur, and he trailed in eleventh of twenty in the Champion Stakes. There was even some talk of him being lily-livered.

Relkino's association with Carson began promisingly. They nearly made all in the $1\frac{1}{4}$ miles Westbury Stakes at Sandown and then won the Lockinge over a mile. Relkino's next outing is best forgotten. At Epsom he was the innocent party in one of the year's major contretemps when Marinsky attempted to savage him during the Diomed Stakes. With the Sussex Stakes imminent, Hern decided to try him in a double-mouthed snaffle. This bit has single rings at each side of the two mouthpieces and, consequently, with nothing in the middle of his mouth to 'lay against' it was hoped Relkino would be more amenable to restraint. The new bit worked, but Relkino was no match for Artaius at a mile. Over the additional $2\frac{1}{2}$ furlongs of the Benson & Hedges Gold Cup, however, Relkino was a revelation. "They went a cracking good gallop," said Hern. "When Willie produced him, having had him beautifully settled, it was just a case of – ping. That was it." Never off a tight rein, Relkino won by four lengths. Although he subsequently had no reply to Flying Water's devastating kick in the Champion Stakes, his York display had shown him to be no jade and, courtesy of Hern's thoroughness, he retired to stud with his reputation enhanced,

Hern's elusive first Derby winner arrived at West Ilsley in late 1977 among the annual consignment of yearlings from the Bally-macoll Stud. He was a bay with three white socks by Petingo out of La Milo, a winning daughter of Pin Prick, another of the Paget mares inherited by Sobell and Weinstock in 1960. Named Troy in deference to the classical pursuits at Oxford of Simon Weinstock, who had suggested the mating of his parents, the colt was the last foal of La Milo. Her chronic arthritis meant she was put down as soon as Troy was weaned. (As Petingo had died in February 1976, Troy could claim orphan status.) Sir Gordon Richards, who acted as racing manager for Sobell as well as Lady Beaverbrook, soon spotted the active Petingo colt on his yearly visit to Ballymacoll. "He didn't fiddle about. He always moved nicely at that age which is a very good sign."

Safely ensconced at West Ilsley, Troy proved a deceptive character. "He was a very quiet, placid horse to be around and he never showed much until approaching the gallops," says Carson. "But then he'd try to run off with me!" Troy was made favourite for each of his first three races. Second at Salisbury over six furlongs, he won the next two over seven furlongs at Newmarket and Goodwood. "He was bloody horrible to ride, very lethargic. He didn't have instant speed, so he needed a distance to show his brilliance. He had to build up his speed and settle into his own pace. He never took hold of the bit and needed a strong pace for his best." Finally, Hern aimed him at the Royal Lodge Stakes over Ascot's round mile, a race assuming increasing significance as a pointer to the following year's classics. Overhauling Lyphard's Wish inside the final furlong, Troy was then caught close home by Ela-Mana-Mou (behind him at Goodwood) and beaten by three-quarters of a length. Largely on the basis of this performance Troy was allotted 9 stone in the Free Handicap, 2lb below Ela-Mana-Mou and one pound below his stablemate More Light, second in the Dewhurst to the leading juvenile Tromos (9st 7lb).

Sir Arnold Weinstock had yet to convince himself of Troy's Derby potential. "But Dick's methods of training the youngsters means that he never drives them to fitness. He brings them along gently. He always does no more than what the horses show him they are capable of. In the spring of 1979 I was hopeful that Troy would be a Derby horse but one is never advised to take a strong view of Dick Hern's three-year-olds early on in the season. He never asks them a big question at home. There is no betting in the stable, and there is no incentive for the horses to be worked flat out on the gallops. They are tried at full tilt only on the racecourses." As the season got underway Carson still leant toward More Light as his Derby mount, but whereas he suffered defeat – by Ela-Mana-Mou – on his reappearance, Troy at least returned victorious from Sandown's Classic Trial. However, he had not impressed for the soft conditions negated his magnificent, free-flowing action.

Providing a third card to Hern's classic hand was the Queen's Milford. As the first foal of Highclere and by a stallion like Mill Reef, the possibility of greatness always lurked within Milford. After he captured the White Rose Stakes at Ascot by eight lengths and the Lingfield Derby Trial by seven lengths it began to look as if the 200th Derby might have a royal ending. Milford became 5/1 joint favourite with Ela-Mana-Mou for the Epsom classic. Joe Mercer had ridden the horse at Lingfield owing to Carson having broken a collar bone at Chester three days previously when his mount Lidgate stumbled during the Roodeye Stakes. More Light's disappointing fourth in the Mecca-Dante Stakes effectively eliminated one name from Carson's calculations, but the stable-jockey had still not committed himself when he resumed riding at Goodwood on 23 May, the day of Troy's dress rehearsal over the full Derby distance in the Predominate Stakes. The going was again soft but Troy stripped much fitter than at Sandown and pulverized pretty moderate opposition to the tune of seven lengths. Carson deflected all requests for the name of his Derby partner, insisting he wanted a night to sleep on it. "I'm very glad it's not me who is making the decision," Hern told reporters. "I don't honestly know which one I would pick. Troy simply had a nice bit of work. It was a delightfully easy race, and I now have two real live Derby hopes. Troy has an ideal temperament and will not be affected in any way by all the hullabaloo at Epsom. He won't care less when the band strikes up. His trainer will be more nervous – that's for sure. Milford is a more excitable type and this is always a slight worry. But he has never done anything actually wrong in a race."

The news that Carson had picked Troy and that Lester Piggott would ride the Queen's colt surprised quite a few people. "I was sure he'd picked the wrong one," said Brian Procter, "but he said, 'Oh no I haven't, that's the one'. Up until that time I'd ridden Milford, who was just the opposite of Troy, who was lazy whereas Milford was always running in your hands. The next time Troy worked I rode him and I thought, 'I'll find out which is the right one' and he worked like a bomb, so I quickly changed my mind. Of all the people I've ridden work with Carson is the best judge of finding a good horse."

For the first time in 1979 Troy got some decent ground on which to show his paces, though it was not all plain sailing for the 6/1 second favourite (to Ela-Mana-Mou) who had to be niggled along to keep his place in the middle of the 23-strong field. "I planned to follow Lyphard's Wish but Troy had no pace early on. They went very fast and I wasn't going anywhere. I needed a pair of binoculars to see the leaders. Coming down the hill I thought, 'Another disappointment, it's not going to be this year either.' Most of the field were in front of me and I had experienced terrible trouble getting past Laska Floko. But turning into Tattenham Corner my fellow started to grab ground like he'd got six-inch nails in his feet. Ahead of me I could see everything slowing up. They'd gone too fast but once mine began to get some breath back he began to motor. He was strong and an athlete. He ate up the ground and just ran away from the others. The whole race ended in four strides and I've had a harder time than he has. This must be the easiest Derby winner of all time."

Whilst Carson's claim was not exactly verifiable due to the paucity of early records, Troy's seven-length margin of victory was surpassed by only one other performance this century – Manna's eight lengths of 1925 – until Shergar won by ten lengths in 1981. The abiding memory of Troy's victory was the stunning manner in which he made up all of fifteen lengths from Tattenham Corner. Drifting off the fence, he stormed up the centre of the track to pounce on the Irish 2000 Guineas' winner Dickens Hill at the furlong marker and then maintained his surge right to the line. Carson actually hit him twice in the last fifty yards. "I was not in the mood to take any chances at all. There is only one Derby and my policy was to keep whipping until I passed the stick. If I had not looked up and seen the winning post, I'd have bloody well hit him again. When I hit the front I thought of Lester two years ago. But he didn't come this time."

Carson's riding was universally praised. "There's only one way to ride a Derby", commented Hern, "and that is the way Willie rode it. Leave nothing – absolutely nothing – to chance." Sir Gordon Richards, laid up with a trapped nerve in his back, watched the race from his Kintbury home. "I don't think I would have won the Derby on Troy. I wouldn't have had the tremendous patience of Willie Carson. He had the courage to wait until the horse did it all for him. I'm certain that as he struggled to go the early pace I would have been tempted to give him a backhander and he would probably have cut his throat after one flick."

After connections had returned from the Royal Box, Dick Hern imbibed the wine of victory, all the sweeter at the fifteenth attempt. "I'm really thrilled. It's every trainer's dream to win this classic. This colt has a marvellous temperament and nothing bothers him. I thought he had plenty to do coming down the hill and I must say he surprised me in the way he quickened." The extent of Hern's delight can be gauged from the fact that when the following day's card was washed out by a freak thunderstorm, he trudged to the Press Room at the very top of the Epsom grandstand in order to share the latest news of his Derby winner with journalists and enjoy a glass of champagne with them. "Troy is very well and had lost only 2lb when I weighed him last night. How many other classic winners have returned so unaffected? He wasn't extended to win and it took nothing out of him. In fact, I shall have to canter him tomorrow morning, otherwise he'll be too fresh." As regards the future, Troy was going to tread the same path as Nijinsky, Grundy and The Minstrel by attempting to add the Irish Derby and King George VI & Queen Elizabeth II Stakes to his Epsom Derby, thus completing what some were calling the midsummer Triple Crown. "We might as well strike while the iron's hot. The Curragh will suit him far better than Epsom – though he didn't do too badly, did he?" continued his trainer. "The owners are keen on a crack at the Arc, so we'll give him a holiday after the King George before taking in an easy one, and then Longchamp."

Troy started a 9/4 favourite to win the Irish Derby. On this occasion he had Rivadon and Brian Procter to undertake the donkey work on his behalf. "He came past me like lightning," said the pacemaker, at the memory of Troy engaging overdrive in order to catch the Irish outsider The Bart. "That fellow in red frightened me for a while because he didn't look like coming back," admitted Carson after it was all over. Yet again, Troy's closest pursuer was Dickens Hill and once the Irish colt gained ample consolation by defeating the older horses in the Eclipse, the prospect of Troy recording his golden treble soared. Ile de Bourbon, the best of the English four-year-olds, had the virus leaving Troy few to beat except the French four-year-old Gay Mecene, second to Ile de Bourbon in the Coronation Cup and the subsequent conqueror of Ela-Mana-Mou (fourth in the Derby) in the Grand Prix de Saint-Cloud. Troy won handily by $1\frac{1}{2}$ lengths from Gay Mecene, but whether his failure to spreadeagle the field in familiar style was due to the shortness of the Ascot straight or the slow pace set by Procter on Road to Glory is difficult to judge. "There's pressure on, all right, when you're pacemaking," says Procter. "I mustn't go too fast because the others will let me go and not take any notice. You see it happen so many times with pacemakers, they're off and gone and wasted their time. I think there were a few criticisms that I went too slow, but for me it was the easiest race Troy had." Road to Glory could not have truly stretched the field because at 2.33.75, on firm ground, this was the slowest King George since 1970 and was some seven seconds off Grundy's track record. Indeed, Road to Glory still retained enough puff to lead into the straight, whereupon Troy, who had slipped on the bend, unleashed a burst between the two and the one furlong marks which was unofficially timed at 11.51 seconds and sealed his victory. This figure is the only recorded sub-twelve seconds penultimate furlong in King George history and settles any arguments concerning Troy's powers of acceleration.

The next day Hern reported that Troy had "eaten up everything and looks as if he could run again tomorrow." Although continuing to stand his ground in the St Leger, Troy was expected to tune up for the Arc with a run in Kempton's September Stakes. Lady Beaverbrook's Niniski and Milford, respectively ninth and tenth in the Derby, represented Hern at Doncaster. The former, who had won the Geoffrey Freer Stakes last time out, actually started joint favourite. He prevailed in the duel of stable companions, but eventually succumbed to the French pair Son of Love and Soleil Noir. Niniski atoned by picking up the Irish and French equivalents – the Irish by ten lengths.

Early in August Hern took the Press by surprise when out of the blue he announced that Troy would contest the Benson & Hedges Gold Cup. Over a distance now short of his best it was distinctly possible that Troy would have an unnecessarily hard race in an event, which, furthermore, had developed a deserved reputation as being a graveyard for hot-pots. Besides the Brigadier (1/3) in the inaugural running of 1972, Rheingold (4/6, 1973), Grundy (4/9, 1975), Trepan (10/11, 1976) and Artaius (8/11, 1978) were other odds-on favourites to be overthrown. Only Dahlia, 15/8 on in 1974, had beaten the bookies. The defeats of Brigadier Gerard and Grundy were attributed to those severe races at Ascot. None of this bothered Hern. "Unlike the other colts Troy won the King George easily and he will win the Benson & Hedges," he declared in such unequivocal tones that the tip should not have been lost on anyone desiring a license to print money.

Against these specialist $1\frac{1}{4}$ milers Troy, as anticipated, found himself under extreme pressure from the outset and was soon a dozen lengths behind the leaders. However, the long York straight is a galloper's heaven. Troy accepted the invitation and, switching into top gear, he tore past Crimson Beau. Then, with barely fifty yards to go, Carson seemed to relax and the eventual margin was a rapidly dwindling three-quarters of a length. "He was doing nothing when he was in front and that usually means he's well clear. So I dropped my hands and was amazed to see how near Crimson Beau was."

Hern was now of a mind to venture that Troy was the best horse he had ever trained. His record for the year read six out of six for £408,424, easily the most money won by a European horse in a single season. He had collected an unprecedented Group I four-timer comprising the Derby, Irish Derby, King George and Benson & Hedges; only the Arc stood between him and equine immortality. He would be Hern's sixth representative following Remand (1969, seventh), Royalty (1971, sixth), Buoy (1973, eighth), Highclere (1974, eighteenth) and Dunfermline (1977, fourth). Accompanying him as pacemakers were Rivadon and Sobell's French-trained Player. Despite the customarily high quality field, Troy looked unbeatable. Even nineteen of the twenty-five racing correspondents in the most important French newspapers tipped him. Every championship pretender was here. The leading French three-year-old colt Top Ville had broken track records at Longchamp (Prix Lupin) and Chantilly (Prix du Jockey-Club). The filly Three Troikas had done likewise in Longchamp's Prix Saint-Alary, one of her four successes, the most recent being the Prix Vermeille. Yet, odds of 11/2 or better could be had about this pair – and others such as Trillion, Le Marmot and Ile de Bourbon – as Troy hardened at 5/4 on.

The afternoon began ominously for West Ilsley when Jakie Astor's filly The Dancer, made favourite for the Criterium des Pouliches, ran abysmally and beat only her pacemaker. It was excusable if Hern cast his mind back to 1977. That year the defeat of Cistus in the Pouliches preceded Dunfermline's unlucky Arc fourth. The Arc card had not been a happy hunting ground for Hern since Sallust's 1972 victory in the Prix du Moulin, apart from Cistus' win in the Prix de l'Opera of 1978. Another potential drawback, and one less rooted in superstition, was the state of the ground – good to soft, dead perhaps – which might inhibit Troy's pounding stride.

Troy looked superb in the paddock and his defeat was a bitter pill to swallow. There could be no recriminations, however. He got the fast pace he craved, the first mile was run in 1.39.20 – two seconds faster than in Mill Reef's record-breaking Arc of 1971 – and he was well enough placed entering the straight. But the acceleration necessary to match Three Troika's – the Epsom variety, for instance – was not forthcoming. Troy ran on gamely to finish third, four lengths behind the winner.

The obvious conclusion to draw was that Troy's fall from grace was due to his amazingly successful, but extremely rigorous, midsummer campaign. Carson's initial reaction was to say: "Remember, Troy has been on the go a long time. The others have been trained specifically for this race and if we'd met them fresh we'd have killed them. I felt we'd win turning for home but there was no bounce in the ground." Later on, when the dust had settled, he argued: "The only reason he didn't win the Arc was the ground. He was such a big, heavy horse he couldn't handle it soft. I suppose you'd say he couldn't be a true champion because he couldn't handle any ground but he was a great horse that day at Epsom."

In phlegmatic mood Hern was forced to agree: "He ran a super race but he has such a magnificent action and the soft going meant that he never bounced off the top of the ground. Never mind. He was a very great racehorse. He has a great temperament, great looks, a fantastic burst of speed and wonderful courage. And I will say this: if sometime during the rest of my life I ever train a horse nearly as good as Troy I will count myself a very, very lucky man."

Alas, Troy did not have much opportunity to pass on those qualities. After the King George he had been syndicated for £7.2 million, a record for a European stallion, but he sired only four crops before dying of a perforated gut at the Highclere Stud on 12 May 1983, having covered the thirty-fifth of his forty-two mates booked that season (Porchester's Bluebell) at 4.30 pm the previous afternoon. His career total of first prize money which amounted to £415,735, a record for a European-based colt – only the fillies Dahlia and Allez France had accumulated more – defied the ravages of inflation until Dancing Brave's year of 1986. Troy's exploits in 1979 deservedly won him twenty-seven of the thirty-two votes for Horse of the Year and were instrumental in Sir Michael Sobell at long last topping the owners' table. Hern, too, had another tremendous season. Henry Cecil pipped him for the trainers' championship even though he had won in excess of £500,000. Add to that a further £155,454 from the classic successes of Troy and Niniski in Ireland and France (three of the stable's six Group I victories) and 1979 had the trappings of a year that Hern could not possibly envisage surpassing in the near future. Yet he would, and in the very next season at that.

The Sobell-Weinstock partnership lost no time finding a suitable replacement for Troy with whom to mount another attack on the Arc. In December they paid £500,000 for Ela-Mana-Mou, who would henceforth run in the colours of Simon Weinstock. They bought the horse, by Pitcairn, a son of Troy's sire Petingo, with Captain Tim Rogers of the Airlie Stud, where the horse would ultimately stand. For a horse considered almost a stone below the best of his generation, who had yet to win a Group I event and had cost only 4,500 guineas as a yearling, this constituted an enormous outlay. But such was the improvement Hern encouraged from Ela-Mana-Mou in 1980 that he was syndicated for £3.2 million, more than six times his market value of a year earlier and six hundred times the price he had fetched at Goffs in 1977. Apart from his victory over Troy in the 1978 Royal Lodge Stakes, the colt's principal success had come in another Group II race, the King Edward VII Stakes at Royal Ascot after he was fourth in Troy's Derby. Second place in the Grand Prix de Saint-Cloud and third in the King George implied that Ela-Mana-Mou might always have to be content with the role of best man rather than groom whenever he competed in Group I class.

Hern had his eye on the Eclipse, by which time Ela-Mana-Mou had run in, and won, two Pattern races: the Earl of Sefton Stakes (Group III) at Newmarket and the Prince of Wales's Stakes (Group II) at Royal Ascot. Ela-Mana-Mou took command halfway up the

Sandown hill to win comfortably, and to elicit *The Sporting Life* headline, "Sizzling Ela eclipses them all." Having broken his Group I duck he became West Ilsley's nominee for the King George VI & Queen Elizabeth II Stakes three weeks afterwards. Facing him were the recent winners of the Irish Derby (Tyrnavos) and French Oaks (Mrs Penny) while Dunette, victress in the 1979 French Oaks from Three Troikas, and Arc runner-up Le Marmot, represented the elder generation. Both of the French raiders had won their previous races in Group I company, the filly dead-heating for the Grand Prix de Saint-Cloud and Le Marmot winning the Prix Ganay.

Neither French challenger got into the firing line. Tyrnavos cut out the running until Carson dashed Ela-Mana-Mou into the lead passing the half-mile pole. "My colt was pulling so hard that I let him get on with it, knowing that he would relax and idle in front." Ela-Mana-Mou scarcely had time to "idle" before Mrs Penny appeared at his quarters with Piggott giving his impersonation of a Greek statue. The race lay between them and victory went to the four-year-old colt who drew on all his maturity and toughness to outstay the filly by three parts of a length.

Carson did not favour a tilt at the Arc, believing the Longchamp going in October was bound to be "too boggy – though he is all heart he might not be strong enough." Hern gave Ela-Mana-Mou a rest, the Benson & Hedges was missed and the horse went to Paris as fresh as a daisy. In his final gallop he easily beat Niniski and the three-year-old Prince Bee, who had finished second in the Irish Derby and won the Gordon Stakes, Great Voltigeur and the Prix Niel. Niniski and his pacemaker Lindoro also made the trip. Lady Beaverbrook's dual Leger winner had begun the season more impressively than Ela-Mana-Mou, but after winning the John Porter Stakes and the Ormonde Stakes he flopped in the Coronation Cup and had not run since.

Despite the luxurious turf Longchamp's going was officially declared firm – so firm that Hern had felt pads fitted under Ela-Mana-Mou's racing plates. For the second successive October Hern provided the Arc favourite, Ela-Mana-Mou, sharing odds of 2/1 on the Pari Mutuel with Le Marmot because Tim Rogers was a shareholder in both horses and thus they had to be coupled for betting purposes. Ela-Mana-Mou ran a cracking race to match Troy's third place and, in effect, besting it, since he was only half a length and a short head away from victory, the closest an English horse had come to winning since Rheingold's success of 1973. Passing the 400-metre cones he was in front and though he held off Three Troikas, Detroit flew past him inside the final fifty and then Argument caught him on the line. Plans to saddle Ela-Mana-Mou for the Champion Stakes had to be abandoned when Hern found him cast in his box a week beforehand. No matter, his rise to international pre-eminence had been one of the surprise packets of the year and he retired with a Timeform rating of 132, 8lb higher than 1979 – further testimony to Hern's skill and touch.

Having waited twenty-one years for his first Derby winner it seemed inconceivable that Hern would win a second only twelve months later, especially as no trainer had won successive Derbys since Frank Butters with Bahram and Mahmoud in 1935-6. Yet Hern not only equalled that feat, but he also won the 1980 Oaks thus becoming the first trainer since Noel Murless in 1957 to land the Epsom classic double. In all honesty it cannot be said that either Henbit or Bireme were on a par with Troy and Dunfermline. "Henbit wasn't in the same class as Troy," says Carson of his partner in what would be an equally memorable Derby, "but he was game. He broke a leg and still won."

The omens for the 1980 season were propitious from the very beginning of the year. In the New Year's Honours List Hern was made a Commander of the Royal Victorian Order. Dating from 1896, the Order is restricted to those who "having rendered extraordinary or important or personal services to the Sovereign merit Royal favour" and is conferred at the personal discretion of the monarch. A few years later Hern would be joined by Fulke Walwyn, National Hunt trainer to the Queen Mother, Grand Master of the Order.

By March it was appreciated by one and all that West Ilsley housed an exceptionally powerful set of classic prospects and as they were freely distributed among Hern's owners it was quite feasible that the stable would be doubly or even trebly represented at Epsom. Hern had already saddled three runners in the 1976 and 1979 Derbys, for instance. This year's hand included Lady Beaverbrook's Rontino, Lord Rotherwick's Water Mill and Sir Michael Sobell's Prince Bee besides Henbit, whose owner Mrs Ettie Plesch had won the 1961 Derby with Psidium. For the Oaks Hern's ammunition included Jakie Astor's The Dancer and Arthur Budgett's Shoot A Line in addition to Dick Hollingsworth's Bireme. How many of these would reach Epsom was anybody's guess, but the bookmakers were not about to take unnecessary risks. Corals quoted Hern at 7/2 to win the Derby, 5/4 to win the Oaks and 7/1 to bring off the double.

The Derby picture took a while to develop. Henbit was the first contender to show his mettle, winning the same Classic Trial at Sandown as Troy and Bustino. At this stage Hern believed he would be seen to better advantage at Chantilly in the French Derby. However, in winning the Chester Vase by four lengths in record time Henbit proved he could handle one notoriously tricky course and persuaded Hern to delay any decision on Epsom until Rontino had run in the Lingfield Derby Trial and Water Mill had made his seasonal debut in the Dante Stakes. Rontino put himself out of contention by finishing only third but, though he also failed to win, Water Mill (third to Hello Gorgeous and Master Willie) did enough to be declared a definite runner. "I was very pleased with the way Water Mill ran at York," said Hern. "He had been back in training only a month and there was obviously a lot of improvement in him." Henbit's participation in the Derby was not finalised until the following Sunday, 18 May, twenty-four hours after the current ante-post favourite, Monteverdi, had run dismally in the Irish 2000 Guineas. As a result, Henbit was installed favourite at odds varying from 7/2 with Ladbrokes and 7/1 with Mecca. The fourth Hern candidate, Prince Bee, had not run as a juvenile and was slow to learn. By his fourth start, the Predominate Stakes, he had begun to get the hang of things and beat Rankin by three-quarters of a length. Epsom might come too soon for him, so he was put by for the Irish Derby on 28 June.

When the final piece of the West Ilsley jigsaw had been inserted Carson was left with a straight choice between Henbit and Water Mill, which, he confessed, was harder to resolve than the previous year's between Troy and Milford. To outsiders the decision seemed relatively simple. Henbit may not have possessed the pedigree of Water Mill (a half-brother to Homing, arguably the best European miler of 1978 and a great-grandson of Musidora, the 1000 Guineas and Oaks winner of 1949), but he was the horse in form. Henbit's dam, Chateaucreek, won half a dozen sprints in the United States, while his sire Hawaii, a top middle-distance racer in South Africa and the United States, had not managed to impress breeders as a stallion. Consequently, Henbit was something unusual in the Hern stable – not fashionably bred for the classics and bought at public auction. He had, in fact, cost a mere $24,000 at the Kentucky Yearling Sales. He ran three times in 1979: finishing fourth in the Chesham Stakes at Royal Ascot, winning a Newbury maiden and fourth again in the Dewhurst behind Monteverdi.

Henbit's elevation to Derby favourite owed as much to the defection or inadequacy of others as to his own ability. The warm favourite had been Nureyev, the controversially disqualified winner of the 2000 Guineas, but he was laid low by a viral chill and his position taken by Monteverdi, whose stint lasted until the Irish 2000 Guineas. That Curragh classic gave Nikoli his third consecutive victory. After some prevarication by his connections he was sent over for the Derby and a glut of late money made him a 4/1 favourite on the day with Henbit at 7s.

The race turned out to be a rough one; "worse than an apprentice race at Tramore", according to Tony Murray, whose mount Tyrnavos was nearly knocked off his feet rounding Tattenham Corner. Nor did Henbit enjoy an easy passage, and Carson was continually obliged to push him along to retain a decent place in the leading bunch. "He stumbled coming down the hill and didn't come down very well but quickened when I asked him in the straight, then stumbled again $1\frac{1}{2}$ furlongs out".

Thus ran Carson's immediate account of the dramatic finale to an eventful race. Henbit had just snatched the lead from Rankin when he visibly faltered to his right. "All I felt was him change legs. The adrenalin was pumping and I didn't cotton on to the fact he was lame until I pulled up, although it showed up on the video. It wasn't until I pulled up after cantering back that I realized something was wrong with him."

Carson instantly corrected Henbit and, with whip in his right hand, drove hard for the line conscious of Master Willie's presence on his outside. He held on by three-quarters of a length. It was the first time a trainer and jockey combination had won consecutive Derbys since John Walls rode Beadsman and Musjid for George Manning in 1858 and 1859. "Henbit was a very brave horse," observed his trainer. "I knew straightaway that the injury was pretty serious and I felt so worried about the horse. It is always a thrill to win a classic but after that race I felt no elation at all. This

injury takes all the gilt off the gingerbread." Hern's reaction to his
horse's courageous effort afforded the public a rare glimpse of the
deep-seated love for the thoroughbred which, as friends knew only
too well, lay at the heart of his life with horses.

The following day Hern was able to issue a favourable bulletin
concerning Henbit's plight.

> There is every chance that Henbit will race again next year. John
> Gray, my veterinary surgeon, X-rayed his off-fore immediately the
> colt got back to West Ilsley. The cannon bone has a 5-inch crack and
> is in plaster cast. But fortunately there is no separation. The horse is
> able to get up and lie down and is eating his food but he is in con-
> siderable pain and is having painkilling tablets. There will be no need
> for screws or plates to be inserted to hold the fracture together.

Henbit was confined to his box for three months. Towards the end
of October Hern was satisfied that all was in order for him to
commence light roadwork and it constituted yet another example
of his trainer's wizardry that Henbit lined up for the start of the
Jockey Club Stakes on 1 May 1981. Sadly, all the patient endeavour
was in vain. Henbit faded as the pressure was applied, a scenario
repeated in the Royal Whip Stakes at the Curragh and Henbit was
retired forthwith.

In the Oaks Carson chose to side with Bireme, a half-sister to
Buoy, instead of Shoot A Line or The Dancer. All three had won
their trials but Bireme's victory in the Musidora from Gift Wrapped,
winner of the Longfield Oaks Trial, and the 1000 Guineas' runner-
up Our Home looked superior to Shoot A Line's Cheshire Oaks and
The Dancer's Sir Charles Clore Memorial Stakes. The Dancer's poor
display at Longchamp on the afternoon of Troy's Arc was blamed
on periodic ophthalmia in her left eye and she was now quite blind
on her near side. Riding her at Epsom would therefore pose a tactical
exercise of some proportion. She needed to break quickly and obtain
a position on the rail. Shoot A Line was more difficult for Carson to
overlook. She had won both her starts (Bireme lost the second of her
juvenile outings) and was as regally bred as Bireme, being a half-
sister to More Light with whom Hern had won the Gordon Stakes
and Jockey Club Stakes. Indeed, the two fillies were distantly related
for Shoot A Line's third dam, Bardia, was a half-sister to Felucca,
the third dam of Bireme. Carson's choice naturally attracted most

support at 9/2 (joint second favourite), with Shoot A Line at 6/1 and
The Dancer on 14/1. Quick as Lightning, the 1000 Guineas winner,
was favourite in spite of never having raced beyond a mile.

The Dancer burst from the stalls to claim the inside running rail
and take the race by the scruff of the neck. She still led with a
quarter of a mile to go and looked as if she might hang on to her
advantage. Shoot A Line, who had played up at the start, never got
into the hunt, but ever so gradually Bireme began to wear down
her stablemate and, ultimately, build a two length cushion. Vielle
relegated The Dancer to third on the line. The Dancer's gallop,
coupled with the firm ground, helped Bireme to a time of 2.34.33,
which lowered Beam's 53-year-old race record.

After such a long and fruitful association with the female members
of the Felucca family it was entirely fitting that Dick Hollingsworth's
first classic success should come in the Oaks where both Ark Royal
and Cutter had filled minor places. Bireme's long-term objective was
the St Leger (for which she was quoted at 7/1), but more immediately
the Irish Oaks assumed priority. However, on the Thursday of Royal
Ascot Hern had bad news of her. "She got loose this morning and
fell on the road, grazing her knee. She had two cuts – one on the
stifle and one on the elbow. It is not serious but there is no chance
of her going to Ireland." As the summer progressed it became
apparent Bireme would not go to Doncaster either and Hern
announced her retirement on 29 July.

Hern's Ascot statement came after Shoot A Line returned to her
best form with a crushing five length success in the Ribblesdale
Stakes. She would now represent the stable at the Curragh and a
bonny job she made of it. Her victory was never in question and it
provided Hern with a slice of Turf history. He became the second
man to train the winner of each English and Irish classic, Vincent
O'Brien having passed this milestone in 1968 upon Sir Ivor's 2000
Guineas victory. Shoot A Line's Irish Oaks was also Hern's fourteenth Pattern race success of the season, and despite losing both
Derby and Oaks winners, he was armed with sufficiently adept
substitutes to collect eight more by the end of the year. Had not the
virus affected a number of West Ilsley's two-year-olds during the
autumn round of juvenile Pattern races, the total might have risen
even higher. Shoot A Line's contribution to this score continued
with the Yorkshire Oaks and the Park Hill Stakes and she went into

winter quarters boasting the consistent record of five wins from six starts as a three-year-old. Timeform rated her the equal of Bireme at 127, while the official handicapper assessed her a pound superior and the best filly in Europe – jointly with Mrs Penny, the Prix de Diane and Prix Vermeille winner.

Among Hern's classic colts, Prince Bee emerged as Henbit's heir apparent. In the Irish Derby he beat all of Henbit's seven Derby victims who participated bar Tyrnavos and then proceeded to register a hat-trick of victories in the Gordon Stakes, Great Voltigeur and Prix Niel. Hern did not regard him as a true stayer (he was by Sun Prince) and selected Water Mill as his St Leger horse. In the Derby Water Mill had been one of the prime sufferers in all the scrimmaging on Tattenham Hill. Possibly he was still nursing the after-effects of his rough ride when next time out he could only dead-heat for third place in the Grand Prix de Paris. Equally, he might not have seen out the one mile seven furlongs. At any rate, Hern was disappointed with his lifeless display ("He did not seem to show the fire I expected") and thereafter put blinkers on him as he had his half-brother Homing. Water Mill responded by winning twice at Goodwood to become, in the words of *The Sporting Life*, "the new Hern classic star" and he started favourite for the St Leger. However, he could never get within striking distance of Light Cavalry who, under a superb ride from Joe Mercer, made all the running and increased the pace as Water Mill tried to get on terms.

Water Mill's defeat was the first spanner to disrupt West Ilsley's well-oiled mechanism all year. This setback, if one can describe it so in such a gloriously successful season, effectively signalled the end of Hern's assault on the £1 million barrier in first prize money. After the wins of Shoot A Line, Prince Bee, Kittyhawk (Lowther Stakes) and Deadly Serious (Galtres Stakes) at York in mid-August his total leapfrogged Henry Cecil's old record and stood at £749,669; contrasted with this, in the final three months of the campaign West Ilsley added less than £100,000 to the total. Hern dispatched eleven runners to Doncaster and won only with Shoot A Line. But, when all is said and done no trainer can cavil at a year which saw four patrons – Simon Weinstock (first), Mrs Ettie Plesch (second), Dick Hollingsworth (eighth) and Arthur Budgett (tenth) – finish high among the leading moneywinners, four of his horses – Ela-Mana-Mou (first), Henbit (second), Bireme (seventh) and Shoot A Line (ninth) – occupy lofty positions in their table, and his stable-jockey win the jockeys' championship.

Hern's own personal achievements were monumental. The fact that he won sixty-five races worth £831,964 to win his third trainers' title and break Henry Cecil's record by almost £150,000 scarcely tells the whole tale. Not since Noel Murless breached the £250,000 mark in 1967 had a trainer so monopolized the quality races. In 1967 Murless won sixty races in England of which twenty-one (plus two more in France) came in events accorded Pattern status in 1980. He won three English classics, the Eclipse and the King George. Thirteen years later Hern collected nineteen English Pattern races through the efforts of Ela-Mana-Mou (four), Shoot A Line (three), Henbit (three), Bireme (two), Prince Bee (two), Niniski (two), More Light (Jockey Club Stakes), Kittyhawk (Lowther Stakes) and Sovereign Rose (Diadem Stakes), quite apart from the Irish Oaks (Shoot A Line), Prix Niel (Prince Bee) and the Prix de la Porte Maillot (Luck of the Draw), which contributed a further £86,775 in stakes. Three classics and three other races at Group I level is no mean haul. If place money was added to these winnings Hern cruised past the £1 million mark, the first trainer to do so.

One particularly satisfying aspect of this *annus mirabilis* was the fact that with Water Mill, Kittyhawk and The Dancer Hern won decent races for Lord Rotherwick, Lord Porchester and Jakie Astor, owners who generally saw far less of the limelight. During the next three years each of this trio would see their colours carried to victory in a Group I race.

By winning the 1981 St Leger, Jakie Astor's Cut Above gave Hern a much needed tonic. In May and June the stable again had to contend with the virus. The number of runners was reduced to a trickle and the invalids were being dosed with a foul-smelling concoction of honey and garlic to aid their recovery. The first four classics passed with West Ilsley's best placing no higher than Church Parade's fifth in the 2000 Guineas. Prince Bee could not outrun Master Willie in the Coronation Cup: Shoot A Line found Ardross far too strong in the Ascot Gold Cup. The winners began to flow again in July but were distinctly small beer. When the York August meeting came round that year Hern had won only three Pattern races compared to the sixteen of 1980. Then, on York's opening day, a worse calamity befell West Ilsley. Silken Knot crashed to the ground in the Yorkshire Oaks giving Carson the sort of accident every flat-race jockey dreads. The filly's forelegs snapped, two gun-shots one after the other, dumping Carson like a silk rag beneath the hooves of the other runners. Unconscious and bleeding from the ears, Hern's jockey was driven straight to hospital. Carson had fractured his skull. He would not ride again for seven months.

Jockeys had to be found for Hern's two principal Leger horses, Lady Beaverbrook's Bustomi, who had won the King Edward VII Stakes and Gordon Stakes, his only outings, and Jakie Astor's Cut Above, a half-brother to Sharp Edge. After two promising runs as a juvenile, the latter had reappeared to win the White Rose Stakes at Ascot in April but subsequently fell foul of the virus. He recovered in time to chase home Shergar in the Irish Derby and then finished third in the Geoffrey Freer which did little to advance hopes of reversing the Curragh form (beaten a leisurely four lengths) in the St Leger. As a 28/1 shot in the field of seven, Cut Above definitely wore the mantle of Hern's weaker contender. Lester Piggott opted for Bustomi (13/2), who was to be paced by Magikin. In a grand reunion of the old triple alliance that had won the 1965 Leger, Joe Mercer was to partner Cut Above.

"I was asked to ride Cut Above because Jakie Astor owned him. Fortunately it came up soft which suited all Cut Above's family, and the longer trip also helped. I was struggling for a long way, third or fourth, but then he began to find a gear. The writing was on the wall for Shergar before the turn. I heard him gurgling – no horse will win a Leger if he can't breathe." Glint of Gold took Bustomi's measure entering the final quarter mile only to be caught out by the dogged challenge of Cut Above, who went on to win decisively by $2\frac{1}{2}$ lengths. The 9/4 on favourite was labouring $11\frac{1}{2}$ lengths back in fourth. "The Old Firm strikes again as Shergar is vanquished," boomed *The Sporting Life* report. Explained Hern: "I thought he could reverse the form of the Irish Derby over a longer trip, especially when the ground came in his favour." A great day was completed when Hern and Mercer teamed up again forty minutes after the Leger to win the May Hill Stakes with the Queen's Height of Fashion. Cut Above's purse of £76,190 helped nudge Hern up to fourth place in the table for 1981 but the big prizes of the summer had eluded a stable just coming out of the doldrums. Hern eventually mustered sixty-four wins but only seven were in Pattern company.

According to the *Racing Specialist* "Lord Rotherwick would easily top any poll to decide who is Britain's most unapproachable owner." The multi-millionaire former chairman of Union Castle and other international shipping lines, Rotherwick verged on being a recluse, which made him the archetypal Hern owner. The best horse to carry his colours since he became a patron of Hern's was Homing. He began 1978 in handicaps but wound up the season with victories in the Prix du Rond-Point (breaking the Longchamp track record) and the Queen Elizabeth II Stakes, either side of a second place in the Prix du Moulin. All told the blinkered Homing ran twelve times in 1978 – almost unheard of exertion for a Hern-trained animal – and earned a Timeform rating of 130, 8lb superior to the 2000 Guineas winner Roland Gardens. The closest Lord Rotherwick had got to winning a classic was Water Mill's second in the St Leger. His three-year-old filly of 1982, called Swiftfoot, was no relation to the aforementioned colts but she was impeccably bred all the same, and it was she with whom Hern would work the miracle to hand yet another longstanding owner his first classic.

Swiftfoot was by the American sire Run the Gantlet out of White-foot, who, trained by Harry Wragg, won the 1970 Musidora Stakes for Mr R.B. Moller. Whitefoot's grandam, Mitrailleuse, won the Park Hill for Lord Astor in 1947 and traced (via Maid of the Mist – like Grey of Falloden) to Sceptre. By winning the Cheshire Oaks Swiftfoot encouraged hopes of an Epsom repeat but she dropped back alarmingly in the straight to finish last. Greville Starkey (Carson preferred Cut Above's half-sister Cut Loose) said she had choked and subsequent blood tests were indeed abnormal. Whatever troubled Swiftfoot at Epsom declined to manifest itself at the Curragh. She made all to win by three lengths. Awaasif had too much acceleration for her in the Yorkshire Oaks, but as her family history illustrated, (besides Mitrailleuse, her maternal cousin Reload won the race in 1973) the extended $1\frac{3}{4}$ miles of the Park Hill Stakes provided exactly the test of stamina she thrived on. Swiftfoot dictated the pace and skated up to such an extent that she was sent back to Ireland to confront the St Leger winner Touching Wood in the Irish version. Although one or two of Hern's string were running poorly due to the virus, the soft going probably undid her and she trailed in a remote third.

Lord Porchester's Kittyhawk was another inmate of West Ilsley to suffer in 1981. She was off the course for three months after the 1000 Guineas (in which she was ninth), making her return in the Stewards' Cup, not a race one normally associates with Hern's animals. Kittyhawk found the Goodwood cavalry charge too hectic, but she did regain winning form at Doncaster in the Kiveton Park Stakes. If Kittyhawk proved a slight disappointment to Lord Porchester in 1981, he at least possessed a colt who not only won a Pattern race but also looked the sort with a future. Little Wolf was a chestnut son of Hiding Place, a half-sister to Queen's Hussar, who won four races as a three-year-old in 1966, including the Nell Gwyn Stakes. As befitted a daughter of the redoubtable broodmare Jojo (twelve winners from fourteen foals) she too became a prolific source of winners. Little Wolf was her ninth in ten foals, the best of whom had been Smuggler, trained by Hern to win the Princess of Wales's Stakes and Gordon Stakes in 1976 and the Yorkshire Cup and Henry II Stakes in 1978. In spite of appearing to hold all the right credentials Smuggler did not contest the Ascot Gold Cup. His owner – at the time chairman of the Jockey Club Flat-Race Pattern Committee – reportedly stated, somewhat controversially, "It even devalues a horse to enter him." Like his half-brother, Little Wolf raced as a five-year-old, but unlike Smuggler he was allowed to compete at Ascot and duly won the Gold Cup.

Once free of the virus Little Wolf won two races as a three-year-old in 1981, the Scottish Derby and the Group III St Simon Stakes, and he proceeded to improve with age. At four he added the Prix Jean de Chaudenay and the Jockey Club Cup, but could not handle the deplorable ground when made favourite for the Prix Royal Oak. Little Wolf's most eye-catching performance was his one race over two miles – the Jockey Club Cup – and with Ardross in retirement the Ascot Gold Cup was now a wide open contest. Little Wolf ran for the Gold Cup and, on the fast ground he yearned for, galloped home by five lengths in a very fast time. Six weeks later he won the Goodwood Cup over two miles five furlongs which suggested Porchester was either misquoted in 1978 or had experienced a remarkable change of heart concerning the impact victory in the Cup races had on stallion potential. Little Wolf, in fact, demonstrated at Goodwood many of the qualities sought by breeders, because he broke down on his near fore some way from the finish and only a combination of guts and class saw him through. "He began to pull himself up three furlongs out and now we know why," said Carson after walking him back to the winner's enclosure. Initially Hern did not regard the injury as too bad. "He was lame pulling up, uneven when he returned but almost sound as he walked away. He'll be fine to go home and we will put a poultice on it." Little Wolf was found to have badly jarred the joint on his near fore and slightly bruised the cartilage. Hern persevered with the horse and brought him back ten months later in anticipation of a second Gold Cup. Little Wolf finished a commendable third in the Henry II Stakes but had sprained a tendon.

For all the heroics of Little Wolf there was no confusion about the identity of Hern's star performer in 1983. Without hesitation that accolade went to Sun Princess. She represented one of the strongest Ballymacoll bloodlines stretching back to Sunny Gulf, the dam of Park Hill winner Sunny Cove and her own grandam Sunland, who was third in the Park Hill of 1968. Sun Princess's dam, Sunny Valley, won in France and her sire, English Prince, won the Irish Derby of 1974. Consequently, she was bred in the mould of nearly all Hern's horses – a relatively late maturing type with no pretensions of a serious juvenile career (particularly as she was also a 18 May foal), one whose sights were firmly locked on the staying classics. Her only outing as a two-year-old came in the Blue Seal Stakes at Ascot on 25 September where she finished a good second to Khaizaraan. West Ilsley made another painfully slow start in 1983: by Royal Ascot two-thirds of Hern's ninety horses had coughs, despite the installation during the winter of air ionisation units which remove airborne particles. Sun Princess was proving a handful on the gallops. Looking short of peak fitness on her seasonal debut at Newbury, she once more filled second place, two lengths behind Ski Sailing. They met each other again in the Oaks. Ski Sailing was second favourite to the French filly Alexandrie, who owed her position in the market to a comfortable victory in the Prix Cleopatre at Maisons-Laffitte. However, such was Hern's Epsom record of late that Sun Princess, though still a maiden, was 6/1 fourth favourite in the betting ahead of fillies like Cormorant Wood, Acclimatise and Shoreline who had all won decent races.

Sun Princess's staggering twelve length triumph was the most prodigious in an English classic since Never Say Die took the 1954 St Leger by a similar margin and left some observers feeling, as others had after watching Pretty Polly, Sun Chariot and Noblesse win their Oaks, that with the 5lb sex allowance Sun Princess could have won the Derby – maiden or no maiden. Mayonaise was credited with a twenty length victory in the 1859 1000 Guineas but Sun Princess was certainly the most authoritative winner of the Oaks as far as records could tell (official distances only date from 1842). Moreover, she was the first maiden to win an English classic since Asmena won the Oaks of 1950. Her lack of experience had only slightly bothered Hern. "I was a bit worried but she'd never run green and was still a maiden only because the ground had been so bad. I thought she'd go very well and Willie told me after Newbury that she would beat Ski Sailing next time. At home, they put in a lot of hard work teaching this filly to settle because she was so free initially that one even wondered whether she would be trainable. She has much more speed than my other two Oaks winners and stays as well as they did." Carson also drew attention to the patience of Joe Storrar, her regular work-rider, who had accomplished the tricky task of getting her to relax. The story of the race is quickly told. Sun Princess went to the front coming down the hill and, still on a tight rein, then bade farewell. "She lost her place in the jostling when Greville Starkey, on Fields of Spring, was knocked back onto Alexandrie and Freddy Head, so I had to go and get a better position on the outside. When I got there, they were all dying and so it was off we go."

Sun Princess bypassed the Irish Oaks in favour of the King George VI & Queen Elizabeth II Stakes where the opposition included the French Derby winner Caerleon, Carlingford Castle (second at Epsom), dual Group I winner Diamond Shoal and the four-year-old mare Time Charter, who had won the Oaks and Champion Stakes in 1982. Sun Princess was fast learning her trade but not quite rapidly enough to win a race of this competitive nature. She fought Carson throughout the early stages, before a strong late challenge brought her into third place three-quarters of a length and one length behind Time Charter and Diamond Shoal. The Yorkshire Oaks showed Sun Princess in a far more level-headed mood and she led all the way to slaughter the Irish Oaks heroine Give Thanks by seven lengths.

Having twice narrowly failed to win a Prix de l'Arc de Triomphe in the preceding four years, the Weinstocks were anxious to ensure third time really would prove to be lucky. Few owners can expect three bites at the cherry with candidates as live as Troy, Ela-Mana-Mou and Sun Princess. The St Leger was obviously an ideal race for the filly but would the final classic sap her strength, thereby diminishing her chances in the Arc? The Weinstocks believed it might and favoured the Prix Vermeille as her Arc preliminary. Hern persuaded them otherwise. He planned to run Sailor's Dance as the pacemaker but instructed Joe Mercer to set nothing more than a moderate gallop. Fifteen hours of rain on the Friday very nearly scuppered Hern's scheme for the following day. With Longchamp in the forefront of their minds, the Weinstocks began to waver and it was not until Hern had walked the course an hour before the St Leger that the trainer finally allayed their fears. "Had she been withdrawn it would have been bad for racing, it would have been bad for the Leger and it would have been unnecessary," explained Hern. In truth, Sun Princess had little to beat and she won handily, although Carson was obliged to wave his whip at her in order to repel Esprit du Nord and Carlingford Castle. The race time emphasized that the gallop had been as slow as Hern intended. "Willie said she did not have a hard race. They did not go very fast and she settled so well that he left her alone. They will go much faster in the Arc and that will suit her." A relieved Simon Weinstock preferred to play his cards closer to his chest: "I was not too keen to run," he told the Press. "I will let you know what I think in three weeks' time in Paris."

Sun Princess provided Hern with his sixth success in the St Leger, a figure exceeded by the amazing total of sixteen standing to John Scott, the nineteenth century's 'Wizard of the North', but only matched in the modern era by Cecil Boyd-Rochfort, another master in the art of training stayers. Besides the Hern pair of Dunfermline and Sun Princess just two fillies, Sun Chariot and Meld, had completed the Oaks-Leger double since the days of Pretty Polly.

Sun Princess travelled to Longchamp on a wave of optimism at the very least equal to those which bore Troy and Ela-Mana-Mou, and quite possibly even a mite stronger. Both colts faced extremely tough opposition. This year's large field of twenty-six reflected the absence of a really dominant personality and Time Charter was sent off favourite at odds of 13/4. Sun Princess came next at around 7/1 – fillies had won the last four Arcs and they occupied eight of the first nine places in the betting. In time-honoured fashion Hern's few comments were guarded. "There is a lot of luck in the Arc. Apart from other factors there is also the draw to be considered." Sun Princess experienced no difficulty breaking from her number five stall near the inside rail to follow Sailor's Dance (from eight), who was again entrusted with the role of hare. The majority of Arcs are characterized by a lung-bursting gallop through the opening mile, but Mercer dictated a sensible rather than furious pace and was still in front with half a mile to run. His job done, he moved off the rail and Carson punched Sun Princess through the gap and into the lead. Challengers were queueing up on her outside. She beat them off one after another until, ten strides from the post, All Along zoomed out of the pack to come between Stanerra and Sun Princess at missile velocity. In those ten strides the filly whom Mercer had rejected out of loyalty to the West Ilsley team caught Sun Princess and went a length clear. "We could have done with easier ground but she ran a marvellous race," said a disappointed Carson. Bearing in mind his comments at Doncaster Simon Weinstock took defeat like a man. "Sun Princess was superb. Her race in the Leger had done her no harm at all."

Sun Princess had shown herself to be the best staying filly of her generation (rated at 130 by Timeform, albeit 3lb below Dunfermline) and she contributed over a third of the prize money that lifted Hern to his fourth title of leading trainer. The stable's four Group I successes also provided the high-spots of Carson's 159 winners which gave him his fifth championship. Sun Princess remained in training for another season but she failed to reproduce the top class form of 1983 in either the Coronation Cup, King George or the Arc – her only three runs.

Despite the magnificence of Sun Princess's exploits in 1983 the headlines were dominated for most of the year – too much so for Hern's peace of mind – by the non-exploits of another West Ilsley inmate. When a horse is blessed with parents who won five classics between them, a regal name with highbrow undertones, good looks and the ability to match so that a track record is shattered the first time it steps onto a racecourse, that horse is either heading for immortality or ignominy.

To Dick Hern's sorrow Fate decreed the latter to be the destiny which awaited Gorytus.

Chapter Eleven

GORYTUS & THE PRESS

'I do not consider my horses to be public business'

PROMINENT PUBLIC FIGURES often suffer rough treatment at the hands of the British Press. Such ordeals, they are
frequently reminded, are the price of fame. Oscar Wilde, who had
good reason to bear the odd grudge as far as the gentlemen of the
fourth estate were concerned, was moved to say: "In the old days
we had the rack, now they have the Press. . . . Journalism justifies
its own existence by the great Darwinian principle of the survival
of the vulgarest." Wilde and Dick Hern hardly strike one as plausible
soul mates. At first glance a common thread is impossible to dis-
tinguish. A love of poetry? Perhaps. Antipathy toward the Press?
Most definitely.

One of the oldest tenets in racing proclaims secrecy to be the
essential prerequisite in the trainer's perennial battle of wits with
the bookmaker and punter. Hern's was not a 'betting' stable but his
strict, almost obsessive, adherence to the code of silence rivalled any
trainer of the old school and not a few practitioners of omerta.
"The Major's comparative silence as far as the Press is concerned,"
explains Ian Cocks, "is all part of his loyalty toward his owners. He
maintains he trains for his owners and not the general public." Of
paramount concern to a trainer like Hern is the overwhelming desire
not to upset owners, nearly all of whom are as diffident, reserved
and private as himself. Besides, to someone imbued with Army
mores, owners constitute the trainer's superiors. They pay the piper,
they call the tune. Their satisfaction is his number one priority –

which is why he found it difficult to accept Willie Carson discussing West Ilsley's runners during televised racing and at one stage put a stop to the practice. Although not exactly beyond criticism, the views and actions of one's superiors are immune to anything other than the most private form of questioning or censure. Hern's unspoken covenant with his owners would be shaken to the core should private dissension be dragged into the public gaze.

Consequently, journalists never have featured highly on Hern's list of priorities. It is one of their jobs to seek and expose the very snippets of information that Hern considered were for his eyes and ears only. If owners were the trainer's superiors, then journalists were certainly his inferiors. Yet they point-blank refused to conform to the rules. Journalists tend to exercise a blatant and unhealthy disregard for protocol and the niceties of hierarchical ritual. They frequently utilize the telephone like a mugger wields a cosh in a darkened alleyway. The get the wrong end of the stick, they misrepresent, and, the last straw, they have the temerity to criticize. "It's a fact of the game that the odd Press man tends to let you down," says David Murray-Smith, who can speak from his own experiences as a trainer in addition to his days as an assistant to Hern and Vincent O'Brien. "They misquote you or something and it puts your back up." Apparently, something like this happened to Hern right at the beginning of his career when training for Major Holliday. The ensuing embarrassment was not easily, if ever, forgotten. Nor were the thousands of words spilled about Joe Mercer's sacking calculated to dilute Hern's wariness.

To make matters worse, Hern was not blessed with the kind of communicative skills which make talking to the Press a natural exercise. "Men prominent in life are mostly hard to converse with," wrote Max Beerbohm. "They lack small-talk, and at the same time one doesn't like to confront them with their own grand themes." Hern eschewed general tittle-tattle, preferring to give a specific answer to a specific question or, better still, issue statements through the Press Association. If an interview was sanctioned, he favoured the formality of his study back in West Ilsley rather than the hurly-burly of the weighing room or winner's enclosure. Even then, the dialogue was liable to be curt and business-like, the interviewer kept at arm's length, fraternization minimal.

Of course, few journalists were granted this privilege. "I once tried to interview Dick Hern simply to ask permission to feature three of his horses in an article," one nameless scribe was quoted as saying, "and he was so rude to me that I wish I hadn't bothered." Hern had an image problem to tax any advertising agency in the world, however many gallons of midnight oil they burnt in his cause. "His public image is quite wrong," insists Ian Cocks. "At home he is a different person, a tremendous host and impeccably mannered," but to outsiders Hern remains remote and prickly. Spirited, full-throated renderings of "Won't You Come Home Bill Bailey" and the like are all very well after dinner in the Mess and at the Old Rectory, or after some celebration in West Ilsley Village Hall, but until these plebeian touches presaged a similar lowering of the boom in public, reports of such bonhomie pared no more than the top few millimetres of ice.

In fact West Ilsley was a closed shop to most of the Press Room, whose members were largely faceless figures to Dick Hern. For instance, one day at Ayr in September 1979, one reporter (with nineteen years in Fleet Street) who was gathering news for ITV that afternoon, approached Hern with an enquiry about Troy's health – it was rumoured he had contracted ringworm – in the build-up to the Arc. He was stopped in his tracks with a brusque: "Who are you?" At the outset of the 1980s only Michael Seely (*The Times*), Peter Scott (*The Daily Telegraph*), John de Moraville (*Daily Express*) and Peter Willet were allegedly *persona grata* with Dick Hern.

This situation led to a quite remarkable outburst in the *Racing Specialist* of 31 March 1983. The paper's "Off the Bit" column, a mixture of gossip and news items, was entitled "Major problems with the media", and concluded with the sentiments: "We feel it's a great pity that such a gulf now exists between one of the greatest Flat trainers of the postwar era and representatives of the media. But perhaps it's fair to think that . . .imaginative reports would not appear in print if Major Hern was to adopt a more open style in handling journalists – as in the manner of, say, Guy Harwood or Henry Cecil."

The blue touchpaper leading to this powderkeg had been sparking for some time. Despite Hern's silence "Off the Bit" kept its readers intimately acquainted with West Ilsley's horses, more so than for any other leading stable in the land. Somehow or other its contributors had penetrated the meticulous security screen erected by the 'Pipe-puffing Major', as they referred to Hern. "There are no secrets these days," Hern was eventually forced to admit. "Every stable has a mole, or even two. If a horse hasn't eaten up in the morning the world seems to know by lunchtime." Events were being related in such detail that one was left pondering whether the source was extraordinarily close to Hern himself. No stable lad could possibly have been privy to such breadth and depth of information. In September 1981 "Off the Bit" hinted that one West Ilsley owner would be asked to remove his horses so Hern could accommodate twenty of Sobell's which were being transferred from France, and six months later the column divulged that Lady Beaverbrook's Bustomi "had met with a serious setback and his future must now be in some doubt" before Hern could reach a telephone to inform the colt's owner. Hern was not amused. He called in Racecourse Security Services to track down West Ilsley's "mole". The investigation led by former Flying Squad member Wally Bridges got nowhere. If anything matters deteriorated... And that's where Gorytus enters the story.

Gorytus was bred in the USA by his owner Mrs Alice Mills of Hickory Tree Farm, in Virginia. He was a beautiful specimen of the thoroughbred, a wonderfully proportioned, strong-limbed bay crowned with a noble head. His sire was the peerless Nijinsky, the lone post-war Triple Crown winner, while his dam, Glad Rags, was also prepared by Vincent O'Brien to win a classic (for Mrs Mills), namely the 1000 Guineas of 1966. Foaled on 7 February 1980, Gorytus – the Latin word for a quiver of arrows – was Glad Rags' ninth living foal of whom five had won races, though only two of them had done so in England. Hatter's Dream won a Newcastle maiden in 1973 and Mirthful Flirt won the Kingsclere Stakes at Newbury and finished second in the Cherry Hinton Stakes of 1974 before she was shipped back to the USA for further success. The best relation of Gorytus to run in America was his full sister Terpsichorist, who won eleven races at the ages of three and four to earn a rating in 1979 just 5lb behind the French mare Trillion, second in the 1978 Arc and ultimately the dam of Triptych.

Once put into training Gorytus soon became the cynosure of all eyes. "In my time with the Major," says Ian Cocks, "Gorytus was the outstanding horse, particularly in his early days on the Trial Ground. He put in more competitive pieces of work there than any other horse I can remember. Consequently, he became the biggest disappointment of my stay at West Ilsley. It was a complete mystery what went wrong with him." His racecourse debut was nothing short of electrifying. York's Acomb Stakes over seven furlongs at the big August meeting was the selected race, one confined to horses sired by stallions that had won over $1\frac{1}{2}$ miles or more and therefore ideally suited to slower developing animals whose classic aspirations were incompatible with an intensive two-year-old campaign. Not surprisingly it was a race Hern liked. His representative had won three of the previous five runnings and back in 1973 the Acomb had given the public its first sight of Bustino.

Despite impressing everyone round the paddock Gorytus started at 5/1 due to the presence in the field of the unbeaten Salieri, "at this stage by far the best of my two-year-olds" according to his trainer Henry Cecil. Those victories incurred Salieri a 7lb penalty. Nevertheless, he was a raging 2/1 on favourite to concede the weight to his thirteen opponents. Salieri led for five of the seven furlongs. Then Carson shook up Gorytus and the handsome colt proceeded to demonstrate that he possessed more than mere looks. One length, two lengths, three lengths clear he shot in a matter of strides. At the post he and Carson had seven lengths to spare over Salieri (admittedly eased when defeat was inevitable) and their time knocked more than a second off the two-year-old track record. Odds of 25/1 about Gorytus for the 1983 Derby were instantly snapped up and by the close of racing he was 20/1 for the Epsom classic and a 16/1 shot for the 2000 Guineas. On his next outing Salieri took the scalp of Horage, unbeaten in nine races (including the Coventry and Gimcrack), when victorious in the Mill Reef Stakes.

Gorytus had ruthlessly dispelled any fears that his ability might not mirror his pedigree and looks. The next objective was the Champagne Stakes at Doncaster and this, too, was also achieved with the minimum of fuss, by five lengths in the best time for fourteen years. "He can do better than that, you'll see," promised Carson on dismounting. "This is the best two-year-old colt I've ever ridden." The ante-post market on the 1983 classics went haywire. The best available prices were 5/1 for the Guineas and 7/1 for the Derby; with some firms Gorytus was as tight as 3/1. Only old-timers could recall the last colt to be quoted at such cramped odds for the Derby during the preceding season. That was Bahram, the winner of his five races in 1934 (culminating with the Middle Park), whose record on retirement read a perfect nine out of nine and included the Triple Crown. Whatever long term ambitions Hern harboured for Gorytus his short range plans were more clear cut: "The Dewhurst, 2000 Guineas and the Derby," he replied to the obligatory inquiries. "I'm very pleased with him. Delighted. He's done everything we have asked of him and his temperament is good."

By 1982 the Dewhurst Stakes had become the single most important staying event in the calendar for two-year-olds. Although a race with a considerable history dating back to 1875 and numbering such luminaries of the Turf as Ormonde, Bayardo, Hyperion, Pinza and Crepello on its roll of honour, the Dewhurst's contemporary kudos dated from 1966 when its first prize was trebled to £9,866 and to 1973 when its value was further enhanced, to nearly £27,000, thanks to sponsorship from the bookmakers William Hill. In 1982 the victor would receive £46,228. Predictably, this Group I contest attracted the leading colts and its winners invariably topped the Free Handicap, to be exact, nine in the sixteen renewals between 1966 and 1981. More significantly, Nijinsky, Mill Reef, Grundy, Wollow and The Minstrel went on to win classics. However, the Dewhurst had never been a happy hunting ground for Dick Hern. Admittedly, he very rarely set his juveniles such a searching examination as the Dewhurst. In twenty-four years as a trainer he had only been represented in the race by five horses: Prime Value (fourth, 1958), King's Favourite (third, 1962), More Light (second, 1978), Henbit (fourth, 1979) and Solaboy (fifth, 1981). The two Holliday horses started favourite, which was also the assured status of Gorytus on Friday, 15 October 1982.

Gorytus frightened off all bar three. Having seen his stable's Proclaim humbled by Gorytus at Doncaster, Guy Harwood elected to take him on with Gordian, the promising winner of a Salisbury maiden who was subsequently an unlucky second in the Somerville Tattersall Stakes. Henry Cecil's standard bearer was the Middle Park winner Diesis, an unlikely runner until he sparkled in a gallop with Cecil's other top two-year-old colts on 9 October. Cecil had some kind of formline on Gorytus via Salieri, but in the Middle Park Diesis had only beaten Hern's Orixo by $2\frac{1}{2}$ lengths and Orixo was streets behind Gorytus at home. The fourth competitor was Tough Commander, a 200/1 no-hoper praying for a miracle. The gravest danger to Gorytus appeared to be the cough lingering at West Ilsley. The stable had not sent out a winner since Little Wolf won the Jockey Club Cup at the last Newmarket fixture a fortnight earlier, and Swiftfoot had performed like a sick animal when running no sort of race in the Irish St Leger the previous Saturday. Hern took the precaution of twice having Gorytus bloodtested before the horse departed for Newmarket on the Thursday afternoon. Both tests proved normal.

By the time Gorytus was delivered to the Links Stables rumours were already circulating to the effect that he was not the cast-iron certainty everyone thought. 'Well-informed backers' had rung William Hill to support Diesis; Gorytus, insisted the grapevine, was coughing. All the leading bookmakers promptly suspended business on the race. Hern, confronted with this 'news' while he was pre-occupied at the Yearling Sales, was understandably reticent and non-committal. However, as the afternoon wore on Hern became more and more irritated. The *Daily Star*'s Fleetwood Jones was on hand to chronicle the trainer's harassment: "Never one to be voted the most forthcoming handler of the year by the race-writing fra-ternity, Hern started off by replying to the question of whether Gorytus would run, 'I don't know, I really can't say.' Later in the day when approached by about the 50th journalist with the same query, he rounded on the unfortunate Press man with: 'Do you own the horse? If not, what has it got to do with you.'" At 5 pm Hern emerged from the peace and tranquillity of the Links Stables, dapperly attired in cavalry twills, tweed jacket and flat cap, to quash all the rumours. "I've just seen Gorytus. He looks a picture. He's travelled very well and I'm 100% satisfied with him." Panic over. On Friday morning Michael Seely was able to write in *The Times* reassuringly, "Immaculate Major gives backers a dressing down," – in marked contrast to the *Daily Star* which spoke of "Hern's D Day poser". Gorytus strode into the paddock radiating health and he was made a 2/1 on favourite to lift Hern's Dewhurst hoodoo.

The following couple of minutes saw the trainer's recurring night-mare become horrific reality. Gordian led from the stalls at a decent clip, tracked by Gorytus and Tough Commander with Diesis bringing up the rear. Three furlongs out Carson asked Gorytus to quicken. Nothing happened. The colt began to labour and lose ground. The jockey thought he was choking, perhaps from swallowing his tongue.

As Diesis swept into the lead in the Dip, Gorytus fell further and further behind. Carson glanced down at his hind legs, causing some stunned spectators to conclude that Gorytus had pulled a muscle or rapped a nerve. An obviously distressed Gorytus passed the post so far adrift that the photo finish camera had been switched off (he trailed Diesis by an estimated forty lengths) and he was visibly shaking when Hern reached him in the area reserved for beaten horses. In the midst of more journalists than were gathering round the winner, Hern was truly run to earth and admitted to being dumbfounded. "He stood like a rock and was as good as gold when I saddled him," he said, staring at the now quivering horse. Nor could Carson shed much light on the situation. "Gorytus was unable to do anything when I asked to go on after about three furlongs," he said, before putting into words what everyone was thinking: "It's just as though he'd been got at. Gorytus ran like a dead horse." The training community's sympathy with Hern's predicament was immediately expressed by Mrs Peter Walwyn. "That was a horrible thing to happen. It's bad for racing, it's bad for everyone." Winning owner Lord Howard de Walden, member of the Jockey Club and thrice Senior Steward, concurred: "That was a terrible thing to happen to Gorytus. But, I'm afraid that it proves the truth of the old saying, 'You should never be afraid of taking on one good horse.'"

As everyone anticipated, the inevitable Stewards' Enquiry failed to discover an explanation:

> Major Hern said that he was unable to account for the poor per-formance of the colt and stated that Gorytus had been blood-tested both on Monday and Wednesday with perfect results. The colt had also eaten-up on the previous evening and on the morning of the race. The colt pulled up extremely distressed after the race and this was confirmed by the vet. Carson stated that Gorytus was unable to produce anything when asked to go on after about three furlongs.

A routine dope test was ordered and as Hern's saddest day as a trainer drew to a close, racegoers – many of them experienced and hardened professionals – filed off the Heath spouting pearls of wisdom born of hindsight: "Everyone knew that Gorytus was wrong except Dick Hern. Why did he run him?"

The heat was only just being turned on. Saturday's *Sporting Life* appeared with the headline, "Hern quizzed as 'great' Gorytus flops."

The *Daily Star* took no prisoners whatsoever and devoted its entire front page to the story. Beneath the dreaded question "Was the Wonder Horse Nobbled?", suitably inscribed in big, bold, black two-inch high lettering, the paper gave priority to the views of jockey and trainer. "The racecourse vet told me that by the time he had got to the stable he thought the horse had just finished in the Grand National," Carson was quoted as saying. The perplexed trainer had little new to add: "My colt is very distressed. I just don't know what to make of it. I've had every test on him prior to the race and he pleased me beforehand – he looked 100%. I don't think it's the virus because Gorytus was blood-tested on Wednesday night and everything was perfectly all right. Willie Carson said the horse just died on him."

In *The Sunday Times*, Brough Scott placed Hern's obsession for secrecy, and its implications for punters, under the microscope. "If Gorytus turns out to have pulled a muscle, burst a blood vessel, choked in his breathing or any other natural explanation, all well and good," wrote Scott. "But if the tests reveal that he suffered from something to do with the rumoured cough, so fiercely denied by his trainer, this episode will show that even in racing's most sacred halls there is a case for candour." Besides that rumour of coughing which had gone the rounds on the day before the Dewhurst, the Newmarket tom-toms also beat out the news that Gorytus had injured a stifle during his final workout. "Rubbish," declared stable secretary Brian Holmes. "Gorytus has never had anything wrong with him physically. The security here is virtually impenetrable but we are anxious as everyone else to get to the bottom of Gorytus's poor running."

Hern, likewise, chose not to mince his words. "I do not consider my horses to be the public's business," he said haughtily. Of Gorytus, he reported: "The colt is now back to normal and we are awaiting the result of the tests. Having the two blood-tests taken was a perfectly normal procedure. Of course I was worried – how could I fail to be when other horses in the yard were coughing." Gorytus lost only 10lb as a result of his traumatic experiences and by Friday – a week after the Dewhurst – had yet to exhibit any symptoms of the cough or a virus. "He looks a picture in the box and he's so well I've had to give him some good exercise," said Hern. "I've got quite a few horses that are coughing, and even those are well in themselves.

But Gorytus is showing no signs of a cough, and even if he did have a virus he should not have stopped as quickly as he did at Newmarket."

The possibility that Gorytus had been 'got-at', however repellent, could not be discounted. For Hern, of all trainers, positive proof of skulduggery would be earth-shaking. He had built his, and West Ilsley's reputation on an old-fashioned ideology of secrecy, security, trust and loyalty. The knowledge that other great trainers had endured this calamitous set of circumstances – Cecil Boyd-Rochfort with Alcide in 1958 and Noel Murless with Pinturischio in 1961, for example – scarcely lifted the gloom or exorcised the devils rattling his brain like trains through a station. The announcement that Gorytus's dope test was negative, and another in December from Racecourse Security Services saying they had uncovered no evidence of foul play did nothing to disperse the smoke which was rapidly beginning to denote an outbreak of fire. And where there's smoke something is liable to blackened. The case of Ribofilio, 15/8 favourite for the 1969 2000 Guineas was too fresh in the memory to allay suspicions that Gorytus might have been "nobbled". Ribofilio looked fine but ran much as Gorytus had, finishing tailed-off. "He couldn't raise a gallop at any stage," said Lester Piggott afterwards and in *The Times* Michael Phillips had pointed out: "Somehow everybody in the ring seemed to know that Ribofilio would not win." Exhaustive tests and enquiries proved inconclusive. Then there was the equally inexplicable display in the 1970 1000 Guineas of Hern's own Highest Hopes. At least she recovered, which is arguably more than Ribofilio did. He started favourite for three more classics and won none of them.

With virtually nothing to go on but their imagination, Journalists began to contemplate the likely causes of Gorytus's downfall. *The Guardian*'s Richard Baerlein recollected being told how Pinturischio had been dosed with a strong purgative called croton oil which was used on constipated elephants. "Gorytus dropped a large excreta as he was led toward the parade ring. A vet standing nearby said no horse could possibly win after such an excretion and would be lucky if he was not finished for life." Gorytus was also seen scouring as he left the paddock and appeared distinctly uncomfortable. The *Daily Star*'s theory was even more fanciful. Gorytus, they suggested, had been exposed to a broken capsule of instant vapour of the sort used as a defence against muggers and rapists. The paper confronted Professor Robert Smith, Chairman of the anti-drug committee which was advising Racecourse Security Services and the Jockey Club, with the idea and quoted him as replying: "This is certainly plausible. The contents of such a capsule would need to be volatile and act in an instant. Chlorine and the original war weapon CN gas readily spring to mind." If successfully administered under the horse's nose before the race, the Professor continued, it would restrict air flow under pressure and, as a respiratory complication, would not show up in a blood-test. When eased, the horse would snort the fumes out and soon recover. "The horse was suddenly gasping for air," Carson admitted, "but I find it hard to believe the horse was tampered with while I was on board. Only two stalls' handlers got near me."

If Gorytus was nobbled who stood to gain? The bookmakers? Backers of Diesis? The only big bet taken on the race itself was laid on Gorytus at £10,000 to £5,000. By contrast, not one four-figure wager was placed on Diesis. If anyone was backing Diesis as if there were no tomorrow they placed their money in such small bets over such a wide area that the operation defies belief. However, that was legal. What about illegal gambling where, in the absence of betting tax, large sums are reputedly laid at slightly generous odds? In these circumstances it might be in a bookmaker's interest to 'stop' a favourite like Gorytus.

As the *Star* was at pains to remind everyone, there was also the ante-post market on the 1983 classics to consider. Before the Dewhurst, Gorytus had already been backed to take £10 million out of the major bookmakers. If, like Pinturischio and Ribofilio, Gorytus was effectively destroyed as a racehorse, argued the *Star*, the bookies would save an awful lot of money. The *Racing Specialist* also voiced its misgivings. "Despite the announcement of a negative dope test a curious afterglow remains," it opined on 5 November. "As the situation stands trainer Dick Hern is left with an awful lot of egg on his face."

Whatever pole-axed Gorytus on 15 October 1982 seems destined to remain a mystery. Could Brian Procter's explanation, uncomplicated and free of intrigue as it is, be as likely to account for the horse's malaise as any loaded with more sinister implications? "At the time a lot of our horses had been coughing but up to the race he hadn't. I just think it hit him on the day, no more than that." Alas,

Above: Derby, 1980: Despite racing on three legs Henbit still secures the prize.
(*Gerry Cranham*)
Below: "The old firm strikes again": Astor, Hern and Mercer win the 1981 St Leger
with Cut Above. (*George Selwyn*)

DAILY STAR

SATURDAY, OCTOBER 16, 1982   15p   ★★

WAS THE WONDER HORSE NOBBLED?

Sensation as Derby favourite comes last

Trainer Hern

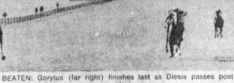

BEATEN: Gorytus (far right) finishes last as Diesis passes post

UNBEATEN: Carson and Gorytus after earlier win

WONDER horse Gorytus was at the centre of a "nobbling" mystery last night after finishing last in a race he was odds-on favourite to win.

His jockey Willie Carson said: "He ran like a horse that had been got at.

"The racecourse vet told me that by the time he had got to the stable he thought the horse had just finished in the Grand National."

The defeat of previously unbeaten Gorytus at Newmarket is the biggest racing shock for years.

He had already been backed with the big bookies to win more than £6 million in next year's 2,000 Guineas and Derby.

He had won his previous two races like a Rolls Royce taking on Minis.

He was hailed as the greatest prospect of the century, ranking with his sire Nijinsky.

But in yesterday's

By FLEETWOOD JONES and GRAHAM GOODE

race, in which he looked a certainty for the £46,000 prize, the horse finished so far behind that the photo-finish camera had been switched off.

He was unofficially estimated at finishing nearly 40 lengths behind the winner.

Gorytus had started the race at 1—2 favourite. But seconds before the off there was a rush of "informed money" for the eventual winner, Diesis, ridden by champion jockey Lester Piggott.

When a distressed

Gorytus struggled past the finishing post, all hell broke loose in the betting ring.

"That can't have been right. Ladbroke's man Mike Dillon said "He wasn't the same horse. Something must have been wrong."

The stewards immediately ordered an inquiry and called in trainer Dick Hern—the Queen's racehorse handler—jockey Carson and the racecourse vet to appear before them.

Hern went off with

Turn to Page 2

You do not need to be a clairvoyant to know Dick Hern's reaction to this kind of press coverage. (*The British Library*)

Above: A rare display of emotion after Sun Princess's 12 length romp in the 1983 Oaks makes her the first maiden to win an English classic since 1950. (*Gerry Cranham*)

Right: Anxiety clearly shows on the face of Willie Carson as he and Sun Princess brave the elements prior to the 1983 St Leger. (*George Selwyn*)

Below: Happier days? Lord Carnarvon and Hern at Royal Ascot, 1977. (*Gerry Cranham*)

Left: "I'd barter 10 years of a peaceable life for a day long when I rode with the Quorn." (*Jim Meads*)
Below: "The thing I miss most is being able to ride with the horses": Messrs Carson and Procter report to Hern's station wagon for debriefing. (*Gerry Selwyn*)

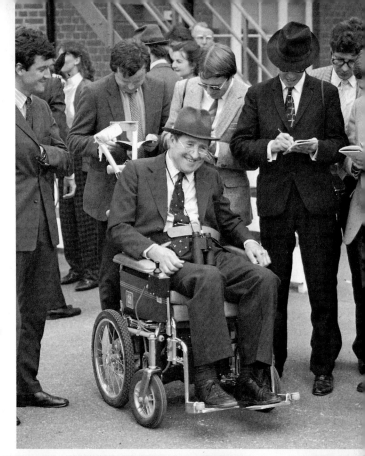

Right: The bad old days seem forgotten as Hern talks to the Press at Newbury in 1987.
(*Gerry Cranham*)
Below: Petoski wears down Oh So Sharp in the King George to provide Hern with a much needed fillip during the summer of 1985.
(*Gerry Cranham*)

Left: In adversity the bond between trainer and jockey grew visibly closer and stronger. (*Times Newspapers Ltd*)
Below: A characteristic Carson drive brings Nashwan home the winner of the 1989 2000 Guineas. (*Ed Byrne*)

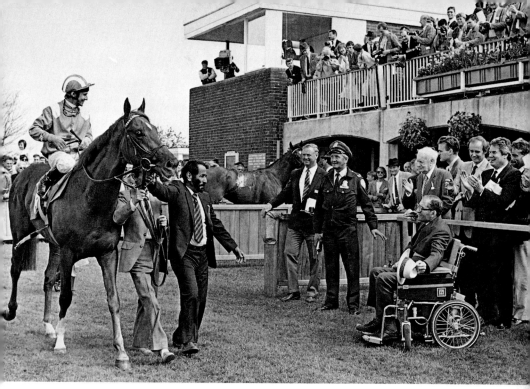

Above: Place the sweep of the panama hat, the looks being exchanged by trainer and jockey and the sea of happy faces into the context of the preceding nine months and you have the reason why this must be the racing photograph of 1989. (*Ed Byrne*)
Below: All smiles at Ascot as the successful trainer accepts his momento from the Queen after Nashwan's thrilling victory in the King George VI & Queen Elizabeth Diamond Stakes. (*George Selwyn*)

Preparing to 'raise the roof' at the HWRA lunch on receiving the Flat Trainer of the Year Award for 1990. The National Hunt recipient, Martin Pipe, is suitably awed. (Racing Post)

one need not be high on cynicism to feel there was more to 'affair' than that.

Naturally, Gorytus went into winter quarters deposed as favourite for the 2000 Guineas and Derby. He received 9st 5lb in the Free Handicap, 2lb below Diesis, and a Timeform rating of 132 which put him on a par with Brigadier Gerard as the best juvenile to pass through Hern's care. Timeform refused to speculate on his classic prospects with any degree of confidence. "If some physical problem was responsible for his dismal display is it likely to recur? And if he was indeed 'got at', will he ever be the same again?"

Eight years later the spectre of doping returned to haunt Hern (and racing as a whole) when Lord Rotherwick's two-year-old colt Bravefoot ran last of five in the Champagne Stakes. Winner of his two previous races Bravefoot, expected to start odds on, had drifted ominously in the market from evens to 11/8. "The lad in charge of Bravefoot sensed that the colt was not quite right in himself," said Hern after the race, "but he had a normal temperature, he was perfectly sound and there seemed no excuse not to run." However, even cantering to post the favourite looked a tired horse, as his rider Walter Swinburn confirmed: "It's unnatural to have to give a two-year-old three cracks down the shoulder to get him out of a trot going to post. I wouldn't have been so surprised had I been riding a ten-year-old chaser." Nine days later the Jockey Club announced that Bravefoot (along with Norwich, favourite for the Kiveton Park Stakes twenty-four hours earlier) had been the victim of a "relatively quick-acting tranquilizer," probably administered about an hour before he ran, i.e. in the racecourse stables.

Hern, who had feared the worst, was understandably incensed. "It has made my blood boil that a horse was got at. This horse is owned by an owner-breeder who is part of a dying breed and he has managed to produce what I think is a decent horse. The first time he runs in a group race, he is got at. It is disheartening." The offending substance was eventually named as Acetylpromazine, the most commonly used tranquilizer in equine medicine. An extremely potent substance which reacts on the central nervous system, one of its symptoms in colts is the prolonged extension of the penis exhibited by Bravefoot before and after his Doncaster race. As little as 0.25 mg could have the desired result, whether given through an injection (15–25 minutes to take effect), a tablet (45 minutes) or possibly a squirt of the drug up the horse's nostrils.

Inevitable reference to Gorytus ensued. "Gorytus was given much more than an ordinary tranquilizer," added Hern. "He finished tailed off and was like a drunken man afterwards. Bravefoot's case was much less severe and he was perfectly all right by the evening."

The story of Gorytus from this point onward became inextricably bound up with the uneasy relationship between Hern and the Press, a relationship at best rarely warmer than frostily cordial and one now plunging toward positively glacial temperatures. Gorytus was being returned to the United States, insisted the bush telegraph unequivocally. No he wasn't, said Hern. The *Racing Specialist* reported:

> Dick Hern has never had a high regard for Fleet Street or its practitioners, but following John McCririck's amazing *Sporting Life* diary item suggesting that 'wonder horse' Gorytus was to be shipped back to America his opinion slumped to an all time low. To add insult to injury, the Galloping Major was further incensed when fearless *Sun* reporter Claude Duval wrote on March 25: 'I can reveal that the Queen and her racing manager Lord Porchester saw Gorytus work impressively on Sunday, leaving his Dewhurst flop miles behind. Sources tell me that Her Majesty saw the controversial colt put in a fabulous gallop.' Unfortunately the Queen in her wisdom, was not anywhere near West Ilsley on the day in question and did not visit the stable until last Saturday when she was an early morning visitor at 7.30 to inspect her trainer's string and watch several horses, including Gorytus, being put through their paces. The morning's most exciting moment was when a scatterbrained filly broke loose and moved horses and humans in all directions.

The inaccuracy of Duval's 'scoop' on this occasion gave Hern due cause for bellyaching, but the veil of secrecy, which had for so long cloaked goings-on at West Ilsley and proved so irksome to many journalists, came under renewed attack. John McCririck used his Diary column in *The Sporting Life* to highlight the iniquity of West Ilsley's 'Closed Shop'. A man who glories unashamedly in his outlandish personality and suitably complimentary garb, the outspoken McCririck is the first to admit he is not high on everyone's Christmas card list. Yet he is seldom wide of the mark, a fact reinforced by his winning the British Press Award as Specialist Writer of the Year in 1978 followed by that as Campaigning Journalist of the Year in

1979. In his opinion, "Racing journalists – and they won't like me for saying so – are the most supine bunch of journalists in the world." Sports journalists as a whole traditionally have attracted more contempt than respect. It has been said that whereas, for instance, political journalists write as if they dislike people they actually like, sports journalists write as if they like people whom they actively despise. The sports writer who desires that exclusive quote next week, runs the argument, had better cross the palm of his subject, whether boxer, footballer, jockey or trainer, with fulsome praise this week. "Some trainers are clearly super sensitive to independent minded press coverage," said the *Racing Specialist* as it reported Hern's refusal for the second year running to grant *The Sporting Life* a pre-season interview. It concluded: "Only write what is expected and everything in the garden is lovely."

What made privileged information in racing circles all the more prized was the possibility of capital gain via the bookmaker. Consequently, racing hacks resisted the temptation to unsheath their swords whatever the provocation, lest self-inflicted damage should result. However, when, in the aftermath of the Racecourse Security Services' investigations at West Ilsley, *Daily Mirror* reporter Charles Fawcus, who for years had ridden out for Hern, was informed he could no longer enjoy the courtesy, McCririck's sabre flashed from its scabbard. On 7 April he wrote: "No one can tell the Major who he should have to dinner. But he is the Queen's trainer and that puts him in a special position regarding the public. He may not care too much about punters or most scribblers. But handling Her Majesty's horses brings with it responsibilities some of them distasteful."

There was never the remotest chance that Dick Hern would be goaded into bandying words with McCririck, particularly, it must be stressed, since Fawcus's banishment from the gallops did not result from his identification as the West Ilsley 'mole', but rather his not being a registered employee. He was no more than an innocent victim of the tighter measures recommended by RSS. The cudgels were quickly picked up on Hern's behalf by Michael Pope. His outraged letter to *The Sporting Life* ran:

I was incensed by McCririck's article decrying Dick Hern's attitude toward members of the media. Dick has been a friend of mine for more than 40 years and before becoming not only one of the leading but also most respected members of the training profession, he served as my assistant for five years and never once was a detrimental word aimed at him either from the Press or indeed any other source. I am not suggesting that if faced with a fatuous question while attending to his job he wouldn't reply with an icy stare or even a few well chosen words. But surely any conscientious trainer is entitled to respond thus. Dick is not only a good trainer but a man of integrity and I feel it most unjust that he should be publicly abused by McCririck in this manner. I am certain my view will be confirmed by Charlie Fawcus and many others.

McCririck was unrepentant and cited other instances of Press Room displeasure with Hern. Pope's form of address, denying McCririck either christian name or even a curt 'Mr', merely emphasized the gulf between officer class and other ranks, which if not the actual root of the problem undoubtedly fertilized it.

Unfortunately for Hern, and the horse's supporters, Gorytus failed to provide the wherewithal to make McCririck choke on his words – despite a torrent of jingoistic bulletins from West Ilsley. "Gorytus galloped this morning and continues to please me," Hern told reporters at Newbury on 16 April, two weeks before the Guineas, when Gorytus should have contested the Greenham Stakes. "I'm glad I decided against running him as the ground is pretty dead out there." Instead, "Off the Bit" gleefully revealed, Gorytus had been galloped a mile at Bath racecourse with Torrey and Orixo, well away from prying eyes. Four days later Hern sent Gorytus to Newmarket to be exercised and walked round the paddock in an attempt to expunge any dark memories the horse might associate with the Rowley Mile. Others, meanwhile, were questioning the colt's courage. Beneath the title "Has Gorytus got the 'bottle' to win the 2000 Guineas" trainer Guy Harwood was quoted in *The Sporting Life*:

> Four years ago I trained a horse called Chrysippos who came from the same family as Gorytus. [He was out of Gorytus's elder half-sister Better Begin.] He looked a world-beater when he won first time out at Salisbury but subsequently proved soft and he failed to win in eight races as a three-year-old. Ten days ago he was tailed off in a Stratford novice chase. There are obviously question marks against Gorytus. He

looked brilliant when beating Salieri at York and I was amazed how easily he trounced Proclaim in the Champagne but he could be a horse who will do it first time and then go downhill. We shall see.

Temporarily promoted to 9/4 favourite forty-eight hours before the Guineas, Gorytus, looking in the pink of condition, was superseded by Diesis on race day itself. Disputing the lead below the Bushes, he faded into fifth, about 3½ lengths behind the winner Lomond but in front of Diesis, whose preparation had been held up by a leg injury. "He just tired like all the others," said Carson, who reckoned the going was worse than the good officially posted.

Gorytus then disappeared for over fifteen weeks. He continued to dominate the headlines, however. Where and when would he run next? Was he coughing? Was he being repatriated so that he could run under the medication permitted in the United States? Hern stuck to his guns as best he could but Gorytus gave him precious little support. "No one is more anxious than I am to run him," he said of the colt's Derby participation. "I could not be more pleased with him. He has come to himself. Gorytus is a horse of the highest class and I would not wish to risk him in conditions that do not suit him." Conditions at Epsom patently would not suit Gorytus; it had been one of the wettest springs on record, so much so that the Derby was in danger of postponement. Gorytus was withdrawn at the overnight stage and the race was won by Teenoso in the slowest time since Common's year of 1891 when a deluge caused the jockeys to draw 2lb overweight on returning to scale. Flak still flew. "For one reason or another Hern never appeared keen to run Gorytus and even if the weather kept dry he may not have run," argued Richard Baerlein. "His whole career since his mishap at Newmarket has been one of continuous bad luck." On this occasion it was Jack Logan who sprang to Hern's defence. His column of 3 June began, "Hern puts Gorytus first and the Derby second" and concluded with a stern rebuke for Baerlein and any other heretics: "Hern, unlike some trainers I could name if I wanted as many writs as election addresses coming through my letter box, is an outstanding example of a trainer who puts the horse first. That is not 'one reason or another'. It is the only reason behind the decision. And you can take it from me that if the going had been good or firm Gorytus would have won."

The ground at last firmed up and Hern's intention was to run Gorytus in the St James's Palace Stakes and the Eclipse rather than the Irish Derby and King George. That plan also collapsed like a pack of cards as, first of all, Gorytus contracted a mild bout of coughing and then, two days before Sandown, the blacksmith committed the cardinal sin of pricking the colt's foot. The Sussex Stakes, on 27 July, also passed without him and the Benson & Hedges Gold Cup on 16 August became the target date. West Ilsley began to beat the drum. "Gorytus is the best he's been all season," said Hern; "Gorytus is an extremely good horse, I'd put him in with the Troys, Brigadier Gerards, Dunfermlines, anything you like," echoed Brian Procter, who was partnering him in his work. "I wouldn't lose faith in him and I'm convinced he'll make that McCririck eat his words." After a super gallop with Torrey three days before the race, Carson quipped sarcastically, "The only thing that can beat us is the blacksmith." Even some rain could not dampen West Ilsley's ardour. Gorytus opened at 8/1 but attracted pots of money to end up 7/2 second favourite. Again he let all and sundry down, finishing about two lengths behind the favourite, Caerleon, in fourth place. "By the time he ran the ground was soft and in the circumstances I was delighted with him," explained Hern, facing the music yet again. "I put him in everything and he'll run when the ground is right. Obviously the Champion Stakes would be a major target – going permitting."

Barely a fortnight later the gods of racing appeared to have relented. The going at Goodwood for the Waterford Crystal Mile on 27 August was good to firm. Of the five rivals awaiting Gorytus one was his stablemate Schuss, another was making a delayed seasonal reappearance due to injury (Sandhurst Prince) and the remaining trio (Adonijah, Montekin and Noalcoholic) were nothing exceptional. For the first time paddock judges found fault with Gorytus ("I'm glad I don't feel like he looks," one leading trainer was overheard to mutter) and the race was a disaster. Gorytus contrived to beat only his stable companion. "I am very disappointed and there are absolutely no excuses", confessed his weary trainer. "I'll need time to think about the future." Four days were all the exercise required. On 31 August Hern announced that Gorytus was returning to Virginia prior to going into training with Woody Stephens. The Jeremiahs were beside themselves. "Gorytus is soft, soft as wet putty," said Richard Baerlein of an animal he had once lauded as "the best ever postwar two-year-old"; "Goodbye Gowrongus," crowed a vindicated McCririck.

Gorytus ran twice inside a week at Hialeah, Florida, in early 1984. He was beaten by half a length in Division I of the Royal Palm Beach Handicap on 31 January and finished fourth in the Grade 2 Bougainvillea Handicap on 4 February. In March he recrossed the Atlantic to stand at the Coolmore Stud in County Tipperary, where despite his handsome looks and regal pedigree his reputation continued to slide. Of his first three crops only Gouriev won a British Pattern race (the Group III Horris Hill Stakes in 1988) and his fee – once as high as IR30,000 guineas – plummeted to IR10,000 guineas by 1988. Gorytus had come to the end of the road. Like many a 'failed' European stallion he was sold for export to Japan. How, indeed, are the mighty fallen.

The career of Gorytus had brought Hern more pain than pleasure, more anguish than elation. Moreover, twelve months of unremitting trial and tribulation had brutally exposed the running sore that marked his relationship with the media – or at least certain sections of it. However much he gave the impression none of the barbs struck home, Hern would have needed to be an exceptionally thick-skinned or arrogant individual not to have been affected by some of the acerbic comments aimed at him in 1982 and 1983.

Yet, Hern was to be dealt a far greater blow in the year to come than any member of the fourth estate could hope to administer. And he would survive that, too.

Chapter Twelve

ACCIDENT & ILLNESS

'He knows not his own strength that hath not met adversity'

"THERE IS A PASSION for hunting," wrote Charles Dickens, "something deeply implanted in the human breast." What was once a necessity, however, had become a luxury cherished by a select minority, a sacred rite involving uniform, ceremony and a shared sense of risk to life and limb which led Surtees to describe hunting as "the image of war without its guilt and only five-and-twenty per cent of its dangers." For a man with the blood of Roy Hern filling his veins, images of the Quantocks colouring his memory and the Army's love of ritual warming his soul, hunting provided a fusion of family, environment and community – three things Dick Hern valued beyond price – with the animals he loved above all others. "Hunting, he was mad about," attests Ian Cocks, a view endorsed by anyone who has ever come into contact with Dick Hern.

Of all the famous Shires' packs, the Quorn (founded in 1753) is arguably the most prestigious. The undulating terrain of east Leicestershire affords splendid vistas in which hounds can be seen to best advantage, decent turf no matter how much rain falls in midwinter and a wealth of hedges and timber as a result of agricultural enclosure. Countryside made by God and shaped by Man for the sole purpose of chasing foxes. It's a matter of local pride that Quorn country has remained largely unchanged while other packs have bent the knee to the ravages of progress: the Belvoir threatened by open-cast mining; the South Oxfordshire, Berkeley and Duke of Beaufort's split up by motorways; the Garth and South Berks swamped by the urban sprawl of Reading, Basingstoke and Wokingham. "I'd barter ten years of a peaceable life for a day long when I rode with the Quorn," said Old Sportsman in the 1884 edition of *Bailey's Magazine*. In 1989 subscriptions for that 'one day' started at £250 and there is no shortage of applications to a Hunt which regularly attracts the Prince of Wales.

For many a year it had also attracted Dick Hern. He kept a couple of hunters with Mrs Barbara Rich at Thorpe Satchville, a few miles south of Melton Mowbray in the heart of Quorn territory, hunting on Mondays and Fridays as often as possible until the start of the Flat. In truth, hunting was Hern's single concession to recreational activity. Ruskin could have had him in mind as he wrote: "When men are rightly occupied their amusement grows out of their work." Or as David Murray-Smith puts it, "When you're training ninety horses to the standard he does you don't get time for much else." Hunting was an escape, of sorts, from the relentless pressures of West Ilsley – the virus, paperwork and the omnipresent dring of the telephone with its threat of a journalist on the other end. Widely acknowledged as "a real goer who wanted to be in the first flight, driving forward to the cry", Hern had always hunted to ride rather than ridden to hunt and, unlike Mr Jorrocks, never regarded a fall "a Hawful thing."

Anyone rash enough to have suggested to Hern that a trainer in his sixty-fourth year should confine himself to less hazardous amusements would undoubtedly have been confronted, in Nelsonian fashion, with the deaf ear he had at his disposal. Having forfeited a number of days at the commencement of the 1984 season owing to Bedtime's expedition to the Japan Cup on 25 November, Hern was keen to make up for lost time. On 29 November he was out with the South Notts (alongside the Prince of Wales) and on Friday, 7 December he was in Leicestershire for the Quorn's meet at Twyford. Since the home pack was suffering from kennel cough, the Fitzwilliam Hounds were invited to do the honours for the day and they soon made their presence felt, catching one fox in the Prince of Wales's Covert at Baggrave and marking another to ground at South Croxton. In the afternoon they found again at Bent's Covert and ran down Queniborough Brook toward Baggrave before retracing their route in the direction of Carr Bridge. Running uphill now, the hounds poured across the lane linking the villages of Hungarton and Lowesby near Whites Barn. It was about 3 pm when Hern approached the hedge beside the lane. His horse swerved, throwing him to the ground.

Sheilah Hern later described exactly what had happened. "They were jumping a fence and they could not see what was on the other side. In front of them was a stone water trough and his horse tried to take avoiding action by jinking in mid-air. On landing the horse stumbled to its knees, firing the Major off." Dr Tom Connors, who was fortunately out with the Quorn, tended the stricken rider until the ambulance arrived to rush Hern the eight miles to the Leicester Royal Infirmary. Within hours he was visited by Barbara Rich, who was able to assure reporters that he was "lying flat out but he was cheerful."

Hern's injuries were grave. He'd broken his neck and was partly paralysed. He had some feeling in one side of his body and could slightly move the other, no more. His accident and subsequent plight cruelly paralleled that of his West Ilsley predecessor Captain Richard Gooch back in the 1920s. On the Saturday Hern was transferred to the Spinal Injury Unit at Stoke Mandeville Hospital in Buckinghamshire. Front page coverage of Hern's ordeal was shared with the news that on the other side of the world in a Hong Kong hospital jockey Brian Taylor was fighting for his life after fracturing his skull in a spill at Sha Tin racecourse. As Hern tried to come to terms with the prognosis of nine weeks in traction, Taylor's tragic death was confirmed. Both men were indulging a passion when tragedy struck. Taylor was 45 years old and on the point of retiring. Facing up to the possibility of not being able to walk again, let alone ride or hunt, was a pitiless method of thinking away the tedium of lying motionless on one's back, but at least Hern was alive. Sheilah Hern's daily visits to Stoke Mandeville throughout the spring of 1985 not only kept up her husband's spirits but, with their news of West Ilsley, also acted as a constant reminder of the life he was anxious to resume. On 25 January she said optimistically: "My husband will be able to resume riding but I don't know whether he will go hunting again. He won't be 100% for several months but the progress is good. Doctors have told me that he should make a full recovery. Luckily there was no damage to his head and he is perfectly au fait with everything that is going on. Last week he was visited by the Queen. It was marvellous of her to spare the time and it was a marvellous boost for him. In fact, the kindness of people has been overwhelming. There is a lot of malice in racing but there hasn't been one who hasn't come forward to offer help."

Hern, who was sharing a ward with a Lebanese golfer hit in the back by a stray bullet whilst playing in Beirut, expected to leave Stoke Mandeville in March.

Hern's dice with death prompted a revision in the plans of Ian Cocks, who had contemplated departing for a more secure job outside racing now that he had a young family to raise. Even though Cocks could count on the skill and loyalty of a backroom brigade without peer in British racing, none of them had an answer to the viral scourge which gripped West Ilsley yet again during the opening weeks of the new season. "The virus is like a thief in the night," Hern reflected upon his return. "You don't see it coming and you don't see it go. This time there was no other symptoms except for a lack of zest in the horse's finishing effort." The air of despondency hanging over the yard merely added to the frustration Hern felt at his own personal lack of progress. After an operation on 13 February, he paid a brief visit to West Ilsley in March before going home for good in April. He remained partially paralysed and could only walk with assistance from either side. However, a set of parallel bars, which soon appeared on the lawn, signposted the way ahead. Refusing to allow his infirmity to get the better of him, he determined to get about under his own steam and began utilizing a walking frame. The inevitable happened. He slipped and broke a leg. With a virus-ridden string and once more immobilized, Hern's armageddon seemed complete.

Only Doctor Time could cure both ills. The first four classics of 1985 came and went with just a single representative (Petoski in the Derby) from the country's most respected classic stable. Indeed, Longboat's victory in the Group III Sagaro Stakes was West Ilsley's solitary Pattern race success, and the treble at a Wolverhampton evening meeting in late June actually doubled the stable's score in one fell swoop. To further aggravate matters, Royal Ascot gossip said Carson was about to leave Hern and join John Dunlop – a rumour denied by both trainers. (Carson had previously rejected a substantial offer from Robert Sangster in 1978.) Then, on 9 July, the tide began to turn. Petoski won the Group II Princess of Wales's Stakes, convincingly reversing his Epsom form with the Derby fifth

Lanfranco, and at the weekend Sir Michael Sobell's Helen Street (a daughter of Troy) landed the Irish Oaks.

Although she had won the 1982 Coronation Cup with her home-bred Easter Sun (trained by Michael Jarvis) Lady Beaverbrook's fortunes in the 1980s had flagged somewhat compared with the dizzy heights achieved by Bustino, Boldboy, Relkino and Niniski. Petoski was the very first yearling by Niniski to be sold at public auction and Lady Beaverbrook went to 90,000 guineas to get him – the greatest outlay for one of that initial crop. A big bay with a white blaze, Petoski concluded his first season with a moderate effort in the Royal Lodge Stakes (3/1 favourite, sixth of eight), after he had completed in a trio of Champagne Stakes: winning at Salisbury and Goodwood (the Lanson) but finishing third in the more important Laurent Perrier version at Doncaster, where he enjoyed anything but a clear passage. Petoski's two runs before the Derby were encouraging (seconds in classic trials at Sandown and Chester), though hardly sufficient to invalidate his 33/1 starting price at Epsom. Petoski ran like a 33/1 shot, beating just two of his rivals. However, in the month between Epsom and Newmarket the West Ilsley magic began to return and Petoski's win in the Princess of Wales hinted he was a solid each-way bet in the King George VI & Queen Elizabeth II Stakes. "Each-way" because to win he would need to defeat five classic winners: the unbeaten filly Oh So Sharp, who had already won the 1000 Guineas and Oaks, Law Society (Irish Derby), Princess Pati (Irish Oaks), Strawberry Road (Australian Derby) and Sirius Symboli (Japanese Derby), besides the easy Coronation Cup (and ultimate Arc) winner Rainbow Quest. Since that Wolverhampton treble a month earlier Hern's horses had collected eleven more races and the trainer knew Petoski would relish the firm ground.

Viewing the race at home on television Hern saw a thrilling contest unfold. August, Rainbow Quest's pacemaker, went off at a blistering gallop, which resulted in the second fastest King George ever, and quickly spread-eagled the field. Infantry swept past the exhausted leader before the turn where Petoski was apparently stranded behind a wall of horses. "Petoski would have been a very unlucky loser," reported Carson. "I was stuck in behind and wondering how the hell to get out. I've never seen so many backsides in my life but once we got clear in the straight we were always going to win." Oh So Sharp had got the better of a protracted struggle with Rainbow Quest

when Petoski, finally seeing daylight, came storming up the wide
outside. Striking the front barely fifty yards out, he battled on
resolutely to beat the odds on favourite by a neck. "The Major has
never lost faith in Petoski and the horse has improved all year," said
Carson. "It might look a surprise result on paper but it was not a
shock to us."

Ten years on Bustino's defeat had been avenged. "I'm 102 but
feel twenty-one," cooed an ecstatic Lady Beaverbrook. "I did not
think it was possible for Petoski to win but I never stopped praying."
The colt was obviously on song for the St Leger but during his
preparation for the Great Voltigeur he jarred a pastern and missed
the rest of the season. Petoski stayed in training. Unhappily the
glory days did not return and after running third in both the Coronation Cup and Princess of Wales he could finish no better than
sixth to Dancing Brave in the 1986 King George and was retired to
the National Stud.

Petoski's renaissance in the summer of 1985 provided Hern with
a timely boost as he continued down his own long road to recovery.
Holidaying at Leet D'Arcy, near West Wittering in Sussex, during
the big Goodwood meeting in August, his spirits were noticeably on
the rise.

> Dr Frankel at Stoke Mandeville said that most people with my con-
> ditions would have to take a year off. I told him that was impossible
> and if I did I would have to retire. And that I have no intention of
> doing. Recently I was seen by both Dr Frankel and Mr Crockford, the
> surgeon who operated on me. They said I was well ahead of schedule.
> I shall always be grateful to them and also Dr Michael Allen, of the
> Jockey Club, for his regular visits. I've had scores of letters from
> complete strangers with the same kind of trouble as mine. It's all given
> me tremendous encouragement. As well as being grateful to the staff
> at Stoke Mandeville I also want to thank Jimmy Savile, who by
> his great efforts manages to keep everyone cheerful. If I've learned
> anything from this at all it is that one's health and strength are the
> most important thing in life . . .

As yet going racing was not on the agenda.

> It would be a great mistake to do so at this stage. I have a two hour
> physio session every day and also go in the swimming pool. What with

watching work, looking at the horses and getting all the paper work done I have not time for anything else. If I started racing again I would have to drop the physio. I can't do that, as I'm determined to assist my recovery in every possible way. As far as what goes on at the races is concerned many meetings are televised. If not, Ian Cocks and Buster Haslam can give me an accurate description of what has happened.

The resurgence in Hern's fortunates signalled by Petoski's mid-summer double was ultimately reflected in a seasonal total of fifty-three winners, only three less than 1984. The famed West Ilsley *esprit de corps* had shone through once more. Ian Cocks says: "West Ilsley is a very tight ship and there is definitely a special atmosphere around the place. It is a self-contained community with very little staff turnover and they all think an awful lot of the Major. He treats them as individuals and takes a lot of notice of what they say. He relies on his staff to a tremendous extent and part of his skill as a trainer is knowing who to listen to. He's a very good listener. He'll talk to each lad after work and gets his opinion. If Brian Procter says this or that after a gallop he accepts it. And he has a great harmony with Geordie Campbell. He took with absolute courage and bravery the news he wouldn't ride again. The broken leg, I think, was a blessing in disguise because he was trying too hard with lots of swimming and physiotherapy."

Cocks left at the end of the year to take up a position with Weatherbys. His place as assistant trainer was filled by 25-year-old Alex Scott, an old boy of Eton and the Harry Thomson Jones academy at Green Lodge. "Don't think about it. Just pack your bag. It will be good for you," a friend advised him when the chance materialized. "I didn't need to be told. Dick was the man I'd always wanted to work with and I never thought I'd have the chance. THE classic middle-distance trainer." It did not take Scott long to appreciate at first hand that unspoken bond of loyalty between Hern and his staff identified by Ian Cocks. "He does have an incredible relationship with a long-standing staff. Of course, it's not roses all the time but ultimately he never fails to win respect from the people he works with. The other crucial point is the creation of an atmosphere in which people aren't afraid to admit their mistakes because the worst things happen when people try to cover up mistakes. If everyone feels free to admit when they've done something wrong it helps the yard run smoothly and it gives the trainer a wonderful feeling of confidence."

Scott also recognized the possibility that Hern "gives even more than a man would who hadn't suffered such an accident." Training horses was more than ever his reason for living now that he could no longer rejoice in riding them to hounds. The job still had to be done in the only fashion Hern knew – the proper fashion – however long it took. The object remained constant even if the game plan had of necessity to be altered. The evolution of a slightly modified approach to training involved a painful period of transition. "The thing I miss most is being able to ride with the horses before and after work. You can see how they are, how they feel, whether they are sweating or starting to think a bit. I can see but it is not the same. You have to adjust. Whereas I could feel a leg in days gone by, now I have to rely on others to do it. Of course, I can still see if a horse is getting a prominent joint or spot any irregularity in his action."

Hern's eyes rapidly assumed the role of his hands and, said Lord Carnarvon (who became the 7th Earl on the death of his father in 1987), they seldom missed a trick. "I sometimes feel that he sees more now than when he was riding horses, being able to touch their skins and feel their legs. He's always had an extraordinary ability to concentrate. And now when the lads ride the horses round him, he can see how they're breathing and how they've taken their exercise. The moment their fast work is finished, his eyes are on the far Downs watching them come back. He'll see if a horse is trotting right or if it is relaxed. And he's always had this knack of being able to notice things that might go wrong. Of course, all top trainers can do this. But he must have to carry so much in his head now. It must be frustrating not to be able to write things down quickly, particularly if you're naturally impatient. The staff have had to become his arms and legs, as well as doing their own jobs. All the work-riders have to come to him afterwards and tell him what's happened. It's all extra responsibility for them. They're fantastic."

Hern echoed Carnarvon's valuation of his staff. "They know what I have done on previous days. We have been lucky enough to have had a lot of good horses at West Ilsley. The work-riders are vastly experienced. If they tell you that a horse has given them a good feel, they know what they are talking about." Brian Procter and Willie Carson were perfectly capable of shouldering the extra responsibility. In the latter's case some of Hern's gritty determination (and, on occasion, not a little of his crustiness) rubbed-off and Carson began to display a degree of statesmanlike *gravitas* one would not previously have dreamt possible. The bond between trainer and jockey grew closer and closer. "His accident changed the lives of so many people apart from himself. Me. The stable staff. Everyone connected with the yard. We all got together and realized we were a back-up for the old man. As a team we did work harder. He still works very, very hard. He's adapted himself so well to what's happened. He's got people around him doing the things he used to do before. Before the accident, if anything was wrong he was always there in the thick of it. Now he can look but he can't touch so he has to use his eyes rather than his hands. He used to walk round every night feeling the horses' legs and feeling their skin. He could learn so much from that, and not being able to do it must be a tremendous disadvantage. But his eyes have taken over and he can look at a horse's coat now and make the judgements he used to make by feeling. They say blind people learn to see through their fingers. Well, this is the same thing in reverse."

However, no one – least of all Hern – believed West Ilsley possessed some form of divine right to continued success. "The competition is keener than ever. There has been an influx of American-bred stock of the highest quality during the past decade." In 1986 Hern's forty-five winners included seven at Pattern race level (one at Group I); the 1987 total of thirty-six included only two Pattern race successes (one at Group I). This was the trainer's lowest tally since the virus epidemic of the late 1960s and his name disappeared from the list of ten leading money earners for the first time since 1969. Hern's phenomenal achievements had been firmly based on the home-bred animals which trundled off the Astor, Sobell, Weinstock, Rotherwick and Hollingsworth production lines. Even Lady Beaverbrook, once the most lavish of spenders, was breeding her own. Most of the choicest sale ring lots were now being purchased by Arab owners, led by the four Maktoum brothers of Dubai, and most of them were lodged with the rising generation of dynamic 'young' trainers, Messrs Cecil, Stoute, Harwood and Cumani.

It was inconceivable that Hern would not be asked to take some Arab-owned horses sooner or later. The Maktoums made a point of personally selecting their trainers (over two dozen individuals) and believed in spreading a wide net. In the summer of 1982 the Queen had owned a big, raking filly named Height of Fashion (a daughter of Highclere), unbeaten in five starts. Winner of the Acomb, May Hill and Hoover Fillies Mile as a two-year-old, she was the top-rated of her sex and favourite for the Oaks until her performance in Goodwood's Lupe Stakes made it plain that her long-striding action would not be seen to advantage at Epsom. Rerouted to the Princess of Wales's Stakes she led throughout and broke the track record standing to her half-brother Milford. Shortly afterwards she was bought by Sheikh Hamdan Al-Maktoum for a sum reported to be between £1.4 and £1.8 million. At first glance the sale of a potential St Leger winner – whatever the price – appeared unwise, but the deal had far wider implications for it helped finance the Queen's acquisition of West Ilsley from Sobell and Weinstock. Hern now had a landlady.

Ironically, on the only two occasions Height of Fashion sported the Sheikh's colours (the King George and the Yorkshire Oaks), she met defeat and she was consigned to the paddocks. Then, in the winter of 1983, Sheikh Hamdan's younger brother Mohammed bought Head for Heights out of Richard Hannon's stable and sent him to Hern. Assessed at a mere 8 stone in the Free Handicap (barely making the top 100) the colt was somehow coaxed by Hern into winning the King Edward VII Stakes and the Princess of Wales's Stakes (both Group II) as a three-year-old. By 1987 nearly a quarter of Hern's horses were in the hands of Arab owners, principally the Maktoums. Some of them cost staggering amounts of money yet produced little or nothing in the way of returns. The likes of Trojan Prince (cost 1.1. million guineas; won once, gelded), Wassl Touch ($5.1 million; won three relatively minor races, sold to Japan), Nobly Born ($2.4 million; ran once), Kinema ($2.2 million; unraced), Laa Etaab ($7 million; unraced) gave ample proof that money cannot automatically buy success. Local Suitor had looked the likeliest contender for major honours. He cost $2 million at the Keeneland July Sales of 1983 and won his first two races. On his final juvenile outing, the Dewhurst, he took command $2\frac{1}{2}$ furlongs out and kept the lead until Kala Dancer and Law Society edged past him in a

thrilling last fifty yards. Beaten two heads, Local Suitor received
9st 5lb in the Free Handicap, 2lb and 1lb behind his two Newmarket
conquerors. On his only subsequent appearance, however, he finished
a disappointing fourth in the Craven Stakes and never ran again.
Another of Sheikh Mohammed's million dollar colts, Sharrood, also
demonstrated early potential before he too failed the classic tests.
Fourth in the 1986 2000 Guineas and eighth in the Derby he was
packed off to the United States, where he developed into a useful
performer.

Bearing in mind this colossal spending there is a certain irony in
the fact that neither of Hern's Group I winners in 1986 and 1987
cost a penny at public auction. Dick Hollingsworth's Longboat –
like Sharp Edge and Cut Above a grandson of Cutter – had been off
the course for eleven months after his narrow defeat in the 1985
Ascot Gold Cup. Now Hern brought him back to collect four Pattern
races, including the Ascot Gold Cup (by five lengths), Goodwood
Cup (by ten) and Doncaster Cup (on the just disqualification of
Petrizzo) – only the sixth occasion the stayers' Triple Crown has
been won since it became possible in 1812. Hern's 1987 Group I
success came in Doncaster's William Hill Futurity with Sir Michael
Sobell's Emmson, whose female line traced to Pretty Polly. Emmson
achieved the notable distinction of providing Hern with his very
first victory in a Group I event for two-year-olds in Britain:
Sun Prince won the Prix Robert Papin in France, while Brigadier
Gerard's Middle Park came one year before the inception of the
Pattern.

In areas where one had grown accustomed to seeing Hern successes
there were none. No winners from only five runners at Royal Ascot;
Dry Dock the sole West Ilsley runner in an English classic (third in
the St Leger). To some onlookers the conclusions were obvious. The
pervasive after-effects of the virus and the trainer's incapacity were
taking their inevitable toll. Conversely, to any optimists, the prospects for 1988 seemed brighter. Besides Emmson, there were Lady
Beaverbrook's pair Charmer and Minster Son (bred by Willie Carson
from a free nomination to Niniski) and Sheikh Hamdan's Unfuwain
(a son of Height of Fashion), all of whom seemed destined to play
meaningful roles in the colts' classics.

First to run was Charmer, in the Ladbroke European Free Handicap, where he found only Lapierre (benefiting from a previous race)

too good for him at the weights. Charmer easily reversed the places in the 2000 Guineas but although finishing like a train he failed to catch Doyoun. Minster Son, meanwhile, had won the Newmarket Stakes over $1\frac{1}{4}$ miles and Unfuwain had made the acquaintance of Epsom when pulverizing his rivals in the Warren Stakes, winning by fifteen lengths. With Charmer being aimed straight at the Derby, Hern's three other candidates were directed at the Chester Vase, York's Mecca-Dante and Goodwood's Predominate Stakes. Unfuwain won the first named by eight lengths. On a less successful note, a burly Emmson did well to finish fourth to Red Glow at York after rearing and falling over backwards in the paddock. Lastly, on 18 May, Minster Son emulated Troy by winning the Predominate, thereby setting Carson the familiar Epsom poser of which horse to ride. Emmson was sent to Chantilly for the French Derby (beaten less than a length into third), leaving a choice of three. He plumped for Minster Son, a decision, he was at pains to stress, that had nothing to do with the fact that he had bred the colt. "This has definitely been the hardest decision I've ever had to make before a classic. Deciding on Bireme instead of Shoot A Line was the most difficult in the past. I said before I made up my mind that I'd have to be pretty sure before I chose him because I wouldn't want anyone saying, 'Oh, he's just riding that one out of sentiment'. You must never knock classic form and with another furlong Charmer would have beaten Doyoun decisively. But will he stay? Unfuwain has got a lot going for him. But there's one snag. He doesn't seem able to change gear quickly. Mine is the form horse of the race: he's beaten the top two in the betting [Red Glow at Newmarket and Unfuwain as a juvenile] and I wouldn't be riding him if I didn't think he could do it again."

As ever Hern played possum but was thought to favour Charmer, at 11/1 the least fancied of his trio, who occupied three of the first five places in the betting.

For once Carson chose incorrectly, although it made no difference. Kahyasi presented the Aga Khan with his second Derby in three years leaving Hern to ruminate: "Unfuwain [seventh] wanted a stronger pace according to Steve Cauthen. Minster Son [eighth] would have been better suited had the rain not come, though I don't want to make excuses. And Charmer did not come down the hill." In actual fact Charmer returned to West Ilsley lame and Minster Son was found to have injured his back. Nevertheless, by the Saturday of Derby week Hern could not carp at the overall form of his horses. Twelve wins from only forty-three runners yielded a 28% success rate second only to Luca Cumani's and placed Hern eighth in the table. With over five months of the season remaining there was much to look forward to.

Lady Luck had other ideas. Hern was experiencing problems with his heart and on 17 June he underwent surgery in Kensington's Cromwell Hospital for the removal of a leaky valve. It fell to Lord Carnarvon to inform the Press.

"Dick is doing very well and the surgeons are very pleased with his condition. I am sure he will be miles better as a result of this operation and we are very much hoping he will be back in charge at West Ilsley again in September. Neil Graham will be coming as deputy trainer and will probably start in the next couple of weeks." Earlier in the month 28-year-old Graham had been appointed to succeed Alex Scott who was embarking on his own training career. Currently in California working with John Gosden, Graham caught the racing bug while at Shrewsbury School. A year as a chartered accountant in the City was enough to convince him where his future lay and he went to Derek Kent prior to joining William Hastings-Bass as an assistant. When Hastings-Bass left for Australia Graham moved to Ian Balding, with whom he spent four seasons before accepting the post with Gosden in March 1987.

Hern was confined to hospital for a month, his homecoming coinciding with Unfuwain's attempt to win the King George VI & Queen Elizabeth II Stakes on 23 July. Sheikh Hamdan's colt was fresh from a fifteen length triumph in the Princess of Wales's Stakes. He led early in the straight but had no answer to the speed of dual Eclipse winner Mtoto inside the final furlong. His trainer was no more fortunate. Within a fortnight he was re-admitted to the Cromwell Hospital for further tests and treatment. "Major Hern is ill but stable," announced a hospital spokesman. "Surgery is not indicated." Jockey Club policy requires a licence holder to be present in the yard and able to direct operations in person at all times. In these circumstances the transference of Hern's licence to Neil Graham, however temporary, was a foregone conclusion, and was confirmed by Sheilah Hern on 1 September: "As his medical advisors have recommended that he takes a two-month rest to recuperate before returning to work, Major Hern, in fairness to his owners, has asked the licensing committee to grant a temporary training licence to Neil Graham for the remainder of the season. It is hoped that Major Hern will be fit to resume training towards the end of the year.''

On behalf of the Queen, Lord Carnarvon expressed every confidence in the ability of Graham and the West Ilsley staff ''to continue the smooth running of the yard.'' The new custodian was similarly enthusiastic: ''It's a terrific challenge and a great responsibility. I spoke to the Major on the telephone this morning and his voice was strong. He was in very good form. I shall have a very good team behind me. Geordie Campbell and Buster Haslam between them have been with the Major for almost seventy years and I think Brian Holmes is in his twelfth season as secretary.'' The racing papers were not slow to spot a story opportunity, however, and the possibility that Hern might retire and be replaced at West Ilsley by William Hastings-Bass, son of the Queen's former trainer Captain Peter Hastings-Bass, brother-in-law of another (Ian Balding) and godson of Lord Carnarvon, was broached in all reports.

Graham got off to a cracking start. Within ten days of receiving his licence he had not only won with his first Pattern race runner but also trained a classic winner, surely some kind of record. Prince of Dance, the first born of Sun Princess, was not unduly troubled in winning the Laurent Perrier Champagne Stakes on the third day of the St Leger meeting. Twenty-four hours later Minster Son put Willie Carson's name into the history books as the first jockey to win a classic on a horse he had bred. Confined to his box by that sore back for two weeks after the Derby, Minster Son was unable to run until the Gordon Stakes. In the process of beating Assatis he again aggravated his back and although spending only four days in his stall this time, came to Doncaster on three weeks' preparation. The odds on favourite was Henry Cecil's little Diminuendo, victress of the Epsom, Irish and Yorkshire Oaks.

Carson knew his colt would stay every inch of the Leger distance. ''He gallops and gallops and I mean for a full mile and six furlongs, and he is very brave. I was going to make the running if I had to but, as it turned out, the fast early pace was just right. The race went exactly as I dreamed it would. I was a bit worried when Diminuendo and Sheriff's Star both headed me but when my fellow got his head back in front I thought, 'That's it'. They were never going to get back at me again. He is not a machine. Not the same horse as Troy but he is very brave. He just keeps galloping and has lots of guts."

With a furlong to go Diminuendo was upsides Minster Son but the colt muscled her out of it to win by a length. Unable to contain her excitement Lady Beaverbrook confessed, "I hardly know if I'm here or there. I am on cloud nine." But her thoughts immediately turned to Dick Hern. "I hope this has done the Major a world of good. He has worked so hard for this horse and brought it all about in the most magical way he has with horses because he really loves them." John Carroll, Minster Son's lad and fourteen years a Hern employee, spoke for everyone at West Ilsley: "I just wish Major Hern could have been there. I would love to have seen his face because he has always had great faith in Minster Son. We are all looking forward to having him back in the yard. He keeps such a strong hold on the place, keeps all of us in shape and doing our jobs properly. All the time he is very fair and you can't help but have the greatest respect for him."

The St Leger upheld Hern's assessment of Minster Son's capabilities. "No one's ever given this horse enough credit. They have always made excuses for every horse we've beaten." Neil Graham understandably wondered whether "it's going to be all downhill from now on." His worries proved groundless because, although Unfuwain (fourth) and Emmson could not land the Arc, Prince of Dance dead-heated for the Dewhurst Stakes and Sheikh Hamdan's Al Hareb captured the William Hill Futurity, the two autumnal Group I events for potential classic colts. From seventy-one runners Graham won eleven races worth £278,232 to finish tenth in the trainers' list. More significantly, if his totals were added to Hern's, West Ilsley's figures read forty-one victories of £516,449 for seventh place in the table. With Unfuwain, Charmer, Emmson and Minster Son due to remain in service and with three-year-olds like Prince of Dance, Al Hareb and a promising chestnut of Sheikh Hamdan's called Nashwan to aim at the classics, Hern needed no greater stimulus to regain his health and resume command of West Ilsley.

"He knows not his own strength that hath not met adversity."

wrote Ben Johnson. Hern had become the living embodiment of the Jacobean playwright's words. During the next six months he would prove the point over and over again as he surmounted yet one more treacherous obstacle sent to frustrate the complete recovery of all that was dear to him.

Chapter Thirteen

EVICTION

'A matter of public concern'

SIXTY-ONE WORDS were all Buckingham Palace needed to confirm one of racing's worst-kept secrets. The official statement of Monday, 13 March 1989 read matter of factly:

> The Queen has appointed Mr William Hastings-Bass to take over the West Ilsley stables when Major Hern's lease runs out in November this year. Major and Mrs Hern will continue to live at the Old Rectory and Mr Hastings-Bass will train from Hodcott House, previously the home of the late Mr Jack Colling, Major Hern's predecessor at West Ilsley.

Ever since Hern's heart surgery it had been whispered that his lease would not be renewed. The bombshell finally burst in the Press on the opening day of the Cheltenham National Hunt Festival but any presumption in royal circles of this coincidence muting its reception was gravely mistaken. From *The Times* to *The Sun*, the Champion Hurdle was booted out of the headlines. Those sixty-one words were merely the opening barrage in a war of words which lasted the best part of two months.

Although the story had been kept pretty securely under wraps throughout the winter it began to emerge on 9 March that something sensational was indeed in the offing. "The Queen's trainer is told to leave," disclosed the *Racing Post*. "Feelings in racing will run high when the news is fully digested. Hern is one of the greatest trainers of the postwar era and West Ilsley's huge success over the past 20 years has been his creation. So the likely consensus will be that the

Queen, swayed by reports of Hern's ill-health, has been put in an embarrassing position." The piece concluded by quoting a nameless insider who put his finger on a further source of potential ridicule: "With the horses he has, Dick Hern could well be champion trainer this season. That would be wonderful but also very embarrassing." Among the 107 horses which made up Hern's strongest team for years were the St Leger winner Minster Son and the classic-placed Emmson and Charmer, not to mention Unfuwain, the two Group 1 winning two-year-olds Prince of Dance and Al Hareb and West Ilsley's 'dark horse' for the classics, Nashwan. Within six months the royal decision could be made to look distinctly more and more stupid.

Lord Carnarvon refused to expand. "Our hands are tied until a statement is issued when matters will be explained and clarified. Until then everything is just speculation." Willie Carson was less tongue-tied and became the first to break cover, expressing unequivocal support for Hern.

> It's terrible news. We have had some really tremendous times together over the years. I'm very disappointed that he has to leave West Ilsley because he has built up such a good team. If he does get another yard I shall be helping him all I can. The team is nearly as good as the one we had in 1980 – all the lads think so – and the Major is in great form. The Major is not down at all. In fact he is in high spirits because he has not been in such good health for a long time. He wanted to go on for two more years and that would have suited me fine. They've made a bad decision. I've nothing against Hastings-Bass, but there's no way he's going to fill the yard like Major Hern did. He'll be a hard act to follow. There could be a lot of people out of work in the village. It's an upheaval. That's the truth and no one can get at you for speaking the truth. It's very disappointing that it's come to this. It's also disappointing for another reason. The Major has come a long way through a very dark tunnel since his accident. And now, just when we were beginning to see the light, it's as though someone has dropped a trap door and shut off that light. It's certainly put my future in jeopardy. If the Major can't find a yard I'll retire.

Barely concealed rancour also manifested itself in the comments of the recently departed Alex Scott, who confessed to being "disillusioned" by the decision. "It is quite clear to me that Major Hern's health is more, not less, likely to deteriorate if he's taken away from those things which have always produced his *raison d'etre:* his gallops; his horses and his owners. I'd sum it up by saying that the loyalty and bond between himself and his staff does not seem to have been reflected in the relationship between landlord and tenant. I feel very sorry for William Hastings-Bass in the position he's in now, through no fault of his own because he would have been crazy to have refused West Ilsley when it was offered. But if a man like Major Hern, for whom everyone in racing has such respect, can be treated in such a fashion, then it doesn't say much for racing."

The 41-year-old Hastings-Bass found himself in mountainous seas. "I am very honoured to have been asked by Her Majesty to take on the lease of the West Ilsley stables," ran his prepared statement. "I realize it will be an enormous challenge to match the success of the Major. I am greatly indebted to the loyalty of my owners and staff during my time at Newmarket. I hope that as many as possible will be able to move with me, and that those who wish to remain at West Ilsley will join in and help me continue the high standards of their famous stables." These were words of someone desperately trying to steady the ship and pretend there was not a tidal wave on the horizon. No one was fooled.

Carson's reference to Hastings-Bass's ability to fill Hern's boots went straight for the jugular. In the season just ended Hastings-Bass had trained the winners of thirty-one races worth £165,694; West Ilsley had sent out forty-one winners for over £500,000. In a twelve year career Hastings-Bass's top score was 44 in 1981 and his success in Pattern races could be counted on fingers. However, he was bred for the job of royal trainer. Due to a tragically early death from cancer, his father Captain Peter Hastings-Bass enjoyed scarcely half a season training for Her Majesty from John Porter's historic Kingsclere yard, which – along with the royal patronage – passed to Ian Balding, who later married Hastings-Bass's sister Emma. Consolidating the royal connection was the figure of Lord Carnarvon, godfather to Hastings-Bass. At the end of 1977, his first year as a licence holder, Hastings-Bass was sent two of the Queen's yearlings.

Apart from wishing the new tenant of West Ilsley "every success" Dick Hern maintained a dignified silence. Any other reaction was unimaginable. The in-fighting could safely be left to others more than willing to plant the stiletto with merciless effect. Jack Logan, typically, wasted little breath: "There is no point pretending that the dismay which most racing people feel will not rub off onto the Queen herself. Most punters in the betting shop will feel Her Majesty should have told her advisors to get lost." In *The Times*, Michael Seely hinted at the unrest simmering away beneath the polite veneer of formal statements, voicing the opinion that "the family of racing is a close-knit one and strong feelings have been expressed that one of its most respected members has been treated with insensitivity. The general consensus seems to be that the Queen has been poorly advised and that the timing of the move is wrong. The royal advisors, including Lord Carnarvon, the Queen's racing manager, must feel, however, that it is time to look to the future."

Unfortunately for those "royal advisors" Dick Hern's future, which seemed all too bleak in August 1988, could not now have looked rosier. Refreshed by a month's holiday in Dubai, Hern was fitter than for some months and full of enthusiasm for the season ahead. What could have been wiser, and more grateful a gesture, than to quietly put the impending change on ice. After all, if the worst came to the worst and Hern did succumb to his disabilities, the West Ilsley team had already demonstrated they were quite capable of 'carrying on' until such time as Hastings-Bass could take over. During the brief period Neil Graham had held the reins the stable had won eleven races (including two Group 1s) worth over £270,000. Hastings-Bass should have inherited the priceless legacy of the Hern staff and its system; this way, many of Hern's staff and horses would leave with him, thereby destroying the very continuity the royal decision was meant to perpetuate. Many of Hern's owners could also be expected to jump ship, taking with them a great number of horses. Of West Ilsley's 107 inmates only eleven actually belonged to the Queen. There could be little doubt where the Beaverbrook and Hollingsworth contingents or the ever increasing Maktoum legions would be heading. Besides a personal loyalty to the man himself, their multi-million pound investment was geared to an operation orchestrated by a particular trainer, and business sense dictates such a relationship ought not to be severed unnecessarily. Once Hern proved incapable of delivering the goods that was another matter. Yet, despite the heart trouble and the $4\frac{1}{2}$ years confined to a wheelchair, Hern's powers showed no sign of diminishing. "I don't want to give up as long as I feel as good as I do now.

It is a way of life and all I know. If I retired, what would I do when
I got up in the morning? Read a book or write my reminiscences?"

In the baffling absence of any justification or further explanation
from the Palace, racing folk – traditionally royalist to a fault – were
left to mull over the mish-mash of fact and rumour and draw their
own conclusions. The columns of *Pacemaker Update* typified racing's
divided loyalties. On one side of the fence was Charles Benson, who
admitted:

> I have known of this situation since last August but maintained my
> silence since I could not believe the monarch and her advisors, prin-
> cipally Lord Carnarvon, could go through with the plan. Well, they
> have, and together with most of the owners in the stable I am appalled.
> Dick has made a great recovery from the terrible physical problems
> which have beset him and his mind is still razor-sharp. Even in the
> dark days of last autumn in hospital, he still kept up his charts and
> knew what each horse was doing.

On the other was Nick Robinson, striking a more sympathetic note:

> Both Dick Hern and Henry Carnarvon have maintained a dignified
> silence over a dispute that may be more in the minds of racing journal-
> ists and others who seem determined to make capital out of a situation
> that has become extremely difficult for the main participants.

If Nigel Dempster's "Mail Diary" was to be believed, the sacking
had even caused ructions within royal circles. "Ma'am's Mum is not
amused," was the peg for a piece which continued: "The Queen
Mother, I understand, has made it known to her racing friends that
she regards the treatment of Hern as deplorable; and her feelings
have been forcefully communicated to both the Queen and Lord
Carnarvon. I am told she feels that what Dick Hern has been subjected to is nothing short of scandalous." It had not gone unnoticed
that the Queen Mother's own trainer, 78-year-old Fulke Walwyn,
had also endured recent illness but not at the cost of his royal
patronage.

Sports pages, front pages, gossip columns: exposure in virtually
every section of the Press merely ratified the affair's status as a *cause
célèbre* of the highest magnitude. If, as Napoleon averred, "Popular
opinion is the thermometer a man should constantly consult," Carnarvon had miscalculated disastrously. In the quest for copy mem-

ories were cast back to November 1933 when the 17th Earl of Derby sacked his 73-year-old trainer George Lambton owing to ill-health, though this was unknown at the time. Lambton had served the Stanley family for forty years and Hyperion's St Leger victory just two months earlier was the eleventh classic he had secured for them. Lambton's rheumatics had been aggravated by a number of falls and he could not possibly be expected, went the Stanley theory, to bear the strain much longer. Like Hern, Lambton rejected thoughts of retirement but otherwise gave little away. However, in a letter to his brother he poured out feelings – with which Hern could empathize – about having his "life's work, my interest in life, my livelihood closed down with five weeks notice. There is only one person for him to have consulted as to my health and that was myself." To his staff, gathered together for the presentation of a silver salver, an emotional Lambton said: "Some of you older men must have wondered why I kept silent – but to tell you the truth I have had neither the strength nor courage to speak to you. It is all too painful and it has nearly broken my heart to break away." Lambton trained for another twelve years until his death at the age of 85.

Had the landlord evicting Hern been anyone other than the reigning monarch there's every reason to suspect he or she would have been the recipient of considerably more venom. One wonders what kind of poison would have flowed had the Weinstocks still controlled the fate of West Ilsley and had they decided to dispense with Hern's services for the same 'business' reasons which saw Joe Mercer axed in favour of a younger prospect. Indeed, although responsible for thirteen of Hern's horses in 1989, the Sobell-Weinstock tandem had already begun spreading its interests: Michael Stoute had eight of their horses, for example. Racing is as unsentimental a business as the next. Training, it might be argued, is a tactile business. The laying-on of hands is paramount; feeling delicate forelegs for telltale signs of strain, gently probing the loins for tenderness or the back for pulled muscles. Dick Hern made his name by carving a well-deserved reputation as a horsemaster: the 'old-fashioned' type of trainer best described, ironically, by that most modern of terms 'hands-on'. Horrid jargon, perhaps, but when applied to the rapport between horse and master not entirely inappropriate. To this type of trainer, as Hern admitted, the wheelchair acts as a prison. To this type of trainer, furthermore, any considerations of accumulating

capital for a rainy day were decidedly secondary to the prime objective in life. Caring for the racehorse and training it to run faster than
its opponents was what made Hern's world go round. Why worship
the false idol of money? Hern's uncomplicated view of life certainly
included no such thing. Enough cash for his hunting and a pipeful
of tobacco was the extent of his homage to the cult. Contempt for
financial accumulation and the power it wields consequently left him
totally naked when 'business' ruthlessly caught up with him. He had
failed to heed the lessons of Joe Mercer's departure. No one is
indispensable.

By 10 April Hern had read and heard enough. So much dirty
washing had been publicly hung out for inspection that he tried to
put an end to it all by releasing a letter to the Press.

> While I very much appreciate all the support and encouragement
> which I have received, I hope the recent correspondence which has
> appeared in the Press about the fact that I shall not be training at
> West Ilsley in 1990 will now cease. For the last 23 years I have had
> the honour of training for Her Majesty the Queen and during that time
> she has always been extremely kind and understanding about the
> problems involved in training racehorses. Although I am planning to
> continue training, I feel sure that the only reason the Queen and her
> advisors decided to terminate my lease was concern for my health. I
> am extremely grateful to Her Majesty for allowing me to continue to
> live in The Old Rectory at West Ilsley for as long as I wish to do so.

As one would expect, the missive was no more than a polite request
for silence in the ranks when even a barked command – the quin-
tessential Hern response in these circumstances – would have been
ignored. There was not the slightest chance of elucidation. When
Hern agreed to be interviewed on Channel 4 immediately after
Nashwan's 2000 Guineas victory he did so on the strict proviso that
Brough Scott would not question him about the West Ilsley tenancy.
The crucial issues would continue to be shirked.

Alas, Hern was once more hoisted on the petard of his own success.
Nashwan was a champion. "Few results have given me more pleasure," confessed Carson at Newmarket. "You could say the timing
of this victory was just perfect." Hern hogged the limelight when he
desperately sought the shadows. Declared Michael Seely in *The
Times*:

This is a time for plain speaking. The sustained applause from thousands and the calling of three cheers for the 69-year-old trainer as he came forward in his wheelchair to receive his trophy signalled not only recognition for an outstanding professional feat. It also showed sympathy for the man they considered to have been badly treated. Unfortunately, the whole business has become a matter of public concern, and it is being discussed and debated outside the narrow confines of the world of racing... although the Palace seldom issues statements, the public desire for an explanation is becoming overwhelming.

Seely could hardly be described as an impartial observer, however. He was a dyed-in-the-wool Hern supporter, as were the majority of those "thousands" applauding in the Newmarket Members' and Tattersalls' enclosures. This was Hern heartland; these patricians were his peers, in thought and beliefs, if not deeds. To impose their view on the country's racing public involved something of a quantum leap on Seely's part. Nevertheless, in *The Sunday Times*, even the more finely balanced pen of Brough Scott concluded: "Whatever the original intentions of the Queen's decision, it has now backfired. There is no action in the whole of racing that would be more popular, or necessary, than a royal change of heart."

The villain of the piece as far as the racing fraternity was concerned was Henry Carnarvon. Grandson of the 5th Earl (he of Tutankhamen's tomb notoriety), his passion for the Turf dated from childhood. "My father was one of the leading amateurs and had horses with Dick Dawson. So I used to see all the old Aga Khan's horses and have breakfast as a boy with Michael Beary. And my mother was a fantastic punter. She nearly broke Ladbrokes ...and then, as always happens, they finally broke her." After war service in Italy with the Royal Horse Guards young Porchester's interest in racing was fanned by riding work on the Epsom-trained champion hurdler National Spirit and being allowed to gallop round Tattenham Corner. The first decent horse he owned was Esquimalt, who won the 1946 Bessborough Stakes at Royal Ascot, although by far the best was Tamerlane, in 1955 the winner of the St James's Palace Stakes and runner-up in the 2000 Guineas. The best horse trained for him at West Ilsley up to 1988 was probably Smuggler, one of the first two-year-olds he sent Hern in 1975, but in 1989 Roseate Tern would dispute that claim by winning the Yorkshire Oaks and finishing third in the Oaks and St Leger.

In 1989 Carnarvon was serving his second term as President of the Thoroughbred Breeders' Association. He was elected to the Jockey Club in 1964 and was Chairman of the Flat Race Planning Committee; he had also been President of the Amateur Riders' Association. His life was not all racing. On leaving the Blues in 1948 he graduated from Cirencester Royal Agricultural College and started farming at Highclere. Thereafter he added a third string to his bow, entering local government as an independent and winding up Chairman of Hampshire County Council. In 1971 he was appointed Chairman of the South East Economic Planning Council; between 1978 and 1982 he ran the Agricultural Research Council and he also sat on the Sports Council.

Carnarvon first went racing with the Queen at Newmarket in 1945 and he was by her side that day she bought Stroma, the grandam of Dunfermline, at Doncaster in 1956. Thirteen years later he was created Her Majesty's racing manager, an entirely new post. Although prone to imparting a whiff of theatricality, any man who could run a county council, who could chair land planning councils covering 17 million people under both Tory and Labour governments and who could work easily and productively with the Queen and with Trade Unionists, had to possess as much inner substance as superficial gloss. But the renewed uproar in the papers following the 2000 Guineas finally got to Carnarvon. On 10 May he angrily told the *Racing Post*:

> I am not prepared to discuss the various opinions on the matter. But I feel sad that it has turned into an unpleasant saga and that the Press are trying to stir up public opinion. It is simply appalling of the Press and they ought to be ashamed of themselves. Whatever they think they may be doing to help one party they must realize they are doing damage to another. It is very unpleasant for everyone concerned. Dick and I have been great friends and I hope will remain so.

Needless to say, all this outburst succeeded in doing was stimulating further copy. Two days later the *Daily Mail's* Colin Mackenzie purported to explain "The true-blue facts of that racing split" in an article headed: "Why Carnarvon and Dick Hern continue to be good friends." Frankly, Mackenzie's 'explanation' was so weak as to make no difference and had all the trappings of a sob-story. "This public furore has created a lot of unhappiness," he confided. "Lady Carnarvon hardly dares pick up a newspaper these days and I understand that the Queen feels deeply wounded. 'Dick and I are good friends – there is no antipathy between us,' said Carnarvon." The one sentence of import was the revelation that Hern was offered the chance to stay at West Ilsley as long as he shared the facilities with his eventual successor. He declined.

That same morning John Oaksey adopted a much more strident line in his *Racing Post* column, "Hern: the heart of the matter." He began by having no truck with Carnarvon's accusations against the Press.

> I firmly believe that the Queen's racing manager is guilty of a grave, if understandable, exaggeration. A delicate, potentially, explosive question has, in fact, been handled with remarkable restraint ...far from trying to 'stir up public opinion' the racing Press has been quite remarkably controlled. They have, if anything, played down a sequence of events in which to Dick Hern's many friends and admirers, one of Britain's most successful and universally respected trainers seems, on the face of it, to have been very harshly treated.

After explaining how a combination of racing's patriotic leanings and respect for Hern's own declared resolve not to say or do anything which could reflect discredit on the Queen had brought about this restraint, Oaksey returned to the attack.

> In racecourse bars, Press Rooms and other similarly enlightened forums it has not been fashionable lately to give Lord Carnarvon the benefit of many doubts. He has been widely held responsible, among other things, for the total absence of explanations or reasons for the Palace's attitudes over West Ilsley. He would, I think, accept that responsibility – but whether you approve of them or not, he has definite reasons for his silence. All medical reports are, of course, confidential but so, it seems, by inflexible tradition, is all counsel given to the Queen by her advisors.

With Hern looking better and stronger by the day and West Ilsley continuing to churn out big winners, the need for an explanation, argued Oaksey, was becoming increasingly urgent.

What needs most explaining is why the Queen, who is famous for her loyalty to royal employees, is sticking to a decision which, however humane, well-meant and justifiable it may have seemed in the first place, now threatens to force an old, valued and devoted friend into a difficult, undignified and uncomfortable position.

In *The Sporting Life*, editor Monty Court also defended the Press against Carnarvon's accusations, although according to James Underwood – never a man averse to swimming against the tide of opinion – in his small circulation magazine *European Racing & Breeding Digest*, the efforts of both Court and the "waffling John Oaksey" were to "no avail". Asserted Underwood: "Racing people surely have the right to demand of their newspapers and journalists that they adequately present both sides of a story and not just indulge in the luxury of going along with what may be informed or possibly utterly uninformed opinion."

In this bitter climate of recrimination punctuated by arctic silences from the wounded principles, Charles Benson reminded avid followers of the 'saga' that the problems were not theirs alone. "Hern's loyal and able staff are thrown onto the horns of a terrible dilemma. To a man they are loyal to the Major but, like most of us, they have commitments – mortgages, hire purchase agreements and the debts of a modern society. It is a cruel plight to face."

Thankfully, media attention eventually switched to the possible location of Hern's new quarters; the favourites were Peter Cundell's Roden House in Compton, on the opposite side of the A34 to West Ilsley, and James Bethell's yard at Chilton, two miles to the north. When asked for his thoughts, Angus Gold, racing manager to Sheikh Hamdan Al-Maktoum, was quoted as saying: "Of course, we're sympathetic to the Major's cause. But we are first going to see how he gets on with his own arrangements." Within a few days the fog began to lift. Authoritative reports appeared "drawing on sources close to the royal family" to the effect that Hastings-Bass and Hern would, after all, share the facilities at West Ilsley but train as separate individuals. Had the royal advisors finally wilted in the gale of public opinion? There was even talk of a knighthood for Hern in the next Honours List. "All sorts of ideas are being discussed but nothing has been decided yet," is all the Press could winkle out of Sheilah Hern, speaking on her husband's behalf. The Palace said even less, yet still managed to give the game away: "We have nothing to say – at the moment." Later that day (17 May) Channel 4 Racing confirmed the accuracy of the previous day's rumour during its transmission from York, thereby getting into hot water with the Palace, who had placed an embargo on publication of the story until midnight. The statement went as follows:

> The Queen has made an offer to Major Hern whereby he can share the West Ilsley stables for 1990 with Mr Hastings-Bass. Major Hern has gratefully accepted the offer in principle. The details of the arrangements to create two yards are now under discussion between the trainers and will be subject to final approval by the Stewards of the Jockey Club. The offer to share the stables was originally made by the Queen, with the knowledge of the officials of the Jockey Club, in November 1988. At the time, however, Major Hern felt unable to accept the terms.

That last sentence left little room for interpretive manoeuvre. This was no royal climb-down. Hern had now accepted an offer he had refused six months earlier on the grounds that he wanted a two-year extension to his lease not one year. "I am not aware of any changes from the offer made last November," said Lord Carnarvon. "In the last fortnight the offer was made again to share the yard." Hern would receive none of the Queen's new intake of yearlings. Any climbing-down had been done by Hern. Out of loyalty to the Queen and a passionate desire to see the controversy dead and buried he had bitten the bullet like a good soldier. "Obviously this has been a very recent offer," he said in apparent contradiction to Carnarvon's reference to the November deal. Or was this a conscious attempt to erase all knowledge of the last six months from his mind? "And you cannot settle something like this overnight. But I hope it will end all speculation about my future. I have about ninety active horses at the moment and will reduce that number to around fifty. I think it's very doubtful if substantial new buildings will be required. This is a breathing space for the future but with a maximum of fifty horses I won't have so much ammunition from which to fire my big guns but I do intend to continue training after 1990."

The two other principal parties made all the right noises. "It seems the best solution to a very difficult situation," said Hastings-Bass. "It was partly my suggestion in the first place back in November.

It will give Major Hern a breathing space. I hope it works and cannot see any reason why it shouldn't, as I've always got on well with Major Hern. There will obviously be enough gallops as over a hundred horses have been trained here in the past." If Carnarvon's reaction had been accompanied by a sigh of relief it would be forgivable. "It has been a very unpleasant time without all the facts from both sides being put on the table. Jockey Club officials have been to West Ilsley and have given their approval in principle. We all met there recently, discussed all the arrangements, agreed and had a drink on it. We are all very pleased."

If "all the facts from both sides" had never been "put on the table" whose fault was that? As the leading protagonists of each "side" Carnarvon and Hern had no one to blame for this "very unpleasant time" but themselves if they chose to withhold certain "facts" instead of making a clean breast of things. There were, indeed, "enough gallops", but enough jobs, no. In September Hern had to issue five redundancy notices, four of them to married men. "It goes against the grain to have to make loyal staff redundant when they've done nothing wrong," he said. "I feel extremely sorry for them and their families but there's nothing I can do about it. I've been training thirty-two years and I've never made a man redundant in my life." With the strength of his number one retaining stable halved Willie Carson also had due cause for misgivings.

> I am very pleased for the Major and the whole team at West Ilsley. This means there will be no upheaval and no unemployment in the village, which will keep its good atmosphere. I hope the Major will have a good team for next year but my plans are fluid and I might retire. I don't want to but I don't want to be chasing around after mounts as a freelance. Everything is up in the air and we shall just have to see. If the Major moves elsewhere he will obviously have a much reduced string, probably fifty or sixty horses which would hardly sustain a top jockey as number one retainer. So where would I go then? I don't know. But of course I'll stick with him as number one if he'll have me.

Referring to the public stand he had made on the Major's behalf the jockey was forced to admit: "It's done me no good at all but I stand by my remarks and I would do the same again. The Major and I are part of a unique team and I will always stand by him, even if it means a premature end to my career."

With hatchets seemingly buried, Hern got on with the job of preparing Nashwan for a triumphal campaign which encompassed the Derby, Eclipse and King George. However, a further instalment of what had teetered on the brink of becoming a soap opera unfolded on 28 September when it was revealed that as of November 1990 Hern would train from a brand new complex to be built on Farncombe Down, some twelve miles and one exit down the M4 from West Ilsley on the Berkshire-Wiltshire border. A private company linked to the Maktoum family had purchased the 180-acre block of farmland and gallops for a sum variously described as £750,000 or £1 million. Known locally as the Windmill gallops, these training grounds dated from the late eighteenth century and were used by Ossie Bell and Marcus Marsh to condition their Derby winners Felstead (1928) and Windsor Lad (1934). The property had been on the market for two years – empty and unused – with a price guide of £850,00. The extensive range of gallops included a one-mile level summer gallop and a one-mile level valley gallop, a 1¼-mile left-handed gallop rising steadily on the collar and a six-furlong all-weather strip, in addition to large areas of canters. The construction of necessary buildings would set the Maktoums back several more millions. "The Maktoum family consider this a good investment," said Angus Gold. "They are delighted the Major has agreed to train from Farncombe, which will not be run as a private yard. The Major will continue to handle horses for other patrons."

Hamdan Al-Maktoum had come to his trainer's aid when others had failed him. Exercising customary restraint, Hern expressed equal delight at the prospect of a fresh start so late in his career. The statement was straight from the Dick Hern manual of not using two words where one will suffice: "I am very grateful to the Maktoum family for asking me to be the first man to train from their new yard at Farncombe Down." For the first time in almost a year Dick Hern could lay his mind to rest.

Notwithstanding Hern's new-found peace of mind the projected move to Farncombe eventually fell through. On 21 February 1990 Hern disclosed that although he would still utilize the Farncombe gallops his actual base from 1991 was going to be Kingswood House, on the edge of Lambourn, which had been acquired from the present occupant Mark Smyly. "It will be a first class establishment, one of the best in the country, and I am looking forward to the move tremendously. Everything will be new, with a modern covered ride and swimming pool for the horses and there will be a bit more room. Hopefully it will be ready by the time I have to leave West Ilsley on November 30." Confirmation of the sale came from Smyly's wife Harriet: "Sheikh Hamdan has bought the main house, lads' hostel, stables and eighty acres of land here, subject to plans for a brand new training complex on the site being approved by Newbury District Council. I understand the planning application involves the existing boxes being demolished to be replaced by about sixty more, plus a new lads' hostel, with the back-up of the existing plans for Farncombe to stand should it be refused. There is a very quiet access from Kingswood to the Farncombe gallops which takes only a quarter of an hour. It will be a great boost to the area to have Major Hern training in Lambourn."

CHAPTER FOURTEEN

NASHWAN

'Be to his virtues ever kind and to his faults a little blind'

"HE MOVES LIKE A PANTHER." The object of Hern's admiration and the apple of his eye during the spring of 1989 was a superbly athletic chestnut with two white socks and a star between his alert eyes. "He has always had such an air, such presence. I felt he was trying to tell us something all last season," added Sheilah Hern. "Above all, I wanted Dick to be up here training him again this year." Up on his beloved gallops Dick Hern could push all thoughts of accident, illness and the tenancy row to the back of his mind and immerse himself in the sights and sounds no money could buy for him or take from him. Back from death's door his eyes feasted on the boundless horizon interrupted only by the snorting minotaurs that are man and horse in flawless harmony, the rhythmic thudding as they passed his grey Mitsubishi station wagon music to his ears. Hern's spirits could afford to soar with the larks presiding over the scene, for this was a year many had not expected him to see. He had every reason to feel full of the joys of spring. Even the name of his new star was Arabic for joyful – Nashwan.

A big, rangy colt with a wonderfully fluent, sweeping stride, beautifully balanced and possessed of a seemingly imperturbable temperament, Nashwan had won both his outings as a juvenile. There was no mistaking his potential. He was bred to be a champion. His sire Blushing Groom had won the French 2000 Guineas and four other Group 1 events and since retiring to Gainsway Farm, Kentucky, had got such European winners as Rainbow Quest (Prix de l'Arc de Triomphe) and Al Bahathri (Irish 1000 Guineas). The fascinating element of Nashwan's pedigree, however, was his dam, for she was Height of Fashion, the mare sold by the Queen to Sheikh Hamdan Al-Maktoum in 1982's so-called 'sale of the century' that financed the Queen's purchase of West Ilsley from Sobell and Weinstock.

One of Sheikh Rashid bin Said Al-Maktoum's four sons, the 44-year-old Hamdan was Dubai's finance minister, to whom money grew on trees. His income is estimated at £1 million a day. Like most Arabs, Hamdan's interest in racing horses (and camels) began at birth and while studying at a Cambridge language school he and younger brother Mohammed would sneak out on Saturdays to Newmarket where they spectated, reputedly, from the cheap Silver Ring enclosure. A shy man with slow, heavily accented English which should not be allowed to disguise the fact that he has a remarkably retentive memory and an encyclopaedic knowledge of breeding, Hamdan's involvement with the Turf developed into a passion outstripping his other pursuits of shooting, falconry and camel racing. Clearly, the combination of unlimited capital and fanatical commitment was guaranteed to reap a spectacular harvest on the English Turf. "Whatever the Maktoums do, they do it supremely well – or they don't do it at all," says one Dubai businessman. By the same token their success, eventually bordering on an unhealthy domination, was also guaranteed to raise a few hackles among xenophobic elements of the racing establishment.

Mohammed set the ball rolling in 1977 by sending Hatta, bought for a mere 6,200 guineas, to John Dunlop. The filly won four races, including the Group III Molecomb Stakes. Thereafter the expenditure became gargantuan. The first horse to run in Hamdan's name was Ghadeer, which cost 625,000 guineas – more than twice the existing record – at Tattersalls in 1979. In the 1980s the Maktoums spent over $370 million on American yearlings alone, while continuing to average £10 million a year at Newmarket. In 1988, for instance, they accounted for nearly a third of the turnover at the Keeneland July Select Sale and the Newmarket Highflyer Sale. Even the Aga Khan was moved to say: "It is difficult to compete with people who do not appear to be inspired by the profit motive." By 1988 their total of horses in training had grown to over 500 in Britain spread among two dozen different trainers. Nashwan's two victories in 1988 contributed toward a total of 287 which included nine of the twenty-three Group I races in England, nine of the twenty-nine Group IIs and seventeen of the fifty-two Group IIIs i.e. 33.7% of the English Pattern. At the same time they built up their interests in studs and stallions.

The case against the 'Maktoum factor' was put virulently by *The Sporting Life* in a special report of 14 November 1988.

> This low-profile family from Dubai looked as though they might be the saviours of a bloodstock industry that had been starved of capital investment. Unfortunately, they never know when to stop spending – and the damage they are now inflicting on the game is beginning to outweigh the massive amount of early good when they helped retrieve lost bloodlines and provided employment on a variety of studs and stables. They and their advisors have failed totally to appreciate the responsibility and duties imposed on them by their staggering wealth.

No other stance could be expected from *The Sporting Life* – the self-styled "Independent Voice of Racing" – because its only rival as a daily racing paper was the Maktoum-financed *Racing Post*. Others were less critical: John Biggs, for the Racehorse Owners' Association, and Richard Mackaness of the National Trainers' Federation, for example. Had not Maktoum patronage extended to race sponsorship, charities and the construction of a new all-weather gallop, the Al Bahathri, at Newmarket? "People tend to get the wrong idea about our attitude to racing," responded Sheikh Mohammed. "We don't want to throw our weight around and we don't try to alter conventions. We enjoy our horses. We don't bet. We run them honestly and fairly and we thoroughly enjoy British racing."

Until the emergence of Nashwan the sweet filly Al Bahathri had been Hamdan's favourite and her Irish 1000 Guineas of 1985 his solitary classic success (though his biggest win had to be the 1986 Melbourne Cup landed by his Derby fourth At Talaq). His brothers Maktoum and Mohammed had, between them, won all the English classics bar the Derby. Winning the Epsom classic, therefore, became a family obsession, and it was with this aim that Height of Fashion was added to Hamdan's band of broodmares. He immediately set about sending her to the best stallions. In 1983 that meant Northern Dancer. The product of that $650,000 marriage was a colt called

Alwasmi with whom Tom Jones won the John Porter Stakes of 1988. By this time his West Ilsley-based full brother Unfuwain was just beginning to show his colours. Although only seventh in the Derby, Unfuwain was the best placed three-year-old in both the King George(second) and the Arc(fourth), thereby earning the title of the middle-distance champion of his generation. It cost Hamdan another $275,000 for Height of Fashion to be covered by Blushing Groom in the spring of 1986 but as soon as the owner/breeder clapped eyes on the resultant chestnut foal careering round a Kentucky paddock a year later he was smitten. "The most beautiful mover," is how Sheikh Hamdan recalled his first meeting with an animal he came to regard as "not part of the family but part of me."

On 15 April 1989 Hern made his first racecourse appearance since the previous Royal Ascot to watch Unfuwain take the John Porter Stakes at Newbury. Reports of Nashwan's progress during the winter had not been auspicious and Ladbrokes were offering 33/1 about him for the 2000 Guineas. "He had a splint in January and we thought he wouldn't be ready in time but he's recovered quickly . . . if he runs at Newmarket he won't have a preliminary race. It's possible to do it on the gallops at West Ilsley as they're very testing." In point of fact, for six weeks Nashwan had accomplished nothing more taxing than a walk and by mid-February was still only trotting. Hern grew worried. "They miss a lot of food when they are only doing that at a time when the others are on full rations. You can't go on stoking a boiler without letting off steam. When Al Hareb disappointed in the Craven, Sheikh Hamdan was keen on going for the Guineas but I was still worried that it would encourage me to do more than I should with him. He is so willing, he always does everything we ask. So, on the testing soft ground in the spring, I worked him only with animals that were very inferior to him, so it wouldn't take too much out of him."

The gallop selected as make-or-break for Nashwan's Guineas prospects was on Saturday, 22 April. The outcome was elevated to instant legend: "normal exaggeration," Brough Scott waxed lyrically in *The Sunday Times*, "having Nashwan actually breaking the sound barrier", and it sent the bookmakers scurrying for cover the moment betting offices opened at 9 am. "It was an extraordinarily good piece of work and I realized then that he was out of the ordinary," confirmed his trainer. Carson filled in the details: "He went with two others, one a four-year-old, and just paralysed them ... whoosh ... about twenty-five lengths clear. When I got back to the Major, I said to him, 'This is some horse', and he said it was the best he'd seen any horse work along the Trial Ground since Brigadier Gerard. So I said, 'Well, Major, you're in the prime position, sitting next to a telephone. If I were you, I'd get on now because all the lads have seen it and they'll be going off like hell on their bikes at breakfast time to ring their punters'."

Overnight Nashwan's price was slashed from 16/1 to 8s and, the subject of further heavy support throughout the next fortnight, these odds shrank to 4/1 (second favourite to Vincent O'Brien's Saratogan) by the first day of the Guineas meeting. "The dogs were really barking. It was very exciting. I knew now he was the best and fastest miler I had trained since Brigadier Gerard and he had a mile and a half pedigree which made it better still." Once Unfuwain and Prince of Dance had won their races on the Friday, Ladbrokes laid Nashwan to lose £250,000 and he became the new favourite at 3/1. "It's not direct encouragement as none of them has worked together," Hern told the Press guardedly, "but as far as it shows that the horses are well it's very encouraging indeed." Carson, typically, was more enthusiastic: "As far as Nashwan is concerned we'll have to see what happens but I'm now beginning to worry whether he might be too fast for the Derby."

If a power above and beyond Nashwan's flying hooves was at work on 2000 Guineas day 1989 it gained racing's universal approval. "Emotion overflowed as Nashwan provided the result the racing world had wanted so much," reported Jonathan Powell in the *Sunday Express*, while in the *Observer* Hugh McIlvanney claimed: "Horse racing has rarely offered deeper pleasure than it did in flooding sunshine at Newmarket yesterday." Nashwan's success, by a length from Exbourne in the fastest electrically-timed Guineas of 1.36.44(just 0.64 seconds outside My Babu's hand-timed record of 1948), was greeted by similar outbursts of joy in virtually every newspaper. Apart from the time the bare form of Nashwan's victory was nothing remarkable. Saratogan, favourably compared by O'Brien to his four previous Guineas winners, faded into a sorry ninth, two places ahead of Shaadi, who had defeated Exbourne in the Craven Stakes and would later prove his Newmarket form all wrong by winning the Irish 2000 Guineas and the St James's Palace

Stakes. The reason for such euphoria was simple. "When you want something badly it seldom ever happens," said Hern, "but luckily God was in His heaven."

Nashwan was never worse than third throughout the race and took up the running before the Bushes. "The fast pace suited us," Carson explained. "My only worry beforehand was that Nashwan might be taken off his legs on the fast ground but he was always laying up and when I kicked three furlongs out I was confident he would keep up the gallop." Hern watched the race on the big television screen in the betting shop beside the weighing room. The pale, hunched figure strapped in the wheelchair seemed to confirm those bleak rumours of the previous autumn, but as Nashwan pounded over the line so did the blood through Hern's veins and a vital gleam shone from his eyes.

The looks – and words – exchanged as Hern welcomed his heroes to the winner's enclosure with a chivalrous sweep of his panama hat, and the rousing three cheers which then rang out, spoke volumes and made it impossible to avoid interpreting this unparalleled reception as a show of discontent from racing's parish at the treatment meted out to Hern by the Queen and her advisors. Carson leapt from his mount and dived through a mêlée of well-wishers to his guv'nor. "You're a good trainer," he laughed. "And you're not a bad jockey, either," shot back the instant reply. "There could have been no more dramatic or convincing demonstration of how exceptional Dick Hern's powers remain," wrote McIlvanney, for Nashwan was the first since Brigadier Gerard to win the Guineas on his seasonal debut. "I don't know what the crowd felt but they gave us an exceptional ovation," mused Hern. "That moment will always be one of the highlights of my life. I think it was a popular result. It certainly gave me enormous pleasure, even more than Brigadier Gerard. It was a bit of a rush to get him ready and we had to put in a lot of work on wet muddy gallops but it has been a great team effort. Willie rode a marvellous race. He just let Nashwan use that wonderful long stride. I shall always be grateful to Sheikh Hamdan for having sent horses like Nashwan and Unfuwain to an old man like me. He could easily have sent them to another trainer."

Scandal-mongers could read what they liked into that last sentence. Thankfully, by the time Nashwan lined up for the Derby the long-awaited 'royal change of heart' had arrived to push the subject of West Ilsley's tenancy into the background.

Nashwan had embarked on a golden eleven-week crusade during which he would pull off an unprecedented clean-sweep of the 2000 Guineas, Derby, Eclipse and King George. He was a firm 2/1 favourite for the Derby even before the Newmarket faithful had dispersed. What could beat him? He had a pedigree crying out for a longer trip, the action to handle the track and a victory in the race which frequently offers the best form guide. "I've no doubt that he will stay," Hern stressed to reporters. "His dam is by Bustino who is such a great influence for stamina and he's got a marvellous temperament. He came down into the Dip all right, didn't he? He's got such a great shoulder that I would think you could ride him down the side of a house. Nashwan is a fabulous mover and he will gallop up or down hill – any way you like. I never get tired of watching him on the Downs and am looking forward to Derby day." Carson was equally optimistic: "He was really digging in at the finish of the Guineas. I have no doubts about his stamina and I would welcome a strongly-run race. He's the one. I've nothing to say about the rest. He's very possibly the best horse I've ridden."

Nashwan came out of his race satisfactorily and having been, in Hern's words, "stone fit on Guineas day", only had to be kept ticking over. Hern's main consideration was the firm going which heralded the beginning of a long, hot summer. Ten days before Epsom was the only occasion when Nashwan (and Prince of Dance) was galloped over the full Derby distance at Newbury racecourse. At home, the glorious springy carpet of West Ilsley's historic old turf came to the rescue yet again. For his final six-furlong workout Nashwan enjoyed a strip of ground that had not felt galloping hooves in four years. However, as if to keep everyone on their toes, Nashwan pulled a plate off at exercise later in the week. "As a precaution he was taken home. The incident was of no consequence, it was only a scare."

A quarter of an inch of rain in the twenty-four hours leading up to the Derby was insufficient to cause Hern any anxiety, though it had not gone unnoticed that all seven of the stable's runners during the preceding fortnight had failed to win. In fact, Hern's last success was the 2000 Guineas. Nashwan entered the stalls as a 5/4 favourite. The market stated he had Guy Harwood's Cacoethes to beat. They had already met once as two-year-olds when Cacoethes (making his debut) lost the argument by $5\frac{1}{2}$ lengths. Subsequently unbeaten, he

came to Epsom fresh from a scintillating victory over the one-time
Derby favourite Pirate Army in Lingfield's Derby Trial, breaking
the track record into the bargain.

With an arrogance rarely seen in a Derby, Nashwan surged away
from Cacoethes in the straight and contemptuously dismissed the
late challenge of the 500/1 outsider Terimon to win by five lengths
in a time of 2.34.90, seldom bettered in the event's history. Carson
confessed: "My heart ruled my head once we hit the front and I went
for home. I didn't plan to go to the front so soon but I did know
that he would stay. He broke very well like he always does, but I
wanted to track Cacoethes because everybody had been telling me
what a great horse he was. So I dropped him back and then I had
to fight a bit to get a position where I could do so. Then, when I got
there Cacoethes almost died too soon, so I thought I ought to go
when I could. He's the tops – the best I've ridden. He would be more
adaptable than Troy and I would definitely put him in front of
Henbit too. Nashwan is a Triple Crown horse but I suppose he'll
have to win the Eclipse before some people are convinced he's a
champion."

Hern viewed his fifteenth success in an English classic (only nine
men have trained more) from Sheikh Hamdan's private chalet. "I
knew Nashwan would go very close but I didn't think he would win
quite so well. He's probably the best I've ever had. Brigadier Gerard
put up a very brilliant display when he beat Mill Reef in the 2000
Guineas. He stayed 1½ miles as a four-year-old but I doubt if he could
have won the Derby at that stage of his career. Nashwan won easier
than Troy, even though his winning margin was seven lengths. Troy
and Henbit would not have had the speed to win the Guineas."
Hern's trusty right arm, Buster Haslam, agreed: "Nashwan is far
better than the other Derby winners Troy and Henbit – he's got
such speed. He's won the race well. I never had any doubts about
him getting the trip as his dam stayed and he has absolutely no
temperament problems." With a 40/1 ante-post voucher safely in
his pocket, Nashwan's lad Allan Thimbleby, who also had care of
Unfuwain and once saw to the needs of Boldboy, was in a mood to
celebrate. "I've looked after some good ones but this fellow is definitely the star. The 2000 Guineas was a bonus. He amazed us with
the speed he showed on the Trial Ground a couple of weeks before
Newmarket and it was only then that it was decided to run him in

the Guineas. When I was asked what would finish second to him in the Guineas I said 'daylight' and I felt the same about today's race. We knew Nashwan was a brilliant horse, it was just a question of proving it to the Press." While Sheikh Hamdan's entourage celebrated at Annabel's nightclub in London, the ecstatic owner spent a quiet evening in his apartment at the family-owned Carlton Tower Hotel watching the race again and again on video. "It was a wonderful moment when he crossed the line. Winning the Derby is not only a life's ambition for me but also for my family. I am very happy, more than happy. It was lovely."

Not since Nijinsky in 1970 had a horse secured the first two colts' classics and put himself in line for the Triple Crown worn by a select group of fifteen. "The horse will stay the extra two furlongs of the Leger." maintained Hern, "But nobody seems to want to know the oldest classic – more's the pity because it has always been a lucky race for me." Before the nettle of St Leger participation had to be grasped there was the question of Nashwan's next race to be settled. Since Nijinsky achieved the hat-trick of the Derby, Irish Derby and King George in 1970 these three mid-summer targets had assumed the guise of a modern Triple Crown for three-year-old colts. Grundy(1975), The Minstrel(1977), Troy(1979) and Shergar(1981) had managed to emulate Nijinsky, and Nashwan now seemed set fair to join them. However, three days before Epsom, Sheikh Mohammed's Old Vic, trained by Henry Cecil, annihilated his field in the Prix du Jockey-Club (the French Derby), winning by seven lengths, and although the brothers had never believed in their horses avoiding each other the likelihood of both Old Vic and Nashwan contesting the Irish Derby was slim. Old Vic it was who competed at the Curragh, defeating Ile de Nisky($6\frac{1}{2}$ lengths) almost as far as Nashwan had at Epsom($7\frac{1}{2}$ lengths), thereby fuelling a debate as to which of the two was the better horse that raged throughout the remainder of 1989.

Nashwan followed the path trod by Mill Reef(1971) and Reference Point(1987) and headed for Sandown and a clash with the elder generation in the Eclipse Stakes. Mill Reef put his seniors in their place but Reference Point found Mtoto too fast for him over this $1\frac{1}{4}$ miles. He had not won a Guineas, however, and although Nashwan had clocked a fast time in the Derby there were many who believed $1\frac{1}{4}$ miles not $1\frac{1}{2}$ miles would see him at his most effective. Carson was less sure. "Personally I would have favoured the Irish Derby route as it would have left more time before the King George. It's a big test coming back in distance to ten furlongs. Although he's the best of his generation, he has still got to prove it against the older horses." The older horses in this instance were the five-year-old grey mare Indian Skimmer (owned by Sheikh Mohammed), winner of five Group I events at around $1\frac{1}{4}$ miles including the Prix de Diane and Champion Stakes, and the four-year-old Warning, Europe's champion colt at a mile in 1988.

The much-touted 'Race of the Century' banner, unfurled on cue, had hardly been run up the flagpole before the issue was thrown into confusion. On the Monday of Eclipse week Nashwan sustained a poisoned foot. "The problem was a nasty scare at the time but my vets John Gray and Barry Park found the poison quickly and he missed only one day's exercise. Even then he was led out three times on that day with a boot on." In addition, neither Indian Skimmer nor Warning was sure to run. The grey mare needed rain; too much rain, on the other hand, would rule out the colt. All these imponderables led Carson to the conclusion that a tactical battle was in the offing. "If Warning runs, he's the only one who'd be suited by a slow gallop. So I imagine that Greensmith is there to try and slow down the pace in front. It doesn't look as though he can stay, both from his style of racing and on his breeding, and the rain's done nothing for his chances of getting the trip. But it shouldn't bother Nashwan too much. He won in soft going as a two-year-old and the going was very soft on Newbury racecourse when he did a particularly convincing trial for the Guineas. Indian Skimmer can't possibly be in top form as we've had dry weather since May. You can't train soft-ground specialists under these conditions. To think that Indian Skimmer is going to run a fantastic race just because we've had some rain is not realistic. It doesn't work that way. She's going to get tired. She's tough and honest but she's beatable. Opening Verse has got no chance on all known form. I hope he's there to make the pace for Indian Skimmer but if he doesn't help me out I might have to make the running myself. Sandown is a front runner's track and therefore doesn't help horses who have to be held for a late run. It's because the finish is uphill and it's very tiring for horses to make up ground. It can be done but it's difficult." Carson's predictions were to prove uncannily accurate.

Greensmith and Opening Verse cut out the early pace on behalf of their stablemates covering the initial six furlongs in a very sharp 1.12.82. The three principals lay well off the pace watching each other like hawks. Rounding the home turn Opening Verse was still galloping strongly in the lead. "I was thinking of doing my Lester Piggott impersonation but I lost my bottle," Carson confessed afterwards. "He was about eight lengths clear of me and I thought for a moment, 'Oh dear, I wonder if I've overdone this,' but from the two furlong marker I had no doubt I would collect him." It required a mighty effort to reduce such a deficit after that frantic early gallop. To a huge roar from the crowd Nashwan caught Opening Verse below the distance and from there on the race was his. Warning had not handled the ground and it was not soft enough for Indian Skimmer, who, just as Carson had foreseen, ran out of steam and failed even to overhaul her own pacemaker. However, it was a very leg-weary Nashwan who passed the post five lengths in front of Opening Verse. The final time was slow and he had really toiled through the last uphill furlong on the rain-softened ground. Carson blamed himself. "I let the pacemaker, who was a very good horse in his own right, get too far away." Nevertheless, no horse since Ballymoss in 1958 had won an Eclipse by as wide a margin and only Blue Peter(1939), Diamond Jubilee(1900) and Flying Fox(1899) had won the 2000 Guineas, Derby and Eclipse in their third year.

"I thought he was most impressive but I didn't think he would win so easily," was the Hern verdict. "He's shown he's the best of the three, four and five-year-old generations and is a charming horse to train. But above all he's very brave. You'd not be surprised if a horse lost 20lb after such a race – they can lose 10lb going to Newbury and back – but he lost only 4lb. I was amazed he lost so little weight." After emptying his manger and trotting out sound, Nashwan was declared a certain runner for the King George thirteen days hence, which appeared at his mercy. Old Vic had won the Irish Derby despite an ugly boil on his back and had yet to resume strong work. The only serious threat was posed by Cacoethes, a Royal Ascot winner since the Derby. The bad news for supporters of Nashwan was the announcement that he would almost definitely be retired to stud at the end of the season. The decision caused profound disappointment in the Racing Press. The *Racing Post*'s Tony Morris, an unabashed disciple of Nashwan, likened the decision to "scrapping Concorde after its maiden flight" and in the same paper John Oaksey devoted his 21 July column to marshalling all the reasons "Why Nashwan should race on". At stud Nashwan would earn £3 million in his first season; on the track he would thus need to win a Group I race once every three weeks. In the face of this seemingly unanswerable case the gist of Oaksey's argument ran: "However strongly the records support a businesslike, cash-register approach, its advocates should not forget that money isn't everything – especially if you own it in large sackfuls." There was, argued Oaksey, plenty left for Nashwan to prove on the racecourse and there was no knowing what he could achieve, particularly if he kept improving. Hern agreed: "There is no reason whatever why he shouldn't train on. In fact, barring accidents, I would be very surprised and dis-appointed if he's not even better at four."

For the present there was Britain's premier all-aged middle-dis-tance championship to be won. Carson's belief in Nashwan was growing by the minute. "I'm sitting on the best horse," he told Julian Wilson on television. "I can make the running or sit last – as long as the horse is 100%. He's a good horse, he doesn't need a jockey." On this occasion Nashwan needed all the assistance his jockey could muster. The Ascot crowd, basking in the hottest tem-peratures for thirteen years – well into the 90's – witnessed a contest run at a muddling pace which culminated in a hell-for-leather last half-mile. As Polemos had undertaken the pacemaking for Nashwan the pedestrian gallop surprised everyone. The situation was ripe for a sudden break. Michael Roberts was the jockey who saw the opportunity first and he drove the 50/1 shot Top Class up on the outside of Polemos to steal a three or four length advantage turning into the short Ascot straight.

Nashwan, tracked by Cacoethes, went off in pursuit but, as in the Eclipse, he was obliged to use a lot of his speed earlier than was advisable. Unlike Opening Verse, however, Top Class could not sustain his charge and Nashwan collared him with a quarter of a mile to race. The ensuing half-minute yielded as pulsating a finale as one could ever wish to see. The fading Top Class hung to his left, bumping Nashwan at the very moment Greville Starkey was launching Cacoethes on the chestnut's outside. With a furlong to go the two were upsides. "The pace was not fast enough and the bump with Top Class cost me half a length but I knew Nashwan would find a bit more. Greville was keeping me tight, preventing me from using my stick but he never actually got past me and I was not forced to give my horse one behind the saddle." Inside the last 100 yards Nashwan forged steadily ahead to win by a neck.

It was a relieved Carson who explained: "Nashwan came back from the Eclipse pretty low. We had only two weeks to get him ready for the King George and when I rode him about a week later I said, 'He can't run; he hasn't recovered.' I had another ride on him and felt he was on the way back but not really back to his old self. We orchestrated our pacemaker to go steady, not flat out, in the belief that Nashwan was the horse with the best turn of foot and that the last thing he wanted was another gruelling race. As it turned out Cacoethes had a better turn of foot on the firm but we still got away with it even though my horse hadn't really come back."

Nashwan's thrilling victory (Hern's fifth in the race – no other trainer has more than three) raised his prize money for the season to a record sum won in Britain of £772,046 (£787,357 in his career altogether) and pushed Hern's total earnings (win and place money) through the £1 million barrier for the second time. Thus it was a very proud trainer who received his diamond-studded momento from the Queen. Nashwan had won Group I races over eight, ten and twelve furlongs on a variety of ground and became the only horse to win the 2000 Guineas, Derby, Eclipse and King George in the same season. "He's won two Group I races in a fortnight and needs a rest," Hern told the Press. "He wasn't quite as relaxed before the race as he was before the Derby and Eclipse but he's done it." Hern had his eyes firmly fixed on the St Leger and the Triple Crown, followed three weeks later by a confrontation with Old Vic in the Prix de l'Arc de Triomphe that would settle once and for all the identity of the current generation's champion.

Sadly, there was to be no Triple Crown for Nashwan, no Arc clash with Old Vic. Indeed, Nashwan did not even figure in the Leger or Arc fields. Despite Hern's repeatedly expressed desire for the Triple Crown the owner, as always, had the last word – which insisted that Nashwan use Longchamp's Prix Niel on 17 September as a springboard to the Arc. It would afford Nashwan valuable experience of the track, Hern was reported as saying. Coming from an avowed traditionalist to whom the Triple Crown meant a diadem beyond price, those words had a hollow ring to them. As Paul Haigh com-

mented in the *Racing Post*: "If someone had said to him when this
season started, 'you'll have a potential Triple Crown winner but you
won't actually run him even though you'll think he could win it' it's
hard not to think that he would have spun round the famous chair
and wheeled it away at full power." After all, Nashwan no more
needed experience of Longchamp before the Arc than he did Epsom
before the Derby. To some, Nijinsky's defeat in the Arc was attribu-
table to his participation in the St Leger and this was also trotted
out in defence of the Sheikh's decision. However, Nijinsky's 'hard'
race at Doncaster owed more to the ringworm he had recently
suffered than the distance of the Leger or its proximity to the Arc.
A hard race in defeat had not stopped Alleged from winning the Arc
in 1977.

Haigh's *Racing Post* colleague Tony Morris went further. Lament-
ing the "Soft option that stops Nashwan from joining the super
elite," he wrote:

> The professionals who surround him believed that he owned the
> stamina and class to win both and the proper course of action was to
> test that belief by allowing him the opportunity ...it behoves the
> owner to exercise his freedom and due regard to the interests of the
> public and the spirit of racing itself. There should never be a time when
> issues get ducked and reputations are protected. The Arc has a winner
> every year: the achievement of the Triple Crown is a once-every-thirty-
> years event. In this case the soft option is the daft option. The sport,
> the public and, not least Nashwan himself are all losers as a result of
> this unadventurous decision.

In the *Observer* Richard Baerlein endorsed Morris's sentiments:
"That Nashwan is not being given the chance to complete his Triple
Crown, a rarely presented opportunity, is one of the tragedies of the
modern approach to racing." Needless to say, the knives were out
at *The Sporting Life*. "The decision to chicken out of running in the
St Leger to try to complete the treasured Triple Crown defies any
sporting explanation," blustered Monty Court predictably. "The
Maktoums have proved that in spite of their colossal wealth a
sporting challenge has no price against their fear of slightly damaging
the market value of a stallion. It's a shame Nashwan's brave heart
is not matched by that of his owner."

History will record that the 1989 St Leger was postponed owing

to the track being declared unsafe in the aftermath of two horrific
incidents involving the falls of four horses during the first three days
of the Doncaster meeting. The abnormally dry summer had cracked
the clay around a number of drains, causing subsidence. The classic
was eventually run at Ayr a week later and, with the gap between
Leger and Arc reduced to only fourteen days, Nashwan would have
been scratched in any event. Consequently, the decision to forgo the
St Leger seemed one blessed in heaven. Not that Nashwan's trip to
France went entirely without a hitch. A flu virus that had decimated
strings throughout Britain meant Nashwan had to pass a French
veterinary examination immediately he landed at Beauvais airport.
So far West Ilsley was unaffected. "I'm pleased with the horse's
condition," was all Hern would say. Allan Thimbleby was more
garrulous. "I promise you he is better than ever – bigger and stronger
since his three week summer break and looking like a four-year-old."
Once passed by the vet Nashwan and his pacemaker Nad Elishba
spent the night at Chantilly. "His one quirk which he shares with
his half brothers Unfuwain and Mukddaam," added Thimbleby, "is
that he does not like strange boxes. At Sandown, before the Eclipse,
I had to walk him around for $4\frac{1}{2}$ hours because he would not enter
the racecourse box, and the plan this weekend is to get him properly
settled before his race." To win the Niel, Nashwan had to concede
weight all round on the softest ground (3.8 on the penetrometer i.e.
between soft and very soft) that he had been asked to negotiate.
The previous September, the Derby winner Kahyasi forfeited his
unbeaten record in this very race when likewise using it as a warm-
up for the Arc.

Nashwan looked superb loping around the stable area before the
race whose outcome proved disastrous. Carson bided his time as Nad
Elishba took the field along at a respectable gallop (over a second
faster at the 1600 metre mark compared to the Prix Foy and Prix
Vermeille, the other Arc 'trials' run on the same card) until overtaken
by French Glory at the top of the straight. Nashwan was breathing
down his neck. Everybody waited for the chestnut's magnificent
stride to lengthen. Instead, he became embroiled in a dire struggle
with French Glory and Golden Pheasant, brought with a steady
run up the centre of the track. Long before the post was reached
Nashwan's fate was sealed. Golden Pheasant, a $2\frac{1}{2}$ length runner-up
to Old Vic in the Chester Vase earlier in the season when trained in

England, proceeded to beat French Glory by $1\frac{1}{2}$ lengths with Nashwan half a length back in third. Although both his conquerors had received 7lb, the soft ground seemed the most logical reason for his downfall. He just could not stretch out in his normal devouring style.

"It's naturally very disappointing for everybody," said a dejected Hern, "but if you go on long enough, every horse has to be beaten. I can't say what happened. He was working well at home and had a perfect flight. Perhaps the next week will reveal something. But there is no point talking about the Arc at the present moment." Interviewed by Brough Scott on Channel 4, Willie Carson looked totally shellshocked and on the verge of tears. "I cannot explain it. Half way up the straight I asked him just to get rid of Pat Eddery on French Glory and he couldn't. So I had to leave him alone and I thought he'd quicken up but he never did. The horse has lobbed through the whole race. I was very happy with him, he wasn't pulling at me, he hasn't changed his legs much – he just didn't fire. I don't know what's gone wrong. The horse has worked well, there's nothing wrong with him, he's travelled well, he's come here and lobbed in the race. The only thing he's done wrong, he hasn't picked up and gone and won the race, which he normally does. He usually grabs the ground and goes. Today he felt like a horse that was tired. He had no energy. It's a shame. I was hoping this horse would never get beaten and I came here thinking that he wouldn't. He was not blowing unduly afterwards and it is a complete mystery. It's an unfair world."

Exhaustive blood tests failed to discover any reason for Nashwan's lack-lustre performance. Hern reported that his temperature was normal, he had not coughed and he had lost only 6lb in weight. "On reflection I wonder if the ground was too dead for him to quicken up." Theories flew round the racing pages like leaves in an autumn wind. Whatever the reason, Nashwan ran – taking the formbook at face value – something like 10lb below his Eclipse and King George displays. Sheikh Hamdan had not abandoned hopes for the Arc (Nashwan remained a 2/1 favourite – with a run) but neither Hern nor Carson exhibited much enthusiasm. "It's the ground as much as anything else which could affect the decision," reasoned Hern, while Carson said warily, "It's a very hard decision and I'm glad I don't have to make it. On balance I'm against going back to a place where he was disappointing. It was very 'puddingy' at Longchamp, unlike Sandown where the ground was soft on top of firm." The announcement on 2 October that Nashwan would miss the Arc and bow out of racing in the Champion Stakes (sponsored by the Maktoums) was therefore not unexpected. Less travelling, a galloping track and better ground were the deciding factors. "I'm sorry that he's not going to Paris but I think it's the right decision," said Carson. "If you get blown up somewhere you don't go back there, do you?"

In Nashwan's absence the Arc was won by the four-year-old Carroll House, who had finished some eleven lengths behind him in the King George on the firmer ground he hated. To the chagrin of Nashwan's supporters his contemporaries and sparring partners Golden Pheasant, French Glory and Cacoethes finished down the field, inflicting further damage to his tarnished reputation: a reputation, moreover, which he would be denied the opportunity of reviving in the Champion Stakes. Coughing finally struck West Ilsley and although Nashwan seemed to have escaped the bug at first, he was found to have a temperature of 102° at evening stables on the Tuesday before the race.

So Nashwan's seven race career ended with a whimper not a bang and syndicated at £18 million off he went to Sheikh Hamdan's Nunnery Stud, near Thetford, for dates with forty-five mares (twenty-three of them Maktoum-owned) at £100,000 a cover, leaving both those close to him and those who had merely marvelled at his glorious summer campaign from afar pondering his true worth. Dick Hern had no qualms about placing Nashwan at the top of the tree.

> It's difficult to compare one generation with another but my impression is that Nashwan is the best I've trained. He won the 2000 Guineas after an interrupted preparation and that was probably his best performance. Then he came back from a hard race in the Eclipse to win the King George. He was unbeaten on firm ground as he was able to bounce off it. Although he had a shorter career than many of the other top horses I have been fortunate to train, I still regard him as the best. 'Be to his virtues ever kind and to his faults a little blind'.

If Hern chose to quote Mr Jorrocks in this most emotional of years he could be excused, but the generosity of his assessment called to mind the lines of the Shakespearean sonnet which go:

O me! what eyes hath love put in my head,
Which have no correspondence with true sight!...
O cunning Love! with tears thou keep'st me blind,
Lest eyes well-seeing thy foul faults should find.

When giving his own valediction Willie Carson pleaded guilty to a similar weakness.

The good horses are what keeps everyone in the game going and when you get into the twilight of your career, you think you're never going to see the like of it again. To win all those races in one year makes him a great horse but there have been lots of doubters recently because of what happened in France and the fact that his form has not always worked out well. But we have seen him all year and he is a very, very special horse so I don't think the word 'great' is misused. For a horse that had got to stay $1\frac{1}{2}$ miles it was a fantastic performance to win the 2000 Guineas and he won the Derby by five lengths. With any horse that wins the Derby by that distance, you've got to be over the moon. Riding Nashwan is like making love. It is absolutely fantastic. Whatever you are thinking, the horse does. You think about quickening up, he quickens; you don't have to ask him to do anything. He is so superior to the horses he works with. It is like going down the motorway and sitting in a car with a Merlin engine in it. It's a great thrill to ride him. Troy was a very good horse – a relentless galloper. He went from A to B quite quickly but he couldn't do it in the same fashion as Nashwan who has a fantastic turn of foot. Nashwan just changed gears – that is why he is possibly the best horse I will ever ride. Never mind what the formbook says, I know what it felt like. He was very good on the days that mattered. If people want to knock him now, that's up to them. Nashwan beat the best around, you can't do more than that. But we 'bottomed' him in the Eclipse – he had to do something fantastic to catch Opening Verse – and after that I was having to look after him in the King George.

The fiercely held views of trainer and jockey strike a vital chord because in cold isolation the formbook can be a harsh judge. Anthony Arkwright, the Jockey Club handicapper responsible for middle-distance horses, felt Nashwan could not be rated the equal of either Dancing Brave(141) or Shergar(140), his top animals of the decade, but he conceded, "I want to try and assess him as high as possible as I have a gut feeling that he's a much better horse than the form will ever show him to be." The International Classification published on 11 January ("The moment I've been dreading since last July," said Arkwright) officially rated Nashwan at 131, not only below Troy(136) and other Derby winners of the 1980s such as Reference Point and Slip Anchor(135) and Golden Fleece and Shahrastani(134), but, controversially, also behind both Old Vic and the champion miler Zilzal, both on 134.

Weak opposition was the 'official' reason cited by senior handicapper Geoffrey Gibbs for Nashwan's lowly rating. "That's the opposition's fault," countered Carson. "The horse won everything he was asked to, except when he went to France, and the ratings are only one man's opinion. Unfortunately, Mr Gibbs has never sat on Nashwan. Otherwise he might have a different opinion. The story of what happened in France has never been told. He didn't like travelling. That's as far as we need go there; he couldn't travel. Nashwan was a horse who knew only one thing, give, give, give. And he couldn't keep giving. He was a machine, an absolute bloody machine. A sprinter and a stayer in one. He could have won from five furlongs to $1\frac{1}{2}$ miles. He could even have given a Quarter Horse a race. He was a true champion and the handicappers got him wrong. Nash-the-Dash was some machine."

Dick Hern picked up Carson's point: "It's all a matter of opinion. They do it all through collateral form, but if the handicappers were always right there would be no bookmakers would there? If Nashwan was taking on Old Vic on decent ground and both horses were at their best, I would be delighted to find that my horse was receiving 3lb."

In their *Racehorses of 1989* publication Timeform awarded Nashwan a rating of 135 (with Old Vic at 136 and Zilzal 137) compared to 140 for Shergar, 139 Reference Point, 137 Troy, 136 Slip Anchor and 135 Shahrastani. Consequently, the Halifax organization regarded Nashwan the same horse as Petoski, also rated 135 as a three-year-old in 1985 largely on the basis of one performance in the King George. Among the decade's other Guineas winners they considered Nashwan inferior to Dancing Brave(141) and El Gran Senor(136) and only the equal of Known Fact and Shadeed. All opinion, it's true. However, for Hern to regard Nashwan as superior to Brigadier Gerard (Timeform 144), a horse who won in the highest class for three seasons rather than three months and is undisputedly one of the Turf's immortals, did suggest a severe bout of "cunning love".

Having manufactured an idol during the heady days of July with a succession of eulogies rich on hyperbole but poor on logic, the Press duly set about destroying it. "Nashwan just a talking horse," boomed the *Daily Star*, while Claude Duval wrote in *The Sun*, "The official handicappers now reckon he beat a cartload of camels." A few scribes stuck to their summer guns and in commencing his *Sunday Times* piece with the phrase "It is the love affair that died" Brough Scott surely provided the most fitting epitaph for a horse whose career spanned the exquisite rollercoaster of emotions associated with any romance.

However contentious Nashwan's merits, there were no reservations about his trainer's. For the first time Hern accumulated £1 million in first prize money, the magic figure being passed on 11 September when the Queen's Trying for Gold took a humble Wolverhampton graduation race worth £1,920 for his thirty-fifth success. By 11 November Hern's score had risen to forty-four worth £1,096,219 (£1,263,932 with place money added). In a poll of seventeen trainers conducted by *The Sporting Life* seven nominated Hern's preparation of Nashwan to win the Guineas on his debut as the training feat of the season. Awards came thick and fast from all directions – though the widely tipped knighthood did not materialize in the New Year's Honours List. In September Hern received the Animal Health Trust's Special Award for services to racing from Princess Michael of Kent. At the ceremony, a luncheon at the Hilton Hotel in Park Lane, Hern – "quite overwhelmed" – heard Dr Andrew Higgins, Director of the Trust, tell the audience how he had fought courageously against the effects of his riding accident. "True to his character, he did not let this stand in the way of his lifelong dedication to horses." In November Hern resumed his seat in the Hilton as one of the twelve 'Men of the Year' chosen by RADAR, the Royal Association for Disability and Rehabilitation. Lastly, on 4 December, he was fêted by the Horserace Writers and Reporters' Association as their Flat Trainer of the Year (having previously won in 1975 and 1980). To the astonishment of the 600 guests present at the Royal Garden Hotel in Kensington Hern, after accepting his trophy of a cut glass decanter from Lord Derby, grabbed the edge of the top table with both hands, hauled himself out of his wheelchair and regaled the audience from his feet. "I am delighted to have won this award for the third time but it has meant more to me this time as part of the Nashwan team of Sheikh Hamdan and Willie Carson. Willie has ridden for me for 12 years now and he and Sheikh Hamdan have been great supporters of mine in recent times and have been a great help." Before sitting down Hern proceeded to raise the roof by relating the contents of one letter of congratulation he had received. "The lady, from Devon, said that many years ago she had nursed me when I was in the Dunedin Nursing Home having a piles operation. I was able to write back and tell her that I had no recurrence of the problem!"

Hern's bravura performance that December day at the Royal Garden Hotel and his stoical demeanour throughout the painful and frequently distressing days of the preceding five years lent startling credibility to the dictum that "Old age and sickness bring out the essential characteristics of a man." The qualities hitherto known only to his friends had finally been revealed to the world outside this relatively select circle.

Appendices

APPENDIX I: DOMESTIC TRAINING RECORD

	Races Won	*Value (£)*	*Position*
1958	40	41,265	5
1959	41	28,434	7
1960	27	14,778	28
1961	37	39,227	9
1962	39	70,206	1
1963	62	39,718	13
1964	43	49,131	9
1965	38	66,416	3
1966	24	9,945	56
1967	60	47,161	6
1968	21	22,172	20
1969	35	26,377	22
1970	50	58,742	5
1971	57	141,531	3
1972	42	206,767	1
1973	62	90,588	8
1974	55	201,850	2
1975	56	90,253	6
1976	69	153,298	5
1977	74	338,471	2
1978	74	253,765	4
1979	61	564,675	2
1980	65	831,964	1
1981	64	342,924	4

	Races Won	Value (£)	Position
1982	44	300,873	5
1983	57	549,598	1
1984	56	406,676	5
1985	53	370,761	6
1986	45	339,010	7
1987	36	208,765	11
1988	30	238,217	15
1989	44	1,096,219	4
1990	30	502,906	9

NB: The 1990 figures exclude All-Weather statistics.

APPENDIX II: DOMESTIC CLASSIC WINS

1000 Guineas: Highclere (1974)
2000 Guineas: Brigadier Gerard (1971), Nashwan (1989)
Derby: Troy (1979), Henbit (1980), Nashwan (1989)
Oaks: Dunfermline (1977), Bireme (1980), Sun Princess (1983)
St Leger: Hethersett (1962), Provoke (1965), Bustino (1974), Dunfermline (1977), Cut Above (1981), Sun Princess (1983)

APPENDIX III: OVERSEAS CLASSIC WINS

(a) IRELAND
1000 Guineas: Gaily (1974)
2000 Guineas: Sharp Edge (1973)
Derby: Troy (1979)
Oaks: Shoot A Line (1980), Swiftfoot (1982), Helen Street (1985)
St Leger: Craighouse (1965), Niniski (1979)

(b) FRANCE
Prix de Diane: Highclere (1974)
Prix Royal-Oak: Niniski (1979)

APPENDIX IV: OTHER PRINCIPAL WINS

Coronation Cup: Buoy (1974), Bustino (1979)
St James's Palace Stakes: Brigadier Gerard (1971), Sun Prince (1972)
Ascot Gold Cup: Little Wolf (1983), Longboat (1986)
King's Stand Stakes: Dayjur (1990)
Eclipse Stakes: Brigadier Gerard (1972), Ela-Mana-Mou (1980), Nashwan (1989), Elmaamul (1990)

July Cup: Galivanter (1961)

King George VI & Queen Elizabeth II Stakes: Brigadier Gerard (1972), Troy (1979), Ela-Mana-Mou (1980), Petoski (1985), Nashwan (1989)

Sussex Stakes: Brigadier Gerard (1971), Sallust (1972)

Benson & Hedges Gold Cup: Relkino (1977), Troy (1979)

Yorkshire Oaks: None Nicer (1958), Shoot A Line (1980), Sun Princess (1983), Roseate Tern (1989)

Nunthorpe Stakes: Dayjur (1990)

Vernons Sprint Cup: Boldboy (1977)

Ladbroke Sprint Cup: Dayjur (1990)

Queen Elizabeth II Stakes: Brigadier Gerard (1971 & 1972), Homing (1978)

Hoover Fillies' Mile: Height of Fashion (1981)

Middle Park Stakes: Brigadier Gerard (1970)

Champion Stakes: Brigadier Gerard (1971 & 1972)

William Hill Futurity Stakes: Emmson (1987)

Phoenix Champion Stakes: Elmaamul (1990)

Prix Robert Papin: Sun Prince (1971)

Prix Vermeille: Highest Hopes (1970)

Prix du Moulin de Longchamp: Sallust (1972)

Prix de l'Abbaye de Longchamp: Dayjur (1990)

APPENDIX V: BEST HORSES TRAINED 1958–89
– BY TIMEFORM ANNUAL RATING (with kind permission)

(a) TWO-YEAR-OLDS

132 Brigadier Gerard (colt, 1970), Gorytus (colt, 1982)

129 Remand (colt, 1967)

128 Local Suitor (colt, 1984), Prince of Dance (colt, 1988)

NB: Top-rated filly: 122 Fortune's Darling (1958)

(b) THREE-YEAR-OLDS

141 Brigadier Gerard (colt, 1971)

137 Troy (colt, 1979)

135 Petoski (colt, 1985), Nashwan (colt, 1989)

134 Hethersett (colt, 1962), Sallust (colt, 1972)

133 Dunfermline (filly, 1977)

131 Galivanter (colt, 1959), Unfuwain (colt, 1988)

130 Provoke (colt, 1965), Royalty (colt, 1971), Bustino (colt, 1974), Homing (colt, 1978), Henbit (colt, 1980), Cut Above (colt, 1981), Sun Princess (filly, 1983), Minster Son (colt, 1988)

129 Highest Hopes (filly, 1970), Highclere (filly, 1974)

NB: Top-rated gelding: 126 Boldboy (1973)

(c) OLDER HORSES

144 Brigadier Gerard (4YO colt, 1972)
136 Bustino (4YO colt, 1975)
132 Ela-Mana-Mou (4YO colt, 1980)
131 Galivanter (5YO horse, 1961), Relkino (4YO colt, 1977)
128 Sea Anchor (4YO colt, 1976), Prince Bee (4YO colt, 1981)
127 Little Wolf (5YO horse, 1983)
126 Sun Prince (4YO colt, 1973), Boldboy (6/7YO gelding, 1976/77)
NB: Top-rated filly: 123 Dunfermline (1978)

Bibliography

The principal sources consulted were as follows:—

BAERLEIN: *Joe Mercer* (Macdonald/Queen Anne Press)
CARR: *Queen's Jockey* (Stanley Paul)
CURLING: *All the Queen's Horses* (Chatto & Windus)
DUVAL: *Willie Carson* (Stanley Paul)
FITZGERALD: *Prix de l'Arc de Triomphe, 1965–82* (Sidgwick & Jackson)
HAWKINS: *The Race of the Century* (George Allen & Unwin)
HISLOP: *The Brigadier* (Secker & Warburg)
HUGHES: *My Greatest Race* (Michael Joseph)
MAGEE & BAYES: *Champions* (Sidgwick & Jackson)
REEVES & ROBINSON: *Decade of Champions* (Oxmoor House)
RICKMAN: *Eight Flat-Racing Stables* (Heinemann)
TANNER: *Teleprompter & Co.* (Private)
TIMEFORM: *Racehorses of 19–*

The Bridgwater Mercury
The British Racehorse
Daily Star
The European Racehorse
Horse and Hound
Pacemaker International
Pacemaker Update International
Racing Post
Racing Specialist
Sporting Chronicle
Stud & Stable
Sunday Express
The Sporting Life
The Sunday Telegraph
The Sunday Times
The Times